Official Google Cloud Certified
Professional Data Engineer
Study Guide

Official Google Cloud Certified
Professional Data Engineer
Study Guide

Dan Sullivan

A Wiley Brand

to Katherine

Acknowledgments

I have been fortunate to work again with professionals from Waterside Productions, Wiley, and Google to create this Study Guide.

Carole Jelen, vice president of Waterside Productions, and Jim Minatel, associate publisher at John Wiley & Sons, continue to lead the effort to create Google Cloud certification guides. It was a pleasure to work with Gary Schwartz, project editor, who managed the process that got us from outline to a finished manuscript. Thanks to Christine O'Connor, senior production editor, for making the last stages of book development go as smoothly as they did.

I was also fortunate to work with Valerie Parham-Thompson again. Valerie's technical review improved the clarity and accuracy of this book tremendously.

Thank you to the Google Cloud subject-matter experts who reviewed and contributed to the material in this book:

Name	Title
Damon A. Runion	Technical Curriculum Developer, Data Engineering
Julianne Cuneo	Data Analytics Specialist, Google Cloud
Geoff McGill	Customer Engineer, Data Analytics
Susan Pierce	Solutions Manager, Smart Analytics and AI
Rachel Levy	Cloud Data Specialist Lead
Dustin Williams	Data Analytics Specialist, Google Cloud
Gbenga Awodokun	Customer Engineer, Data and Marketing Analytics
Dilraj Kaur	Big Data Specialist
Rebecca Ballough	Data Analytics Manager, Google Cloud
Robert Saxby	Staff Solutions Architect
Niel Markwick	Cloud Solutions Architect
Sharon Dashet	Big Data Product Specialist
Barry Searle	Solution Specialist - Cloud Data Management
Jignesh Mehta	Customer Engineer, Cloud Data Platform and Advanced Analytics

My sons James and Nicholas were my first readers, and they helped me to get the manuscript across the finish line.

This book is dedicated to Katherine, my wife and partner in so many adventures.

About the Author

 **Dan Sullivan** is a principal engineer and software architect. He specializes in data science, machine learning, and cloud computing. Dan is the author of the *Official Google Cloud Certified Professional Architect Study Guide* (Sybex, 2019), *Official Google Cloud Certified Associate Cloud Engineer Study Guide* (Sybex, 2019), *NoSQL for Mere Mortals* (Addison-Wesley Professional, 2015), and several LinkedIn Learning courses on databases, data science, and machine learning. Dan has certifications from Google and AWS, along with a Ph.D. in genetics and computational biology from Virginia Tech.

About the Technical Editor

Valerie Parham-Thompson   has experience with a variety of open source data storage technologies, including MySQL, MongoDB, and Cassandra, as well as a foundation in web development in software-as-a-service (SaaS) environments. Her work in both development and operations in startups and traditional enterprises has led to solid expertise in web-scale data storage and data delivery.

Valerie has spoken at technical conferences on topics such as database security, performance tuning, and container management. She also often speaks at local meetups and volunteer events.

Valerie holds a bachelor's degree from the Kenan Flagler Business School at UNC-Chapel Hill, has certifications in MySQL and MongoDB, and is a Google Certified Professional Cloud Architect. She currently works in the Open Source Database Cluster at Pythian, headquartered in Ottawa, Ontario.

Follow Valerie's contributions to technical blogs on Twitter at @dataindataout.

Contents at a Glance

Contents

Introduction

The Google Cloud Certified Professional Data Engineer exam tests your ability to design, deploy, monitor, and adapt services and infrastructure for data-driven decision-making. The four primary areas of focus in this exam are as follows:

- Designing data processing systems
- Building and operationalizing data processing systems
- Operationalizing machine learning models
- Ensuring solution quality

Designing data processing systems involves selecting storage technologies, including relational, analytical, document, and wide-column databases, such as Cloud SQL, BigQuery, Cloud Firestore, and Cloud Bigtable, respectively. You will also be tested on designing pipelines using services such as Cloud Dataflow, Cloud Dataproc, Cloud Pub/Sub, and Cloud Composer. The exam will test your ability to design distributed systems that may include hybrid clouds, message brokers, middleware, and serverless functions. Expect to see questions on migrating data warehouses from on-premises infrastructure to the cloud.

The building and operationalizing data processing systems parts of the exam will test your ability to support storage systems, pipelines, and infrastructure in a production environment. This will include using managed services for storage as well as batch and stream processing. It will also cover common operations such as data ingestion, data cleansing, transformation, and integrating data with other sources. As a data engineer, you are expected to understand how to provision resources, monitor pipelines, and test distributed systems.

Machine learning is an increasingly important topic. This exam will test your knowledge of prebuilt machine learning models available in GCP as well as the ability to deploy machine learning pipelines with custom-built models. You can expect to see questions about machine learning service APIs and data ingestion, as well as training and evaluating models. The exam uses machine learning terminology, so it is important to understand the nomenclature, especially terms such as model, supervised and unsupervised learning, regression, classification, and evaluation metrics.

The fourth domain of knowledge covered in the exam is ensuring solution quality, which includes security, scalability, efficiency, and reliability. Expect questions on ensuring privacy with data loss prevention techniques, encryption, identity, and access management, as well ones about compliance with major regulations. The exam also tests a data engineer's ability to monitor pipelines with Stackdriver, improve data models, and scale resources as needed. You may also encounter questions that assess your ability to design portable solutions and plan for future business requirements.

In your day-to-day experience with GCP, you may spend more time working on some data engineering tasks than others. This is expected. It does, however, mean that you should be aware of the exam topics about which you may be less familiar. Machine learning questions can be especially challenging to data engineers who work primarily on ingestion and storage systems. Similarly, those who spend a majority of their time developing machine learning models may need to invest more time studying schema modeling for NoSQL databases and designing fault-tolerant distributed systems.

What Does This Book Cover?

This book covers the topics outlined in the Google Cloud Professional Data Engineer exam guide available here:

    cloud.google.com/certification/guides/data-engineer

Chapter 1: Selecting Appropriate Storage Technologies   This chapter covers selecting appropriate storage technologies, including mapping business requirements to storage systems; understanding the distinction between structured, semi-structured, and unstructured data models; and designing schemas for relational and NoSQL databases. By the end of the chapter, you should understand the various criteria that data engineers consider when choosing a storage technology.

Chapter 2: Building and Operationalizing Storage Systems   This chapter discusses how to deploy storage systems and perform data management operations, such as importing and exporting data, configuring access controls, and doing performance tuning. The services included in this chapter are as follows: Cloud SQL, Cloud Spanner, Cloud Bigtable, Cloud Firestore, BigQuery, Cloud Memorystore, and Cloud Storage. The chapter also includes a discussion of working with unmanaged databases, understanding storage costs and performance, and performing data lifecycle management.

Chapter 3: Designing Data Pipelines   This chapter describes high-level design patterns, along with some variations on those patterns, for data pipelines. It also reviews how GCP services like Cloud Dataflow, Cloud Dataproc, Cloud Pub/Sub, and Cloud Composer are used to implement data pipelines. It also covers migrating data pipelines from an on-premises Hadoop cluster to GCP.

Chapter 4: Designing a Data Processing Solution   In this chapter, you learn about designing infrastructure for data engineering and machine learning, including how to do several tasks, such as choosing an appropriate compute service for your use case; designing for scalability, reliability, availability, and maintainability; using hybrid and edge computing architecture patterns and processing models; and migrating a data warehouse from on-premises data centers to GCP.

Chapter 5: Building and Operationalizing Processing Infrastructure   This chapter discusses managed processing resources, including those offered by App Engine, Cloud Functions, and Cloud Dataflow. The chapter also includes a discussion of how to use

Stackdriver Metrics, Stackdriver Logging, and Stackdriver Trace to monitor processing infrastructure.

Chapter 6: Designing for Security and Compliance   This chapter introduces several key topics of security and compliance, including identity and access management, data security, encryption and key management, data loss prevention, and compliance.

Chapter 7: Designing Databases for Reliability, Scalability, and Availability   This chapter provides information on designing for reliability, scalability, and availability of three GPC databases: Cloud Bigtable, Cloud Spanner, and Cloud BigQuery. It also covers how to apply best practices for designing schemas, querying data, and taking advantage of the physical design properties of each database.

Chapter 8: Understanding Data Operations for Flexibility and Portability   This chapter describes how to use the Data Catalog, a metadata management service supporting the discovery and management of data in Google Cloud. It also introduces Cloud Dataprep, a preprocessing tool for transforming and enriching data, as well as Data Studio for visualizing data and Cloud Datalab for interactive exploration and scripting.

Chapter 9: Deploying Machine Learning Pipelines   Machine learning pipelines include several stages that begin with data ingestion and preparation and then perform data segregation followed by model training and evaluation. GCP provides multiple ways to implement machine learning pipelines. This chapter describes how to deploy ML pipelines using general-purpose computing resources, such as Compute Engine and Kubernetes Engine. Managed services, such as Cloud Dataflow and Cloud Dataproc, are also available, as well as specialized machine learning services, such as AI Platform, formerly known as Cloud ML.

Chapter 10: Choosing Training and Serving Infrastructure   This chapter focuses on choosing the appropriate training and serving infrastructure for your needs when serverless or specialized AI services are not a good fit for your requirements. It discusses distributed and single-machine infrastructure, the use of edge computing for serving machine learning models, and the use of hardware accelerators.

Chapter 11: Measuring, Monitoring, and Troubleshooting Machine Learning Models   This chapter focuses on key concepts in machine learning, including machine learning terminology and core concepts and common sources of error in machine learning. Machine learning is a broad discipline with many areas of specialization. This chapter provides you with a high-level overview to help you pass the Professional Data Engineer exam, but it is not a substitute for learning machine learning from resources designed for that purpose.

Chapter 12: Leveraging Prebuilt ML Models as a Service   This chapter describes Google Cloud Platform options for using pretrained machine learning models to help developers build and deploy intelligent services quickly. The services are broadly grouped into sight, conversation, language, and structured data. These services are available through APIs or through Cloud AutoML services.

Interactive Online Learning Environment and TestBank

Learning the material in the *Official Google Cloud Certified Professional Engineer Study Guide* is an important part of preparing for the Professional Data Engineer certification exam, but we also provide additional tools to help you prepare. The online TestBank will help you understand the types of questions that will appear on the certification exam.

The sample tests in the TestBank include all the questions in each chapter as well as the questions from the assessment test. In addition, there are two practice exams with 50 questions each. You can use these tests to evaluate your understanding and identify areas that may require additional study.

The flashcards in the TestBank will push the limits of what you should know for the certification exam. Over 100 questions are provided in digital format. Each flashcard has one question and one correct answer.

The online glossary is a searchable list of key terms introduced in this Study Guide that you should know for the Professional Data Engineer certification exam.

To start using these to study for the Google Cloud Certified Professional Data Engineer exam, go to www.wiley.com/go/sybextestprep and register your book to receive your unique PIN. Once you have the PIN, return to www.wiley.com/go/sybextestprep, find your book, and click Register, or log in and follow the link to register a new account or add this book to an existing account.

Additional Resources

People learn in different ways. For some, a book is an ideal way to study, whereas other learners may find video and audio resources a more efficient way to study. A combination of resources may be the best option for many of us. In addition to this Study Guide, here are some other resources that can help you prepare for the Google Cloud Professional Data Engineer exam:

The Professional Data Engineer Certification Exam Guide:

https://cloud.google.com/certification/guides/data-engineer/

Exam FAQs:

https://cloud.google.com/certification/faqs/

Google's Assessment Exam:

https://cloud.google.com/certification/practice-exam/data-engineer

Google Cloud Platform documentation:

https://cloud.google.com/docs/

Cousera's on-demand courses in "Architecting with Google Cloud Platform Specialization" and "Data Engineering with Google Cloud" are both relevant to data engineering:

www.coursera.org/specializations/gcp-architecture

https://www.coursera.org/professional-certificates/gcp-data-engineering

QwikLabs Hands-on Labs:

https://google.qwiklabs.com/quests/25

Linux Academy Google Cloud Certified Professional Data Engineer video course:

https://linuxacademy.com/course/google-cloud-data-engineer/

The best way to prepare for the exam is to perform the tasks of a data engineer and work with the Google Cloud Platform.

 Exam objectives are subject to change at any time without prior notice and at Google's sole discretion. Please visit the Google Cloud Professional Data Engineer website (https://cloud.google.com/certification/data-engineer) for the most current listing of exam objectives.

Objective Map

Objective	Chapter
Section 1: Designing data processing system	
1.1 Selecting the appropriate storage technologies	1
1.2 Designing data pipelines	2, 3
1.3 Designing a data processing solution	4
1.4 Migrating data warehousing and data processing	4
Section 2: Building and operationalizing data processing systems	
2.1 Building and operationalizing storage systems	2
2.2 Building and operationalizing pipelines	3
2.3 Building and operationalizing infrastructure	5

Assessment Test

1. You are migrating your machine learning operations to GCP and want to take advantage of managed services. You have been managing a Spark cluster because you use the MLlib library extensively. Which GCP managed service would you use?

    A. Cloud Dataprep

    B. Cloud Dataproc

    C. Cloud Dataflow

    D. Cloud Pub/Sub

2. Your team is designing a database to store product catalog information. They have determined that you need to use a database that supports flexible schemas and transactions. What service would you expect to use?

    A. Cloud SQL

    B. Cloud BigQuery

    C. Cloud Firestore

    D. Cloud Storage

3. Your company has been losing market share because competitors are attracting your customers with a more personalized experience on their e-commerce platforms, including providing recommendations for products that might be of interest to them. The CEO has stated that your company will provide equivalent services within 90 days. What GCP service would you use to help meet this objective?

    A. Cloud Bigtable

    B. Cloud Storage

    C. AI Platform

    D. Cloud Datastore

4. The finance department at your company has been archiving data on premises. They no longer want to maintain a costly dedicated storage system. They would like to store up to 300 TB of data for 10 years. The data will likely not be accessed at all. They also want to minimize cost. What storage service would you recommend?

    A. Cloud Storage multi-regional storage

    B. Cloud Storage Nearline storage

    C. Cloud Storage Coldline storage

    D. Cloud Bigtable

5. You will be developing machine learning models using sensitive data. Your company has several policies regarding protecting sensitive data, including requiring enhanced security on virtual machines (VMs) processing sensitive data. Which GCP service would you look to for meeting those requirements?

   A. Identity and access management (IAM)

   B. Cloud Key Management Service

   C. Cloud Identity

   D. Shielded VMs

6. You have developed a machine learning algorithm for identifying objects in images. Your company has a mobile app that allows users to upload images and get back a list of identified objects. You need to implement the mechanism to detect when a new image is uploaded to Cloud Storage and invoke the model to perform the analysis. Which GCP service would you use for that?

   A. Cloud Functions

   B. Cloud Storage Nearline

   C. Cloud Dataflow

   D. Cloud Dataproc

7. An IoT system streams data to a Cloud Pub/Sub topic for ingestion, and the data is processed in a Cloud Dataflow pipeline before being written to Cloud Bigtable. Latency is increasing as more data is added, even though nodes are not at maximum utilization. What would you look for first as a possible cause of this problem?

   A. Too many nodes in the cluster

   B. A poorly designed row key

   C. Too many column families

   D. Too many indexes being updated during write operations

8. A health and wellness startup in Canada has been more successful than expected. Investors are pushing the founders to expand into new regions outside of North America. The CEO and CTO are discussing the possibility of expanding into Europe. The app offered by the startup collects personal information, storing some locally on the user's device and some in the cloud. What regulation will the startup need to plan for before expanding into the European market?

   A. HIPAA

   B. PCI-DSS

   C. GDPR

   D. SOX

9. Your company has been collecting vehicle performance data for the past year and now has 500 TB of data. Analysts at the company want to analyze the data to understand performance differences better across classes of vehicles. The analysts are advanced SQL users, but not all have programming experience. They want to minimize administrative overhead by using a managed service, if possible. What service might you recommend for conducting preliminary analysis of the data?

    A. Compute Engine

    B. Kubernetes Engine

    C. BigQuery

    D. Cloud Functions

10. An airline is moving its luggage-tracking applications to Google Cloud. There are many requirements, including support for SQL and strong consistency. The database will be accessed by users in the United States, Europe, and Asia. The database will store approximately 50 TB in the first year and grow at approximately 10 percent a year after that. What managed database service would you recommend?

    A. Cloud SQL

    B. BigQuery

    C. Cloud Spanner

    D. Cloud Dataflow

11. You are using Cloud Firestore to store data about online game players' state while in a game. The state information includes health score, a set of possessions, and a list of team members collaborating with the player. You have noticed that the size of the raw data in the database is approximately 2 TB, but the amount of space used by Cloud Firestore is almost 5 TB. What could be causing the need for so much more space?

    A. The data model has been denormalized.

    B. There are multiple indexes.

    C. Nodes in the database cluster are misconfigured.

    D. There are too many column families in use.

12. You have a BigQuery table with data about customer purchases, including the date of purchase, the type of product purchases, the product name, and several other descriptive attributes. There is approximately three years of data. You tend to query data by month and then by customer. You would like to minimize the amount of data scanned. How would you organize the table?

    A. Partition by purchase date and cluster by customer

    B. Partition by purchase date and cluster by product

    C. Partition by customer and cluster by product

    D. Partition by customer and cluster by purchase date

13. You are currently using Java to implement an ELT pipeline in Hadoop. You'd like to replace your Java programs with a managed service in GCP. Which would you use?

    A. Data Studio

    B. Cloud Dataflow

    C. Cloud Bigtable

    D. BigQuery

14. A group of attorneys has hired you to help them categorize over a million documents in an intellectual property case. The attorneys need to isolate documents that are relevant to a patent that the plaintiffs argue has been infringed. The attorneys have 50,000 labeled examples of documents, and when the model is evaluated on training data, it performs quite well. However, when evaluated on test data, it performs quite poorly. What would you try to improve the performance?

    A. Perform feature engineering

    B. Perform validation testing

    C. Add more data

    D. Regularization

15. Your company is migrating from an on-premises pipeline that uses Apache Kafka for ingesting data and MongoDB for storage. What two managed services would you recommend as replacements for these?

    A. Cloud Dataflow and Cloud Bigtable

    B. Cloud Dataprep and Cloud Pub/Sub

    C. Cloud Pub/Sub and Cloud Firestore

    D. Cloud Pub/Sub and BigQuery

16. A group of data scientists is using Hadoop to store and analyze IoT data. They have decided to use GCP because they are spending too much time managing the Hadoop cluster. They are particularly interested in using services that would allow them to port their models and machine learning workflows to other clouds. What service would you use as a replacement for their existing platform?

    A. BigQuery

    B. Cloud Storage

    C. Cloud Dataproc

    D. Cloud Spanner

17. You are analyzing several datasets and will likely use them to build regression models. You will receive additional datasets, so you'd like to have a workflow to transform the raw data into a form suitable for analysis. You'd also like to work with the data in an interactive manner using Python. What services would you use in GCP?

    A. Cloud Dataflow and Data Studio

    B. Cloud Dataflow and Cloud Datalab

    C. Cloud Dataprep and Data Studio

    D. Cloud Datalab and Data Studio

18. You have a large number of files that you would like to store for several years. The files will be accessed frequently by users around the world. You decide to store the data in multi-regional Cloud Storage. You want users to be able to view files and their metadata in a Cloud Storage bucket. What role would you assign to those users? (Assume you are practicing the principle of least privilege.)

    A. roles/storage.objectCreator

    B. roles/storage.objectViewer

    C. roles/storage.admin

    D. roles/storage.bucketList

19. You have built a deep learning neural network to perform multiclass classification. You find that the model is overfitting. Which of the following would not be used to reduce overfitting?

    A. Dropout

    B. L2 Regularization

    C. L1 Regularization

    D. Logistic regression

20. Your company would like to start experimenting with machine learning, but no one in the company is experienced with ML. Analysts in the marketing department have identified some data in their relational database that they think may be useful for training a model. What would you recommend that they try first to build proof-of-concept models?

    A. AutoML Tables

    B. Kubeflow

    C. Cloud Firestore

    D. Spark MLlib

21. You have several large deep learning networks that you have built using TensorFlow. The models use only standard TensorFlow components. You have been running the models on an n1-highcpu-64 VM, but the models are taking longer to train than you would like. What would you try first to accelerate the model training?

    A. GPUs

    B. TPUs

    C. Shielded VMs

    D. Preemptible VMs

22. Your company wants to build a data lake to store data in its raw form for extended periods of time. The data lake should provide access controls, virtually unlimited storage, and the lowest cost possible. Which GCP service would you suggest?

    A. Cloud Bigtable

    B. BigQuery

    C. Cloud Storage

    D. Cloud Spanner

23. Auditors have determined that your company's processes for storing, processing, and transmitting sensitive data are insufficient. They believe that additional measures must be taken to prevent sensitive information, such as personally identifiable government-issued numbers, are not disclosed. They suggest masking or removing sensitive data before it is transmitted outside the company. What GCP service would you recommend?

    A. Data loss prevention API

    B. In-transit encryption

    C. Storing sensitive information in Cloud Key Management

    D. Cloud Dataflow

24. You are using Cloud Functions to start the processing of images as they are uploaded into Cloud Storage. In the past, there have been spikes in the number of images uploaded, and many instances of the Cloud Function were created at those times. What can you do to prevent too many instances from starting?

    A. Use the `--max-limit` parameter when deploying the function.

    B. Use the `--max-instances` parameter when deploying the function.

    C. Configure the `--max-instance` parameter in the resource hierarchy.

    D. Nothing. There is no option to limit the number of instances.

25. You have several analysis programs running in production. Sometimes they are failing, but there is no apparent pattern to the failures. You'd like to use a GCP service to record custom information from the programs so that you can better understand what is happening. Which service would you use?

    A. Stackdriver Debugger

    B. Stackdriver Logging

    C. Stackdriver Monitoring

    D. Stackdriver Trace

26. The CTO of your company is concerned about the rising costs of maintaining your company's enterprise data warehouse. The current data warehouse runs in a PostgreSQL instance. You would like to migrate to GCP and use a managed service that reduces operational overhead and one that will scale to meet future needs of up to 3 PB. What service would you recommend?

    A. Cloud SQL using PostgreSQL

    B. BigQuery

    C. Cloud Bigtable

    D. Cloud Spanner

Answers to Assessment Test

1. B. Cloud Dataproc is a Hadoop and Spark managed service. Option A is incorrect; Cloud Dataprep is service for preparing data for analysis. Option C is incorrect; Cloud Dataflow is an implementation of Apache Beam, a stream and batch processing service. Option D is incorrect; Cloud Pub/Sub is a messaging service that can buffer data in a topic until a service is ready to process the data.

2. C. Cloud Firestore is a managed document database that supports flexible schemas and transactions. Option A is incorrect; Cloud SQL does not support flexible schemas. Option B is incorrect; BigQuery is an analytical database, not a NoSQL database with a flexible schema. Option D is incorrect; Cloud Storage is an object storage system, not a NoSQL database.

3. C. The AI Platform is a managed service for machine learning, which is needed to provide recommendations. Options A and B are incorrect because, although they are useful for storing data, they do not provide managed machine learning services. Option D is incorrect; Cloud Datastore is a NoSQL database.

4. C. Cloud Storage Coldline is the lowest-cost option, and it is designed for data that is accessed less than once a year. Options A and B are incorrect because they cost more than Coldline storage. Option D is incorrect because Cloud Bigtable is a low-latency, wide-column database.

5. D. Shielded VMs are instances with additional security controls. Option A is incorrect; IAM is used for managing identities and authorizations. Option B is incorrect; the Cloud Key Management Service is a service for managing encryption keys. Option C is incorrect; Cloud Identity is used for authentication.

6. A. Cloud Functions is a managed serverless product that is able to respond to events in the cloud, such as creating a file in Cloud Storage. Option B is incorrect; Cloud Storage Nearline is a class of object storage. Option C is incorrect; Cloud Dataflow is a stream and batch processing service that does not respond to events. Option D is incorrect; Cloud Dataproc is a managed Hadoop and Spark service.

7. B. A poorly designed row key could be causing hot spotting. Option A is incorrect; more nodes in a cluster will not increase latency. Option C is incorrect; the number of column families on its own would not lead to higher latency. Option D is incorrect; Bigtable does not have indexes.

8. C. The General Data Protection Regulation (GDPR) is a European Union regulation protecting personal information of persons in and citizens of the European Union. Option A is incorrect; HIPAA is a U.S. healthcare regulation. Option B is incorrect; PCI-DSS is a self-imposed global security standard by major brands in the credit card industry, not a government regulation. Although not necessarily law, the standard may be applicable to the start-up in Europe if it accepts payment cards for brands that require PCI-DSS compliance. Option D is a U.S. regulation that applies to all publicly traded companies in the United States, and wholly-owned subsidiaries and foreign companies that are publicly traded and do business in the United States - the company may be subject to that regulation already, and expanding to Europe will not change its status.

9. **C.** BigQuery is an analytical database that supports SQL. Options A and B are incorrect because, although they could be used for ad hoc analysis, doing so would require more administrative overhead. Option D is incorrect; the Cloud Functions feature is intended for running short programs in response to events in GCP.

10. **C.** Cloud Spanner is a globally scalable, strongly consistent relational database that can be queried using SQL. Option A is incorrect because it will not scale to the global scale as Cloud Spanner will, and it does not support storing 50 TB of data. Option B is incorrect; the requirements call for a transaction processing system, and BigQuery is designed for analytics and data warehousing. Option D is incorrect; Cloud Dataflow is a stream and batch processing service.

11. **B.** Cloud Firestore stores data redundantly when multiple indexes are used, so having more indexes will lead to greater storage sizes. Option A is incorrect; Cloud Firestore is a NoSQL document database that supports a denormalized data model without using excessive storage. Option C is incorrect; you do not configure nodes in Cloud Firestore. Option D is incorrect; column families are not used with document databases such as Cloud Firestore.

12. **A.** Partitioning by purchase date will keep all data for a day in a single partition. Clustering by customer will order the data in a partition by customer. This strategy will minimize the amount of data that needs to be scanned in order to answer a query by purchase date and customer. Option B is incorrect; clustering by product does not help reduce the amount of data scanned for date and customer-based queries. Option C is incorrect because partitioning by customer is not helpful in reducing the amount of data scanned. Option D is incorrect because partitioning by customer would spread data from one date over many partitions, and that would lead to scanning more data than partitioning by purchase date.

13. **B.** Cloud Dataflow is a stream and batch processing managed service that is a good replacement for Java ELT programs. Option A is incorrect; Data Studio is a reporting tool. Option C is incorrect; Cloud Bigtable is a NoSQL, wide-column database. Option D is incorrect; BigQuery is an analytical database.

14. **D.** This is a case of the model overfitting the training data. Regularization is a set of methods used to reduce the risk of overfitting. Option A is incorrect; feature engineering could be used to create new features if the existing set of features was not sufficient, but that is not a problem in this case. Option B is incorrect; validation testing will not improve the quality of the model, but it will measure the quality. Option C is incorrect; the existing dataset has a sufficient number of training instances.

15. **C.** Cloud Pub/Sub is a good replacement for Kafka, and Cloud Firestore is a good replacement for MongoDB, which is another document database. Option A is incorrect; Cloud Dataflow is for stream and batch processing, not ingestion. Option B is incorrect; there is no database in the option. Option D is incorrect; BigQuery is analytical database and not a good replacement for a document database such as MongoDB.

16. C. Cloud Dataproc is a managed Hadoop and Spark service; Spark has a machine learning library called MLlib, and Spark is an open source platform that can run in other clouds. Option A is incorrect; BigQuery is a managed data warehouse and analytical database that is not available in other clouds. Option B is incorrect; Cloud Storage is used for unstructured data and not a substitute for a Hadoop/Spark platform. Option D is incorrect; Cloud Spanner is used for global transaction-processing systems, not large-scale analytics and machine learning.

17. B. Cloud Dataflow is well suited to transforming batch data, and Cloud Datalab is a Jupyter Notebook managed service, which is useful for ad hoc analysis using Python. Options A, B, and C are incorrect. Data Studio is a reporting tool, and that is not needed in this use case.

18. B. The `roles/storage.objectViewer` role allows users to view objects and list metadata. Option A is incorrect; `roles/storage.objectCreator` allows a user to create an object only. Option C is incorrect; the `roles/storage.admin` role gives a user full control over buckets and objects, which is more privilege than needed. Option D is incorrect; there is no such role as `roles/storage.bucketList`.

19. D. Logistic regression is a binary classifier algorithm. Options A, B, and C are all regularization techniques.

20. A. AutoML Tables is a service for generating machine learning models from structured data. Option B is incorrect; Kubeflow is an orchestration platform for running machine learning workloads in Kubernetes, which is more than is needed for this use case. Option C is incorrect; Cloud Firestore is a document database, not a machine learning service. Option D is incorrect because Spark MLlib requires more knowledge of machine learning than AutoML Tables, and therefore it is not as good an option for this use case.

21. B. TPUs are the correct accelerator because they are designed specifically to accelerate TensorFlow models. Option A is incorrect because, although GPUs would accelerate the model training, GPUs are not optimized for the low-precision matrix math that is performed when training deep learning networks. Option C is incorrect; shielded VMs have additional security controls, but they do not accelerate model training. Option D is incorrect; preemptible machines cost less than non-preemptible machines, but they do not provide acceleration.

22. C. Cloud Storage is an object storage system that meets all of the requirements. Option A is incorrect; Cloud Bigtable is a wide-column database. Option B is incorrect; BigQuery is an analytical database. Option D is incorrect; Cloud Spanner is a horizontally scalable relational database.

23. A. A data loss prevention API can be used to remove many forms of sensitive data, such as government identifiers. Option B is incorrect; encryption can help keep data from being read, but it does not remove or mask sensitive data. Option C is incorrect; Cloud Key Management is a service for storing and managing encryption keys. Option D is incorrect; Cloud Dataflow is a batch and stream processing service.

24. B. The `--max-instances` parameter limits the number of concurrently executing function instances. Option A is incorrect; `--max-limit` is not a parameter used with function deployments. Option C is incorrect; there is no `--max-instance` parameter to set in the resource hierarchy. Option D is incorrect; there is a way to specify a limit using the `--max-instances` parameter.

25. B. Stackdriver Logging is used to collect semi-structured data about events. Option A is incorrect; Stackdriver Debugger is used to inspect the state of running code. Option C is incorrect because Stackdriver Monitoring collects performance metrics, not custom data. Option D is incorrect; Stackdriver Trace is used to collect information about the time required to execute functions in a call stack.

26. B. BigQuery is a managed service that is well suited to data warehousing, and it can scale to petabytes of storage. Option A is incorrect; Cloud SQL will not scale to meet future needs. Option C is incorrect; Bigtable is a NoSQL, wide-column database, which is not suitable for use with a data warehouse design that uses a relational data model. Option D is incorrect; Cloud Spanner is a transactional, scalable relational database.

Chapter

1

Selecting Appropriate Storage Technologies

GOOGLE CLOUD PROFESSIONAL DATA ENGINEER EXAM OBJECTIVES COVERED IN THIS CHAPTER INCLUDE THE FOLLOWING:

1. Designing data processing systems

✓ **1.1 Selecting the appropriate storage technologies**

- Mapping storage systems to business requirements
- Data modeling
- Tradeoffs involving latency, throughput, transactions
- Distributed systems
- Schema design

Data engineers choose how to store data for many different situations. Sometimes data is written to a temporary staging area, where it stays only seconds or less before it is read by an application and deleted. In other cases, data engineers arrange long-term archival storage for data that needs to be retained for years. Data engineers are increasingly called on to work with data that streams into storage constantly and in high volumes. Internet of Things (IoT) devices are an example of streaming data.

Another common use case is storing large volumes of data for batch processing, including using data to train machine learning models. Data engineers also consider the range of variety in the structure of data. Some data, like the kind found in online transaction processing, is highly structured and varies little from one datum to the next. Other data, like product descriptions in a product catalog, can have a varying set of attributes. Data engineers consider these and other factors when choosing a storage technology.

This chapter covers objective 1.1 of the Google Cloud Professional Data Engineer exam—Selecting appropriate storage technologies. In this chapter, you will learn about the following:

- The business aspects of choosing a storage system
- The technical aspects of choosing a storage system
- The distinction between structured, semi-structured, and unstructured data models
- Designing schemas for relational and NoSQL databases

By the end of this chapter, you should understand the various criteria data engineers consider when choosing a storage technology. In Chapter 2, "Building and Operationalizing Storage Systems," we will delve into the details of Google Cloud storage services.

From Business Requirements to Storage Systems

Business requirements are the starting point for choosing a data storage system. Data engineers will use different types of storage systems for different purposes. The specific storage system you should choose is determined, in large part, by the stage of the data lifecycle for which the storage system is used.

The data lifecycle consists of four stages:

- Ingest
- Store
- Process and analyze
- Explore and visualize

Ingestion is the first stage in the data lifecycle, and it entails acquiring data and bringing data into the Google Cloud Platform (GCP). The *storage stage* is about persisting data to a storage system from which it can be accessed for later stages of the data lifecycle. The *process and analyze stage* begins with transforming data into a usable format for analysis applications. *Explore and visualize* is the final stage, in which insights are derived from analysis and presented in tables, charts, and other visualizations for use by others.

Ingest

The three broad ingestion modes with which data engineers typically work are as follows:

- Application data
- Streaming data
- Batch data

Application Data

Application data is generated by applications, including mobile apps, and pushed to back-end services. This data includes user-generated data, like a name and shipping address collected as part of a sales transaction. It also includes data generated by the application, such as log data. Event data, like clickstream data, is also a type of application-generated data. The volume of this kind of data depends on the number of users of the application, the types of data the application generates, and the duration of time the application is in use. This size of application data that is sent in a single operation can vary widely. A clickstream event may have less than 1KB of data, whereas an image upload could be multiple megabytes. Examples of application data include the following:

- Transactions from an online retail application
- Clickstream data from users reading articles on a news site
- Log data from a server running computer-aided design software
- User registration data from an online service

Application data can be ingested by services running in Compute Engine, Kubernetes Engine, or App Engine, for example. Application data can also be written to Stackdriver Logging or one of the managed databases, such as Cloud SQL or Cloud Datastore.

Streaming Data

Streaming data is a set of data that is typically sent in small messages that are transmitted continuously from the data source. Streaming data may be sensor data, which is data generated at regular intervals, and event data, which is data generated in response to a particular event. Examples of streaming data include the following:

- Virtual machine monitoring data, such as CPU utilization rates and memory consumption data
- An IoT device that sends temperature, humidity, and pressure data every minute
- A customer adding an item to an online shopping cart, which then generates an event with data about the customer and the item

Streaming data often includes a timestamp indicating the time that the data was generated. This is often called the *event time*. Some applications will also track the time that data arrives at the beginning of the ingestion pipeline. This is known as the *process time*. Time-series data may require some additional processing early in the ingestion process. If a stream of data needs to be in time order for processing, then late arriving data will need to be inserted in the correct position in the stream. This can require buffering of data for a short period of time in case the data arrives out of order. Of course, there is a maximum amount of time to wait before processing data. These and other issues related to processing streaming data are discussed in Chapter 4, "Designing a Data Processing Solution."

Streaming data is well suited for Cloud Pub/Sub ingestion, which can buffer data while applications process the data. During spikes in data ingestion in which application instances cannot keep up with the rate data is arriving, the data can be preserved in a Cloud Pub/Sub topic and processed later after application instances have a chance to catch up. Cloud Pub/Sub has global endpoints and uses GCP's global frontend load balancer to support ingestion. The messaging service scales automatically to meet the demands of the current workload.

Batch Data

Batch data is ingested in bulk, typically in files. Examples of batch data ingestion include uploading files of data exported from one application to be processed by another. Examples of batch data include the following:

- Transaction data that is collected from applications may be stored in a relational database and later exported for use by a machine learning pipeline
- Archiving data in long-term storage to comply with data retention regulations
- Migrating an application from on premises to the cloud by uploading files of exported data

Google Cloud Storage is typically used for batch uploads. It may also be used in conjunction with Cloud Transfer Service and Transfer Appliance when uploading large volumes of data.

Once data enters the GCP platform through ingestion, it can be stored for longer-term access by other applications or services.

Store

The focus of the storage stage of the data lifecycle is to make data available for transformation and analysis. Several factors influence the choice of storage system, including

- How the data is accessed—by individual record (row) or by an aggregation of columns across many records (rows)
- The way access controls need to be implemented, at the schema or database level or finer-grained level
- How long the data will be stored

These three characteristics are the minimum that should be considered when choosing a storage system; there may be additional criteria for some use cases. (Structure is another factor and is discussed later in this chapter.)

Data Access Patterns

Data is accessed in different ways. Online transaction processing systems often query for specific records using a set of filtering parameters. For example, an e-commerce application may need to look up a customer shipping address from a data store table that holds tens of thousands of addresses. Databases, like Cloud SQL and Cloud Datastore, provide that kind of query functionality.

In another example, a machine learning pipeline might begin by accessing files with thousands of rows of data that is used for training the model. Since machine learning models are often trained in batch mode, all of the training data is needed. Cloud Storage is a good option for storing data that is accessed in bulk.

If you need to access files using filesystem operations, then Cloud Filestore is a good option.

Access Controls

Security and access control in particular also influence how data is stored.

Relational databases, like Cloud SQL and Cloud Spanner, provide mechanisms to restrict access to tables and views. Some users can be granted permission to update data, whereas others can only view data, and still others are not allowed any direct access to data in the database. Fine-grained security can be implemented at the application level or by creating views that limit the data available to some users.

Some access controls are coarse grained. For example, Cloud Storage can limit access based on bucket permissions and access control lists on objects stored in a bucket. If a user has access to a file in the bucket, then they will have access to all the data in that file. Cloud Storage treats files as atomic objects; there is no concept of a row of data, for example, in Cloud Storage as there is in a relational database.

In some cases, you may be able to use other security features of a service along with access controls. BigQuery, for example, is an analytical database used for data warehousing, data analytics, and machine learning. Data is organized into datasets, which are groups of tables and views. At the current time, BigQuery supports dataset-level access controls but not access controls on tables or views directly. One way to work around these limitations is to create authorized views in one dataset that reference tables in another dataset. The dataset with the authorized views can have one set of access controls whereas the dataset with the source tables can have more restrictive access controls.

When choosing a data store, it is important to consider access control requirements and how well a storage system supports those requirements.

Time to Store

Consider how long data will be stored when choosing a data store. Some data is transient. For example, data that is needed only temporarily by an application running on a Compute Engine instance could be stored on a local solid-state drive (SSD) on the instance. As long as the data can be lost when the instance shuts down, this could be a reasonable option.

Data is often needed longer than the lifetime of a virtual machine instance, so other options are better fits for those cases. Cloud Storage is a good option for long-term storage, especially if you can make use of storage lifecycle policies to migrate older data to Nearline or Coldline storage. For long-lived analytics data, Cloud Storage or BigQuery are good options, since the costs are similar.

Nearline storage is used for data that is accessed less than once per 30 days. Coldline storage is used to store data accesses less than once per year.

Data that is frequently accessed is often well suited for either relational or NoSQL databases. As data ages, it may not be as likely to be accessed. In those cases, data can be deleted or exported and archived. If the data is not likely to be used for other purposes, such as machine learning, and there are no regulations that require you to keep the older data, then deleting it may be the best option. In cases where the data can be useful for other purposes or you are required to retain data, then exporting and storing it in Cloud Storage is an option. Then, if the data needs to be accessed, it can be imported to the database and queried there.

Process and Analyze

During the process and analyze stage, data is transformed into forms that make the data readily available to ad hoc querying or other forms of analysis.

Data Transformations

Transformations include data cleansing, which is the process of detecting erroneous data and correcting it. Some cleansing operations are based on the data type of expected data.

For example, a column of data containing only numeric data should not have alphabetic characters in the column. The cleansing process could delete rows of data that have alphabetic characters in that column. It could alternatively keep the row and substitute another value, such as a zero, or treat the value as NULL.

In other cases, business logic is applied to determine incorrect data. Some business logic rules may be simple, such as that an order date cannot be earlier than the date that the business began accepting orders. An example of a more complex rule is not allowing an order total to be greater than the credit limit assigned to a customer.

The decision to keep the row or delete it will depend on the particular use case. A set of telemetry data arriving at one-minute intervals may include an invalid value. In that case, the invalid value may be dropped without significantly affecting hour-level aggregates. A customer order that violates a business rule, however, might be kept because orders are significant business events. In this case, the order should be processed by an exception-handling process.

Transformations also include normalizing or standardizing data. For example, an application may expect phone numbers in North America to include a three-digit area code. If a phone number is missing an area code, the area code can be looked up based on the associated address. In another case, an application may expect country names specified using the International Organization for Standardization (ISO) 3166 alpha-3 country code, in which case data specifying Canada would be changed to CAN.

Cloud Dataflow is well suited to transforming both stream and batch data. Once data has been transformed, it is available for analysis.

Data Analysis

In the analyze stage, a variety of techniques may be used to extract useful information from data. Statistical techniques are often used with numeric data to do the following:

- Describe characteristics of a dataset, such as a mean and standard deviation of the dataset.
- Generate histograms to understand the distribution of values of an attribute.
- Find correlations between variables, such as customer type and average revenue per sales order.
- Make predictions using regression models, which allow you to estimate one attribute based on the value of another. In statistical terms, regression models generate predictions of a dependent variable based on the value of an independent variable.
- Cluster subsets of a dataset into groups of similar entities. For example, a retail sales dataset may yield groups of customers who purchase similar types of products and spend similar amounts over time.

Text data can be analyzed as well using a variety of techniques. A simple example is counting the occurrences of each word in a text. A more complex example is extracting entities, such as names of persons, businesses, and locations, from a document.

Cloud Dataflow, Cloud Dataproc, BigQuery, and Cloud ML Engine are all useful for data analysis.

Explore and Visualize

Often when working with new datasets, you'll find it helpful to explore the data and test a hypothesis. Cloud Datalab, which is based on Jupyter Notebooks (http://jupyter.org), is a GCP tool for exploring, analyzing, and visualizing data sets. Widely used data science and machine learning libraries, such as pandas, scikit-learn, and TensorFlow, can be used with Datalab. Analysts use Python or SQL to explore data in Cloud Datalab.

Google Data Studio is useful if you want tabular reports and basic charts. The drag-and-drop interface allows nonprogrammers to explore datasets without having to write code.

As you prepare for the Google Cloud Professional Data Engineer exam, keep in mind the four stages of the data lifecycle—ingestion, storage, process and analyze, and explore and visualize. They provide an organizing framework for understanding the broad context of data engineering and machine learning.

Technical Aspects of Data: Volume, Velocity, Variation, Access, and Security

GCP has a wide variety of data storage services. They are each designed to meet some use cases, but certainly not all of them. Earlier in the chapter, we considered data storage from a business perspective, and in this section, we will look into the more technical aspects of data storage. Some of the characteristics that you should keep in mind when choosing a storage technology are as follows:

- The volume and velocity of data
- Variation in structure
- Data access patterns
- Security requirements

Knowing one of these characteristics will not likely determine the single storage technology you should use. However, a single mismatch between the data requirements and a storage service's features can be enough to eliminate that service from consideration.

Volume

Some storage services are designed to store large volumes of data, including petabyte scales, whereas others are limited to smaller volumes.

Cloud Storage is an example of the former. An individual item in Cloud Storage can be up to 5 TB, and there is no limit to the number of read or write operations. Cloud Bigtable, which is used for telemetry data and large-volume analytic applications, can store up to 8 TB per node when using hard disk drives, and it can store up to 2.5 TB per node when using SSDs. Each Bigtable instance can have up to 1,000 tables. BigQuery, the managed data warehouse and analytics database, has no limit on the number of tables in a dataset, and it may have up to 4,000 partitions per table. Persistent disks, which can be attached to Compute Engine instances, can store up to 64 TB.

Single MySQL First Generation instances are limited to storing 500 GB of data. Second Generation instances of MySQL, PostgreSQL, and SQL Server can store up to 30 TB per instance. In general, Cloud SQL is a good choice for applications that need a relational database and that serve requests in a single region.

The limits specified here are the limits that Google has in place as of this writing. They may have changed by the time you read this. Always use Google Cloud documentation for the definitive limits of any GCP service.

Velocity

Velocity of data is the rate at which it is sent to and processed by an application. Web applications and mobile apps that collect and store human-entered data are typically low velocity, at least when measured by individual user. Machine-generated data, such IoT and time-series data, can be high velocity, especially when many different devices are generating data at short intervals of time. Here are some examples of various rates for low to high velocity:

- Nightly uploads of data to a data
- Hourly summaries of the number of orders taken in the last hour
- Analysis of the last three minutes of telemetry data
- Alerting based on a log message as soon as it is received is an example of real-time processing

If data is ingested and written to storage, it is important to match the velocity of incoming data with the rate at which the data store can write data. For example, Bigtable is designed for high-velocity data and can write up to 10,000 rows per second using a 10-node cluster with SSDs. When high-velocity data is processed as it is ingested, it is a good practice to write the data to a Cloud Pub/Sub topic. The processing application can then use a pull subscription to read the data at a rate that it can sustain. Cloud Pub/Sub is a scalable, managed messaging service that scales automatically. Users do not have to provision resources or configure scaling parameters.

At the other end of the velocity spectrum are low-velocity migrations or archiving operations. For example, an organization that uses the Transfer Appliance for large-scale migration may wait days before the data is available in Cloud Storage.

Variation in Structure

Another key attribute to consider when choosing a storage technology is the amount of variation that you expect in the data structure. Some data structures have low variance. For example, a weather sensor that sends temperature, humidity, and pressure readings at regular time intervals has virtually no variation in the data structure. All data sent to the storage system will have those three measures unless there is an error, such as a lost network packet or corrupted data.

Many business applications that use relational databases also have limited variation in data structure. For example, all customers have most attributes in common, such as name and address, but other business applications may have name suffixes, such as M.D. and Ph.D., stored in an additional field. In those cases, it is common to allow NULL values for attributes that may not be needed.

Not all business applications fit well into the rigid structure of strictly relational databases. NoSQL databases, such as MongoDB, CouchDB, and OrientDB, are examples of document databases. These databases use sets of key-value pairs to represent varying attributes. For example, instead of having a fixed set of attributes, like a relational database table, they include the attribute name along with the attribute value in the database (see Table 1.1).

TABLE 1.1   Example of structured, relational data

First_name	Last_name	Street_Address	City	Postal_Code
Michael	Johnson	334 Bay Rd	Santa Fe	87501
Wang	Li	74 Alder St	Boise	83701
Sandra	Connor	123 Main St	Los Angeles	90014

The data in the first row would be represented in a document database using a structure something like the following:

```
{
'first_name': 'Michael',
'last_name': 'Johnson'.
'street'_address': '334 Bay Rd',
'city': 'Santa Fe',
'postal_code': '87501'
}
```

Since most rows in a table of names and addresses will have the same attributes, it is not necessary to use a data structure like a document structure. Consider the case of a product catalog that lists both appliances and furniture. Here is an example of how a dishwasher and a chair might be represented:

```
{
{'id': '123456',
'product_type': 'dishwasher',
'length': '24 in',
'width': '34 in',
'weight': '175 lbs',
'power': '1800 watts'
}
{'id':'987654',
'product_type': 'chair',
'weight': '15 kg',
'style': 'modern',
'color': 'brown'
}
}
```

In addition to document databases, wide-column databases, such as Bigtable and Cassandra, are also used with datasets with varying attributes.

Data Access Patterns

Data is accessed in different ways for different use cases. Some time-series data points may be read immediately after they are written, but they are not likely to be read once they are more than a day old. Customer order data may be read repeatedly as an order is processed. Archived data may be accessed less than once a year. Four metrics to consider about data access are as follows:

- How much data is retrieved in a read operation?
- How much data is written in an insert operation?
- How often is data written?
- How often is data read?

Some read and write operations apply to small amounts of data. Reading or writing a single piece of telemetry data is an example. Writing an e-commerce transaction may also entail a small amount of data. A database storing telemetry data from thousands of sensors that push data every five seconds will be writing large volumes, whereas an online transaction processing database for a small online retailer will also write small individual units of data but at a much smaller rate. These will require different kinds of databases. The telemetry data, for example, is better suited to Bigtable, with its low-latency writes, and the retailer transaction data is a good use case for Cloud SQL, with support for sufficient I/O operations to handle relational database loads.

Cloud Storage supports ingesting large volumes of data in bulk using tools such as the Cloud Transfer Service and Transfer Appliance. (Cloud Storage also supports streaming transfers, but bulk reads and writes are more common.) Data in Cloud Storage is read at the object or the file level. You typically don't, for example, seek a particular block within a file as you can when storing a file on a filesystem.

It is common to read large volumes of data in BigQuery as well; however, in that case we often read a small number of columns across a large number of rows. BigQuery optimizes for these kinds of reads by using a columnar storage format known as Capacitor. *Capacitor* is designed to store semi-structured data with nested and repeated fields.

Data access patterns can help identify the best storage technology for a use case by highlighting key features needed to support those access patterns.

Security Requirements

Different storage systems will have different levels of access controls. Cloud Storage, for example, can have access controls at the bucket and the object level. If someone has access to a file in Cloud Storage, they will have access to all the data in that file. If some users have access only to a subset of a dataset, then the data could be stored in a relational database and a view could be created that includes only the data that the user is allowed to access.

Encrypting data at rest is an important requirement for many use cases; fortunately, all Google Cloud storage services encrypt data at rest.

When choosing a storage technology, the ability to control access to data is a key consideration.

Types of Structure: Structured, Semi-Structured, and Unstructured

For the purposes of choosing a storage technology, it is helpful to consider how data is structured. There are three widely recognized categories:

- Structured
- Semi-structured
- Unstructured

These categories are particularly helpful when choosing a database.

Structured Data   *Structured data* has a fixed set of attributes that can be modeled in a table of rows and columns.

Semi-Structured Data   *Semi-structured data* has attributes like structured data, but the set of attributes can vary from one instance to another. For example, a product description of an appliance might include length, width, height, weight, and power consumption. A chair in the same catalog might have length, width, height, color, and style as attributes. Semi-structured data may be organized using arrays or sets of key-value pairs.

Unstructured Data   *Unstructured data* does not fit into a tabular structure. Images and audio files are good examples of unstructured data. In between these two extremes lies semi-structured data, which has characteristics of both structured and unstructured.

Structured: Transactional vs. Analytical

Structured data can be represented in tables of columns and rows, where columns are attributes and rows are records or entities. Table 1.1 showed an example of structured data. Structured data may be oriented to transactional processes or analytical use cases.

Transactional structured data is often operated on one row at a time. For example, a business application may look up a customer's account information from a customer table when displaying data about the customer's shipping address. Multiple columns from a single row will be used, so it is efficient to store all row attributes together in a data block. Retrieving a single data block will retrieve all the needed data. This is a common pattern in transactional databases such as Cloud SQL and Cloud Spanner, which use row-oriented storage.

Now consider a data warehousing example. A business analyst is working with a sales data mart and wants to understand how sales last month compare to the same period last year. The data mart has one row for each product on each date, which include the following attributes in addition to product and date: number of units sold, total revenue for units sold, average unit price, average marginal revenue, and total marginal revenue. The analyst is only interested in the monthly sums of total revenue for units sold for each product. In this case, the analyst would query many rows and only three columns. Instead of retrieving the full row for all rows selected, it is more efficient to retrieve only the date, product, and total revenue of units sold columns. This is a common pattern in analytical applications and the reason why BigQuery uses a column-oriented storage mechanism.

Semi-Structured: Fully Indexed vs. Row Key Access

Semi-structured data, as noted earlier, does not follow a fixed tabular format and instead stores schema attributes along with the data. In the case of document databases, this allows developers to add attributes as needed without making changes to a fixed database schema. Two ways of storing semi-structured data are as documents or as wide columns. An important distinction between the two is how data is retrieved from them.

Fully Indexed, Semi-Structured Data

Let's consider the simple product catalog example again. There are many ways that shoppers might want to search for information about products. If they are looking for a dishwasher, for example, they might want to search based on size or power consumption. When searching for furniture, style and color are important considerations.

```
{
{'id': '123456',
'product_type': 'dishwasher',
'length': '24 in',
'width': '34 in',
'weight': '175 lbs',
'power': '1800 watts'
}
{'id':'987654',
'product_type': 'chair',
'weight': '15 kg',
'style': 'modern',
'color': 'brown'
}
}
```

To search efficiently by attributes, document databases allow for indexes. If you use Cloud Datastore, for example, you could create indexes on each of the attributes as well as a combination of attributes. Indexes should be designed to support the way that data is queried. If you expect users to search for chairs by specifying style and color together, then you should create a style and color index. If you expect customers to search for appliances by their power consumption, then you should create an index on power.

Creating a large number of indexes can significantly increase the amount of storage used. In fact, it is not surprising to have total index storage greater than the amount of storage used to store documents. Also, additional indexes can negatively impact performance for insert, update, and delete operations, because the indexes need to be revised to reflect those operations.

Row Key Access

Wide-column databases usually take a different approach to querying. Rather than using indexes to allow efficient lookup of rows with needed data, wide-column databases organize data so that rows with similar row keys are close together. Queries use a row key, which is analogous to a primary key in relational databases, to retrieve data. This has two implications.

Tables in wide-column databases are designed to respond to particular queries. Although relational databases are designed according to forms of normalization that minimize the risk of data anomalies, wide-column databases are designed for low-latency reads and writes at high volumes. This can lead to duplication of data. Consider IoT sensor data stored in a wide-column database. Table 1.2 shows IoT data organized by sensor ID and timestamp (milliseconds since January 1, 1970 00:00:00 UTC). Future rows would feature the same sensor ID but different corresponding timestamps, and the row key would be determined by both.

TABLE 1.2   IoT data by sensor ID and timestamp

Sensor ID	Timestamp	Temperature	Relative humidity	Pressure
789	1571760690	40	35	28.2
790	1571760698	42.5	50	29.1
791	1571760676	37	61	28.6

Table 1.2 is organized to answer queries that require looking up data by sensor ID and then time. It is not well suited for looking up data by time—for example, all readings over the past hour. Rather than create an index on timestamp, wide-column databases duplicate data in a different row key order. Table 1.3, for example, is designed to answer time range queries. Note that a new table must be created with the desired schema to accomplish this—there is no index that is used to support the query pattern.

TABLE 1.3   IoT data by timestamp and sensor ID

Timestamp	Sensor ID	Temperature	Relative humidity	Pressure
1571760676	791	37	61	28.6
1571760690	789	40	35	28.2
1571760698	790	42.5	50	29.1

Unstructured Data

The distinguishing characteristic of unstructured data is that it does not have a defined schema or data model. Structured data, like relational database tables, has a fixed data model that is defined before data is added to the table. Semi-structured databases include a schema with each row or document in the database. Examples of unstructured data include the following:

- Text files of natural language content
- Audio files
- Video files
- Binary large objects (BLOBs)

It should be pointed out that data is considered unstructured if it does not have a schema that influences how the data is stored or accessed. Unstructured data may have an internal structure that is not relevant to the way it is stored. For example, natural language is highly structured according to the syntax rules of languages. Audio and video files may have an internal format that includes metadata as well as content. Here again, there is structure within the file, but that structure is not used by storage systems, and that is the reason why this kind of data is classified as unstructured.

Google's Storage Decision Tree

Google has developed a decision tree for choosing a storage system that starts with distinguishing structured, semi-structured, and unstructured data. Figure 1.1 is based on the decision tree published at https://cloud.google.com/solutions/data-lifecycle-cloud-platform.

FIGURE 1.1   Choosing a storage technology in GCP

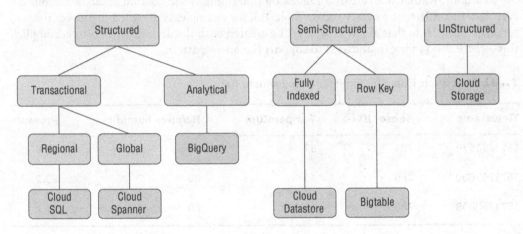

Schema Design Considerations

Structured and semi-structured data has a schema associated with it. Structured data is usually stored in relational databases whereas semi-structured data is often stored in NoSQL databases. The *schema* influences how data is stored and accessed, so once you have determined which kind of storage technology to use, you may then need to design a schema that will support optimal storage and retrieval.

The distinction between relational and NoSQL databases is becoming less pronounced as each type adopts features of the other. Some relational databases support storing and querying JavaScript Object Notation (JSON) structures, similar to the way that document databases do. Similarly, some NoSQL databases now support ACID (atomicity, consistency, isolation, durability) transactions, which are a staple feature of relational databases.

Relational Database Design

Data modeling for relational databases begins with determining which type of relational database you are developing: an online transaction processing (OLTP) database or an online analytical processing (OLAP) database.

OLTP

Online transaction processing (OLTP) databases are designed for transaction processing and typically follow data normalization rules. There are currently 10 recognized forms of normalization, but most transaction processing systems follow no more than three of those forms:

- The *first form of normalization* requires that each column in the table have an atomic value, no repeating groups, and a primary key, which is one or more ordered columns that uniquely identify a row.

- The *second form of normalization* includes the first form and creates separate tables for values that apply to multiple rows and links them using foreign keys. A *foreign key* is one or more ordered columns that correspond to a primary key in another table.

- The *third form of normalization*, which includes the second form, eliminates any columns from a table that does not depend on the key.

These rules of normalization are designed to reduce the risk of data anomalies and to avoid the storage of redundant data. Although they serve those purposes well, they can lead to high levels of I/O operations when joining tables or updating a large number of indexes. Using an OLTP data model requires a balance between following the rules of normalization to avoid anomalies and designing for performance.

Denormalization—that is, intentionally violating one of the rules of normalization—is often used to improve query performance. For example, repeating customer names in both the customer table and an order table could avoid having to join the two tables when printing invoices. By denormalizing, you can reduce the need to join tables since the data that would have been in another table is stored along with other data in the row of one table.

OLAP

Online analytical processing (OLAP) data models are often used for data warehouse and data mart applications. OLAP models are also called *dimensional models* because data is organized around several dimensions. OLAP models are designed to facilitate the following:

- Rolling up and aggregating data
- Drilling down from summary data to detailed data
- Pivoting and looking at data from different dimensions—sometimes called *slicing and dicing*

OLAP can be implemented in relational database or in specialized multidimensional data stores.

SQL Crash Course

In-depth knowledge of SQL is not necessarily required to pass the Google Cloud Professional Data Engineer exam, but knowledge of SQL may help if a question includes a SQL statement.

SQL has three types of statements that developers use:

- *Data definition language (DDL) statements*, which are used to create and modify database schemas

- *Data manipulation language (DML) statements*, which are used to insert, update, delete, and query data

- *Data query language (DQL) statements*, which is a single statement: SELECT

Table 1.4 shows examples of data definition statements and their function. Table 1.5 shows data manipulation examples, and Table 1.6 shows query language examples.

TABLE 1.4 Data definition language examples

DDL statement	Example	Explanation
CREATE TABLE	CREATE TABLE address (address_id INT PRIMARY KEY, street_name VARCHAR(50), city VARCHAR(50), state VARCHAR(2));	Creates a table with four columns. The first is an integer and the primary key; the other three are variable-length character strings.
CREATE INDEX	CREATE INDEX addr_idx ON address(state);	Creates an index on the state column of the address table.
ALTER TABLE	ALTER TABLE address ADD (zip VARCHAR(9));	Adds a column called zip to the address table. ALTER is also used to modify and drop entities.
DROP INDEX	DROP INDEX addr_idx;	Deletes the index addr_idx.

TABLE 1.5   Data manipulation language examples

Data Manipulation Language

DML Statement	Example	Explanation
INSERT	INSERT INTO address VALUES (1234, '56 Main St', 'Seattle', 'WA');	Adds rows to the table with the specified values, which are in column order
UPDATE	UPDATE address SET state = 'OR'	Sets the value of the state column to 'OR' for all rows
DELETE	DELETE FROM address WHERE state = 'OR'	Removes all rows that have the value 'OR' in the state column

TABLE 1.6   Data query language examples

Data Query Language

DDL statement	Example	Explanation
SELECT … FROM	SELECT address_id, state FROM address	Returns the address_id and state values for all rows in the address table
SELECT … FROM … WHERE	SELECT address_id, state FROM address WHERE state = 'OR'	Returns the address_id and state values for all rows in the address table that have the value 'OR' in the state column
SELECT … FROM … GROUP BY	SELECT state, COUNT(*) FROM address GROUP BY state	Returns the number of addresses in each state
SELECT … FROM … GROUP BY … HAVING	SELECT state, COUNT(*) FROM address GROUP BY state HAVING COUNT(*) > 50	Returns the number of addresses in each state that has at least 50 addresses

NoSQL Database Design

NoSQL databases are less structured than relational databases, and there is no formal model, like relational algebra and forms of normalization, that apply to all NoSQL databases. The four types of NoSQL databases available in GCP are

- Key-value
- Document
- Wide column
- Graph

Each type of NoSQL database is suited for different use cases depending on data ingestion, entity relationships, and query requirements.

Key-Value Data Stores

Key-value data stores are databases that use associative arrays or dictionaries as the basic datatype. Keys are data used to look up values. An example of key-value data is shown in Table 1.7, which displays a mapping from names of machine instances to names of partitions associated with each instance.

TABLE 1.7   Examples of key-value data

Key	Value
Instance1	PartitionA
Instance2	PartitionB
Instance3	PartitionA
Instance4	PartitionC

Key-value data stores are simple, but it is possible to have more complex data structures as values. For example, a JSON object could be stored as a value. This would be reasonable use of a key-value data store if the JSON object was only looked up by the key, and there was no need to search on items within the JSON structure. In situations where items in the JSON structure should be searchable, a document database would be a better option.

Cloud Memorystore is a fully managed key-value data store based on Redis, a popular open source key-value datastore. As of this writing, Cloud Memorystore does not support persistence, so it should not be used for applications that do not need to save data to persistent storage. Open source Redis does support persistence. If you wanted to use Redis for a key-value store and wanted persistent storage, then you could run and manage your own Redis service in Compute Engine or Kubernetes Engine.

Document Databases

Document stores allow complex data structures, called *documents*, to be used as values and accessed in more ways than simple key lookup. When designing a data model for *document databases*, documents should be designed to group data that is read together.

Consider an online game that requires a database to store information about players' game state. The player state includes

- Player name
- Health score
- List of possessions
- List of past session start and end times
- Player ID

The player name, health score, and list of possessions are often read together and displayed for players. The list of sessions is used only by analysts reviewing how players use the game. Since there are two different use cases for reading the data, there should be two different documents. In this case, the first three attributes should be in one document along with the player ID, and the sessions should be in another document with player ID.

When you need a managed document database in GCP, use Cloud Datastore. Alternatively, if you wish to run your own document database, MongoDB, CouchDB, and OrientDB are options.

Wide-Column Databases

Wide-column databases are used for use cases with the following:

- High volumes of data
- Need for low-latency writes
- More write operations than read operations
- Limited range of queries—in other words, no ad hoc queries
- Lookup by a single key

Wide-column databases have a data model similar to the tabular structure of relational tables, but there are significant differences. Wide-column databases are often sparse, with the exception of IoT and other time-series databases that have few columns that are almost always used.

Bigtable is GCP's managed wide-column database. It is also a good option for migrating on-premises Hadoop HBase databases to a managed database because Bigtable has an HBase interface. If you wish to manage your own wide column, Cassandra is an open source option that you can run in Compute Engine or Kubernetes Engine.

Graph Databases

Another type of NoSQL database are *graph databases*, which are based on modeling entities and relationships as nodes and links in a graph or network. Social networks are a good example of a use case for graph databases. People could be modeled as nodes in the graph, and relationships between people are links, also called *edges*. For example, Figure 1.2 shows an example graph of friends showing Chengdong with the most friends, 6, and Lem with the fewest, 1.

FIGURE 1.2   Example graph of friends

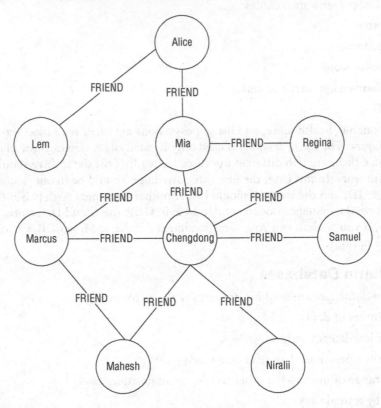

Data is retrieved from a graph using one of two types of queries. One type of query uses SQL-like declarative statements describing patterns to look for in a graph, such as the following the Cypher query language. This query returns a list of persons and friends of that person's friends:

```
MATCH (n:Person)-[:FRIEND]-(f)
MATCH (n)-[:FRIEND]-()-[:FRIEND]-(fof)
RETURN n, fof
```

The other option is to use a traversal language, such as Gremlin, which specifies how to move from node to node in the graph.

GCP does not have a managed graph database, but Bigtable can be used as the storage backend for HGraphDB (https://github.com/rayokota/hgraphdb) or JanusGraph (https://janusgraph.org).

Exam Essentials

Know the four stages of the data lifecycle: ingest, storage, process and analyze, and explore and visualize.   Ingestion is the process of bringing application data, streaming data, and batch data into the cloud. The storage stage focuses on persisting data to an appropriate storage system. Processing and analyzing is about transforming data into a form suitable for analysis. Exploring and visualizing focuses on testing hypotheses and drawing insights from data.

Understand the characteristics of streaming data.   Streaming data is a set of data that is sent in small messages that are transmitted continuously from the data source. Streaming data may be telemetry data, which is data generated at regular intervals, and event data, which is data generated in response to a particular event. Stream ingestion services need to deal with potentially late and missing data. Streaming data is often ingested using Cloud Pub/Sub.

Understand the characteristics of batch data.   Batch data is ingested in bulk, typically in files. Examples of batch data ingestion include uploading files of data exported from one application to be processed by another. Both batch and streaming data can be transformed and processed using Cloud Dataflow.

Know the technical factors to consider when choosing a data store.   These factors include the volume and velocity of data, the type of structure of the data, access control requirements, and data access patterns.

Know the three levels of structure of data.   These levels are structured, semi-structured, and unstructured. Structured data has a fixed schema, such as a relational database table. Semi-structured data has a schema that can vary; the schema is stored with data. Unstructured data does not have a structure used to determine how to store data.

Know which Google Cloud storage services are used with the different structure types.   Structured data is stored in Cloud SQL and Cloud Spanner if it is used with a transaction processing system; BigQuery is used for analytical applications of structured data. Semi-structured data is stored in Cloud Datastore if data access requires full indexing; otherwise, it can be stored in Bigtable. Unstructured data is stored in Cloud Storage.

Know the difference between relational and NoSQL databases.   Relational databases are used for structured data whereas NoSQL databases are used for semi-structured data. The four types of NoSQL databases are key-value, document, wide-column, and graph databases.

Review Questions

You can find the answers in the appendix.

1. A developer is planning a mobile application for your company's customers to use to track information about their accounts. The developer is asking for your advice on storage technologies. In one case, the developer explains that they want to write messages each time a significant event occurs, such as the client opening, viewing, or deleting an account. This data is collected for compliance reasons, and the developer wants to minimize administrative overhead. What system would you recommend for storing this data?

    A. Cloud SQL using MySQL

    B. Cloud SQL using PostgreSQL

    C. Cloud Datastore

    D. Stackdriver Logging

2. You are responsible for developing an ingestion mechanism for a large number of IoT sensors. The ingestion service should accept data up to 10 minutes late. The service should also perform some transformations before writing the data to a database. Which of the managed services would be the best option for managing late arriving data and performing transformations?

    A. Cloud Dataproc

    B. Cloud Dataflow

    C. Cloud Dataprep

    D. Cloud SQL

3. A team of analysts has collected several CSV datasets with a total size of 50 GB. They plan to store the datasets in GCP and use Compute Engine instances to run RStudio, an interactive statistical application. Data will be loaded into RStudio using an RStudio data loading tool. Which of the following is the most appropriate GCP storage service for the datasets?

    A. Cloud Storage

    B. Cloud Datastore

    C. MongoDB

    D. Bigtable

4. A team of analysts has collected several terabytes of telemetry data in CSV datasets. They plan to store the datasets in GCP and query and analyze the data using SQL. Which of the following is the most appropriate GCP storage service for the datasets?

    A. Cloud SQL

    B. Cloud Spanner

    C. BigQuery

    D. Bigtable

5. You have been hired to consult with a startup that is developing software for self-driving vehicles. The company's product uses machine learning to predict the trajectory of persons and vehicles. Currently, the software is being developed using 20 vehicles, all located in the same city. IoT data is sent from vehicles every 60 seconds to a MySQL database running on a Compute Engine instance using an n2-standard-8 machine type with 8 vCPUs and 16 GB of memory. The startup wants to review their architecture and make any necessary changes to support tens of thousands of self-driving vehicles, all transmitting IoT data every second. The vehicles will be located across North America and Europe. Approximately 4 KB of data is sent in each transmission. What changes to the architecture would you recommend?

   A. None. The current architecture is well suited to the use case.

   B. Replace Cloud SQL with Cloud Spanner.

   C. Replace Cloud SQL with Bigtable.

   D. Replace Cloud SQL with Cloud Datastore.

6. As a member of a team of game developers, you have been tasked with devising a way to track players' possessions. Possessions may be purchased from a catalog, traded with other players, or awarded for game activities. Possessions are categorized as clothing, tools, books, and coins. Players may have any number of possessions of any type. Players can search for other players who have particular possession types to facilitate trading. The game designer has informed you that there will likely be new types of possessions and ways to acquire them in the future. What kind of a data store would you recommend using?

   A. Transactional database

   B. Wide-column database

   C. Document database

   D. Analytic database

7. The CTO of your company wants to reduce the cost of running an HBase and Hadoop cluster on premises. Only one HBase application is run on the cluster. The cluster currently supports 10 TB of data, but it is expected to double in the next six months. Which of the following managed services would you recommend to replace the on-premises cluster in order to minimize migration and ongoing operational costs?

   A. Cloud Bigtable using the HBase API

   B. Cloud Dataflow using the HBase API

   C. Cloud Spanner

   D. Cloud Datastore

8. A genomics research institute is developing a platform for analyzing data related to genetic diseases. The genomics data is in a specialized format known as FASTQ, which stores nucleotide sequences and quality scores in a text format. Files may be up to 400 GB and are uploaded in batches. Once the files finish uploading, an analysis pipeline runs, reads the data in the FASTQ file, and outputs data to a database. What storage system is a good option for storing the uploaded FASTQ data?

   A. Cloud Bigtable

   B. Cloud Datastore

   C. Cloud Storage

   D. Cloud Spanner

9. A genomics research institute is developing a platform for analyzing data related to genetic diseases. The genomics data is in a specialized format known as FASTQ, which stores nucleotide sequences and quality scores in a text format. Once the files finish uploading, an analysis pipeline runs, reads the data in the FASTQ file, and outputs data to a database. The output is in tabular structure, the data is queried using SQL, and typically queries retrieve only a small number of columns but many rows. What database would you recommend for storing the output of the workflow?

A. Cloud Bigtable

B. Cloud Datastore

C. Cloud Storage

D. BigQuery

10. You are developing a new application and will be storing semi-structured data that will only be accessed by a single key. The total volume of data will be at least 40 TB. What GCP database service would you use?

A. BigQuery

B. Bigtable

C. Cloud Spanner

D. Cloud SQL

11. A group of climate scientists is collecting weather data every minute from 10,000 sensors across the globe. Data often arrives near the beginning of a minute, and almost all data arrives within the first 30 seconds of a minute. The data ingestion process is losing some data because servers cannot ingest the data as fast as it is arriving. The scientists have scaled up the number of servers in their managed instance group, but that has not completely eliminated the problem. They do not wish to increase the maximum size of the managed instance group. What else can the scientists do to prevent data loss?

A. Write data to a Cloud Dataflow stream

B. Write data to a Cloud Pub/Sub topic

C. Write data to Cloud SQL table

D. Write data to Cloud Dataprep

12. A software developer asks your advice about storing data. The developer has hundreds of thousands of 1 KB JSON objects that need to be accessed in sub-millisecond times if possible. All objects are referenced by a key. There is no need to look up values by the contents of the JSON structure. What kind of NoSQL database would you recommend?

A. Key-value database

B. Analytical database

C. Wide-column database

D. Graph database

13. A software developer asks your advice about storing data. The developer has hundreds of thousands of 10 KB JSON objects that need to be searchable by most attributes in the JSON structure. What kind of NoSQL database would you recommend?

    A. Key-value database

    B. Analytical database

    C. Wide-column database

    D. Document database

14. A data modeler is designing a database to support ad hoc querying, including drilling down and slicing and dicing queries. What kind of data model is the data modeler likely to use?

    A. OLTP

    B. OLAP

    C. Normalized

    D. Graph

15. A multinational corporation is building a global inventory database. The database will support OLTP type transactions at a global scale. Which of the following would you consider as possible databases for the system?

    A. Cloud SQL and Cloud Spanner

    B. Cloud SQL and Cloud Datastore

    C. Cloud Spanner only

    D. Cloud Datastore only

Chapter

2

Building and Operationalizing Storage Systems

GOOGLE CLOUD PROFESSIONAL DATA ENGINEER EXAM OBJECTIVES COVERED IN THIS CHAPTER INCLUDE THE FOLLOWING:

1. Designing data processing systems

✓ 1.2 **Designing data pipelines. Considerations include:**

- Data publishing and visualization (e.g., BigQuery)

- Batch and streaming data (e.g., Cloud Dataflow, Cloud Dataproc, Apache Beam, Apache Spark and Hadoop ecosystem, Cloud Pub/Sub, Apache Kafka)

- Online (interactive) vs. batch predictions

- Job automation and orchestration (e.g., Cloud Composer)

Not only are data engineers expected to understand when to use various ingestion and storage technologies, but they should also be familiar with deploying and operating those systems. In this chapter, you will learn how to deploy storage systems and perform data management operations, such as importing and exporting data, configuring access controls, and doing performance tuning. The services included in this chapter are as follows:

- Cloud SQL
- Cloud Spanner
- Cloud Bigtable
- Cloud Firestore
- BigQuery
- Cloud Memorystore
- Cloud Storage

The chapter also includes a discussion of working with unmanaged databases, storage costs and performance, and data lifecycle management.

Cloud SQL

Cloud SQL is a fully managed relational database service that supports MySQL, PostgreSQL, and SQL Server databases. As of this writing, SQL Server is in beta release. A managed database is one that does not require as much administration and operational support as an unmanaged database because Google will take care of core operational tasks, such as creating databases, performing backups, and updating the operating system of database instances. Google also manages scaling disks, configuring for failover, monitoring, and authorizing network connections.

Cloud SQL supports regional-level databases of up to 30 TB. If you need to store more data or need multi-regional support, consider using Cloud Spanner.

Cloud SQL currently offers First Generation and Second Generation instances. Second Generation instances are generally faster, larger, and less costly than First Generation instances. Support for First Generation ended on January 30, 2020. Unless otherwise stated, the following will describe Second Generation features and operations.

Configuring Cloud SQL

The first step to deploying a Cloud SQL database is choosing which of the three relational database management systems (RDBMSs) you will use. The configuration process is similar for the various types of databases and include specifying the following:

- An instance ID
- A password
- A region and zone
- A database version

   With Cloud SQL, you can choose your machine type, which determines the number of virtual CPUs (vCPUs) and the amount of memory available. Second Generation instances support up to 64 CPUs and 416 GB of memory. Note that these limits may have changed by the time you read this (see Figure 2.1).

FIGURE 2.1   Basic Cloud SQL configuration

   Optionally, you can also specify the use of a public or private IP address for the instance; a public IP is assigned by default. When using a public IP, you will need to specify one or more external networks that connect to the database instance. Alternatively, you could connect to the database using Cloud SQL Proxy, which provides secure access to Second Generation instances without having to create allow lists or to configure SSL. The proxy manages authentication and automatically encrypts data.

Cloud SQL will perform daily backups, and you can specify a four-hour time window during the time that the backup will occur. You can also specify the day and time for a maintenance window. Backups are deleted when an instance is deleted. Keep in mind that you cannot restore individual tables from a backup. To maintain a copy of the data after an instance is deleted or to restore individual tables or databases, use exports, which are discussed in a moment.

Although Google manages the creation of a database, you do have the option of specifying database flags, which are RDBMS specific (see Figure 2.2).

FIGURE 2.2 Optional configuration parameters in Cloud SQL

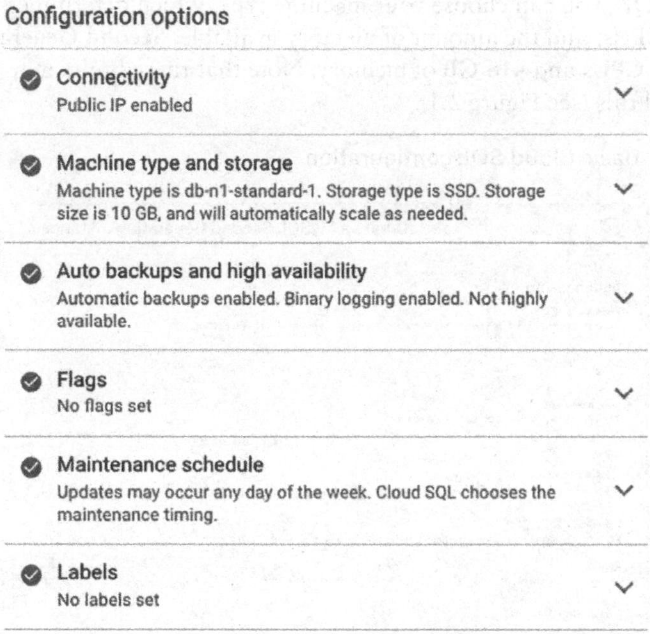

Configuration options

✓ **Connectivity**
Public IP enabled   ⌄

✓ **Machine type and storage**
Machine type is db-n1-standard-1. Storage type is SSD. Storage   ⌄
size is 10 GB, and will automatically scale as needed.

✓ **Auto backups and high availability**
Automatic backups enabled. Binary logging enabled. Not highly   ⌄
available.

✓ **Flags**
No flags set   ⌄

✓ **Maintenance schedule**
Updates may occur any day of the week. Cloud SQL chooses the   ⌄
maintenance timing.

✓ **Labels**
No labels set   ⌄

By default, a Cloud SQL instance is created with one instance in a single zone. If you want to be sure that your application can still access data when a single instance is down for any reason, which is recommended for production systems, you should choose the High Availability option. That will create a second instance in a second zone and synchronously replicate data from the primary instance to the standby instance. If the primary instance becomes nonresponsive, Cloud SQL will fail over or switch to using the secondary instance.

It is a good practice to shard your data into smaller databases rather than have a single monolithic database. The best way to shard will depend on the use case. If data is often queried using time as a selection criterion, sharding by time makes sense. In other cases, sharding by some other attribute, such as geographic region, might make more sense. Smaller databases are easier to manage. Also, if there is an incident involving one instance, the impact is limited to data on the one instance.

Databases should not have more than 10,000 tables. All tables should have a primary key to facilitate row-based replication.

Improving Read Performance with Read Replicas

You can improve the performance of read-heavy databases by using read replicas. A *read replica* is a copy of the primary instance's data that is maintained in the same region as the primary instance. Applications can read from the read replica and allow the primary instance to handle write operations. Here are some things to keep in mind about read replicas:

- Read replicas are not designed for high availability; Cloud SQL does not fail over to a read replica.

- Binary logging must be enabled to support read replicas.

- Maintenance on read replicas is not limited to maintenance windows—it can occur at any time and disrupt operations.

- A primary instance can have multiple read replicas, but Cloud SQL does not load-balance between them.

- You cannot perform backups on a read replica.

- Read replicas can be promoted to a standalone Cloud SQL. The operation is irreversible.

- The primary instance cannot be restored from backup if a read replica exists; it will have to be deleted or promoted.

- Read replicas must be in the same region as the primary instance.

Importing and Exporting Data

Data can be imported and exported from Cloud SQL databases. Each RDBMS has an import and an export program.

- MySQL provides mysqldump.

- PostgreSQL provides pg_dump.

- SQL Server provides bcp, which stands for bulk copy program.

In general, data is imported from and exported to Cloud Storage buckets. Files can be in either CSV or SQL dump format.

It should be noted that when you are using the command line to export a database, you must use particular flags to create a file that can later be imported. For Cloud SQL to import correctly, you will need to exclude views, triggers, stored procedures, and functions. Those database objects will have to be re-created using scripts after a database has been imported.

Both SQL Dump and CSV formats can be compressed to save on storage costs. It is possible to import from a compressed file and export to a compressed file.

Cloud SQL is well suited for regional applications that do not need to store more than 30 TB of data in a single instance. Cloud Spanner is used for more demanding database systems.

Cloud Spanner

Cloud Spanner is Google's relational, horizontally scalable, global database. It is a relational database, so it supports fixed schemas and is ANSI SQL 2011 compliant. Cloud Spanner provides strong consistency, so all parallel processes see the same state of the database. This consistency is different from NoSQL databases, which are generally eventually consistent, allowing parallel processes to see different states of the database.

Cloud Spanner is highly available and does not require failover instances in the way that Cloud SQL does. It also manages automatic replication.

Configuring Cloud Spanner

Cloud Spanner configuration is similar to Cloud SQL. When creating a Cloud Spanner instance, you specify the following:

- An instance name
- An instance ID
- Regional or Multi-Regional
- Number of nodes
- Region in which to create the instance

The choice of regional or multi-regional and the number of nodes determines the cost of an instance. A single node in a regional instance in us-west1 currently costs $0.90/hour, whereas a multi-regional instance in nam-eur-asia1 costs $9.00/hour. The number of nodes you choose is usually dictated by your workload requirements. Google recommends keeping CPU utilization below 65 percent in regional instances and below 45 percent in multi-regional instances. Also, each node can store up to 2 TB of data (see Figure 2.3).

FIGURE 2.3   Configuring Cloud Spanner

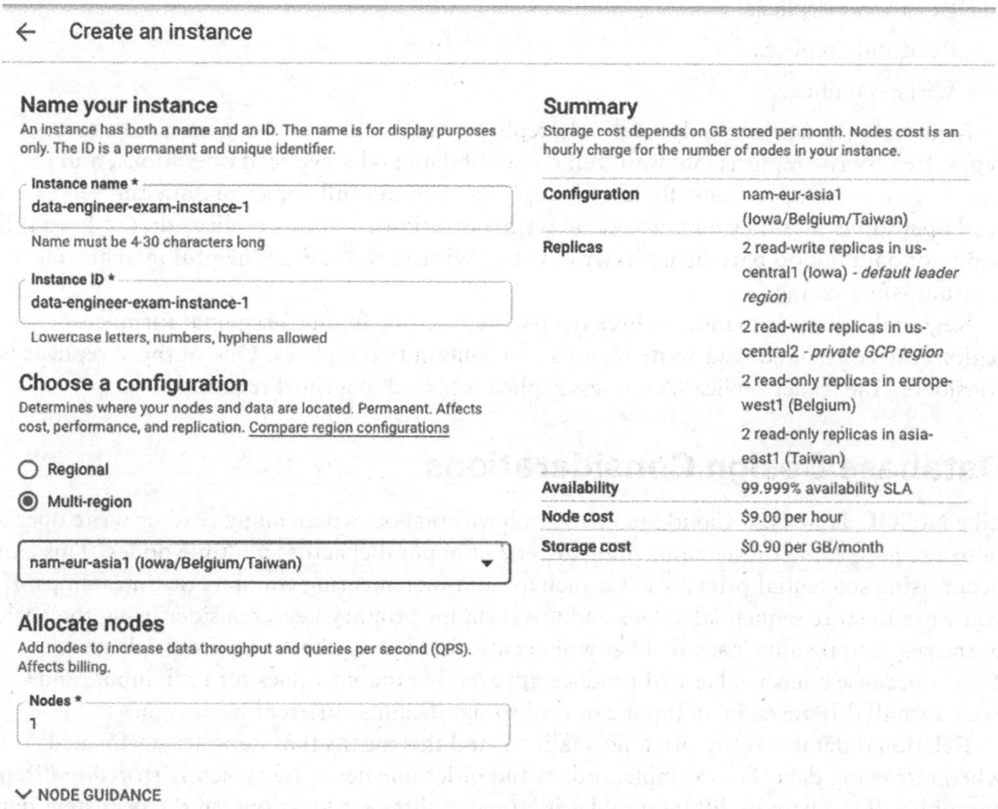

← Create an instance

Name your instance

An instance has both a **name** and an ID. The name is for display purposes only. The ID is a permanent and unique identifier.

Instance name *
data-engineer-exam-instance-1

Name must be 4-30 characters long

Instance ID *
data-engineer-exam-instance-1

Lowercase letters, numbers, hyphens allowed

Choose a configuration

Determines where your nodes and data are located. Permanent. Affects cost, performance, and replication. Compare region configurations

○ Regional

◉ Multi-region

nam-eur-asia1 (Iowa/Belgium/Taiwan)   ▼

Allocate nodes

Add nodes to increase data throughput and queries per second (QPS). Affects billing.

Nodes *
1

⌄ NODE GUIDANCE

Summary

Storage cost depends on GB stored per month. Nodes cost is an hourly charge for the number of nodes in your instance.

Configuration	nam-eur-asia1 (Iowa/Belgium/Taiwan)
Replicas	2 read-write replicas in us-central1 (Iowa) - *default leader region*
	2 read-write replicas in us-central2 - *private GCP region*
	2 read-only replicas in europe-west1 (Belgium)
	2 read-only replicas in asia-east1 (Taiwan)
Availability	99.999% availability SLA
Node cost	$9.00 per hour
Storage cost	$0.90 per GB/month

Replication in Cloud Spanner

Cloud Spanner maintains multiple replicas of rows of data in multiple locations. Since Cloud Spanner implements globally synchronous replication, you can read from any replica to get the latest data in a row. Rows are organized into splits, which are contiguous blocks of rows that are replicated together. One of the replicas is designated the leader and is responsible for write operations. The use of replicas improves data availability as well as reducing latency because of geographic proximity of data to applications that need the data. Again, the benefit of adding nodes should be balanced with the price of those additional nodes.

The distributed nature of Cloud Spanner creates challenges for writing data. To keep all replicas synchronized, Cloud Spanner uses a voting mechanism to determine writes. Cloud Spanner uses a voting mechanism to determine the latest write-in case of a conflict value.

There are three types of replicas in Cloud Spanner:

- Read-write replicas
- Read-only replicas
- Witness replicas

Regional instances use only read-only replicas; multi-regional instances use all three types. Read-write replicas maintain full copies of data and serve read operations, and they can vote on write operations. Read-only replicas maintain full copies of data and serve read operations, but they do not vote on write operations. Witness replicas do not keep full copies of data but do participate in write votes. Witness replicas are helpful in achieving a quorum when voting.

Regional instances maintain three read-write replicas. In multi-regional instances, two regions are considered read-write regions and contain two replicas. One of those replicas is considered the leader replica. A witness replica is placed in a third region.

Database Design Considerations

Like NoSQL databases, Cloud Spanner can have hotspots where many read or write operations are happening on the same node instead of in parallel across multiple nodes. This can occur using sequential primary keys, such as auto-incrementing counters or timestamps. If you want to store sequential values and use them for primary keys, consider using the hash of the sequential value instead. That will evenly distribute writes across multiple nodes. This is because a hash value will produce apparently random values for each input, and even a small difference in an input can lead to significantly different hash values.

Relational databases are often normalized, and this means that joins are performed when retrieving data. For example, orders and order line items are typically stored in different tables. If the data in different tables is stored in different locations on the persistent data store, the database will spend time reading data blocks from two different areas of storage. Cloud Spanner allows for interleaving data from different tables. This means that an order row will be stored together with order line items for that order. You can take advantage of interleaving by specifying a parent-child relationship between tables when creating the database schema.

Please note that row size should be limited to 4 GB, and that includes any interleaved rows.

Importing and Exporting Data

Data can be imported to or exported from Cloud Storage into Cloud Spanner. Exported files use the Apache Avro or CSV file formats. The export process is implemented by a Cloud Dataflow connector.

The performance of import and export operations is affected by several factors, including the following:

- Size of the database
- Number of secondary indexes

- Location of data
- Load on Cloud Spanner and number of nodes

Since Cloud Spanner can use the Avro format, it is possible to import data into Cloud Spanner from a file that was created by another application.

If you prefer to export data to CSV format, you can run a Dataflow job using the Cloud Spanner to Cloud Storage Text template.

Cloud Bigtable

Cloud Bigtable is a wide-column NoSQL database used for high-volume databases that require low millisecond (ms) latency. Cloud Bigtable is used for IoT, time-series, finance, and similar applications.

Configuring Bigtable

Bigtable is a managed service, but it is not a NoOps service: like Cloud SQL and Cloud Spanner, you have to specify instance information.

In addition to providing an instance name and instance ID, you will have to choose if you are deploying a production or development cluster. A production cluster provides high availability and requires at least three nodes. A development cluster is a lower-cost option for developing and testing your applications (see Figure 2.4).

FIGURE 2.4   Configuring a Bigtable cluster

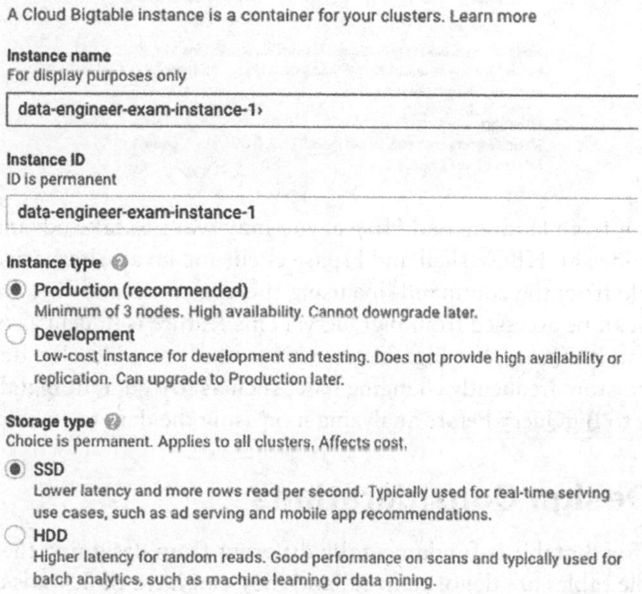

A Cloud Bigtable instance is a container for your clusters. Learn more

Instance name
For display purposes only

data-engineer-exam-instance-1

Instance ID
ID is permanent

data-engineer-exam-instance-1

Instance type ❔
⦿ Production (recommended)
Minimum of 3 nodes. High availability. Cannot downgrade later.
◯ Development
Low-cost instance for development and testing. Does not provide high availability or replication. Can upgrade to Production later.

Storage type ❔
Choice is permanent. Applies to all clusters. Affects cost.
⦿ SSD
Lower latency and more rows read per second. Typically used for real-time serving use cases, such as ad serving and mobile app recommendations.
◯ HDD
Higher latency for random reads. Good performance on scans and typically used for batch analytics, such as machine learning or data mining.

When creating a cluster, you will have to provide a cluster ID, region, zone, and number of nodes. Bigtable performance scales linearly with the number of nodes. For example, a three-node production cluster using SSDs can read and write 30,000 rows per second. Doubling the number of nodes to six increases read and write performance to 60,000 operations per second.

For multi-regional high availability, you can create a replicated cluster in another region. All data is replicated between clusters. In the event that a cluster becomes unresponsive, it can fail over either manually or automatically. Bigtable instances have an application profile, also called an *app profile*, which specifies how to handle incoming requests. If all requests are routed to single cluster, you will have to perform a manual failover. If the app profile uses multicluster routing, then an automatic failover occurs.

Be aware that Bigtable is an expensive service. As shown in Figure 2.5, the cost of a three-node production cluster is over $1,500 a month, or over $2 an hour.

FIGURE 2.5   Cost of a three-node Bigtable production cluster

Cost estimate

Monthly resource costs

Monthly costs reflect Bigtable resources only. Network traffic (replication and internet egress) costs are dependent on the location of your clusters and application request behavior. Learn more

Try another storage size (per cluster)

1000	GB

Item	Estimated cost
▶ 1 cluster	$1,423.50/month
▶ 1000 GB SSD	$170.00/month
Total	$1,593.50/month

Node charges are for provisioned resources, regardless of node usage. The same node charges apply even if your instance is inactive. Learn more

Summary

Monthly charge: $1,593.50 per month (1,000 GB data, 3 nodes)
Effective hourly rate: $2.18

When migrating from Hadoop and HBase, you may want to take advantage of the fact that Bigtable provides an HBase shell and HBase client for Java. Alternatively, you can work with Bigtable from the command line using the cbt command-line utility.

Bigtable tables can be accessed from BigQuery. (This feature is in beta as of this writing). Data is not stored in BigQuery, but Bigtable data is accessed from a table external to BigQuery. This enables you to store frequently changing data, such as IoT data, in Bigtable and not have to export the data to BigQuery before analyzing it or using the data from machine learning.

Database Design Considerations

Designing tables for Bigtable is fundamentally different from designing them for relational databases. Bigtable tables are denormalized, and they can have thousands of columns.

There is no support for joins in Bigtable or for secondary indexes. Data is stored in Bigtable lexicographically by *row-key*, which is the one indexed column in a Bigtable table. Keeping related data in adjacent rows can help make reads more efficient.

All operations are atomic at the row level, not a transaction level. For example, if an application performs operations on two rows, it is possible for one of those operations to succeed and another one to fail. This can leave the database in an inconsistent state. To avoid this, store all the data that needs to be updated together in the same row.

Since Bigtable does not have secondary indexes, queries are executed using either row-key–based lookups or full table scans. The latter are highly inefficient and should be avoided. Instead, row-key lookups or a range of row-key lookups should be used. This requires carefully planning the row-key around the way that you will query the data. The goal when designing a row-key is to take advantage of the fact that Bigtable stores data in a sorted order.

Characteristics of a good row-key include the following:

- Using a prefix for multitenancy. This isolates data from different customers. This makes scans and reads more efficient since data blocks will have data from one customer only and customers query only their own data.

- Columns that are not frequently updated, such as a user ID or a timestamp.

- Nonsequential value in the first part of the row-key, which helps avoid hotspots.

Another way to improve performance is to use *column families*, which are sets of columns with related data. They are stored together and retrieved together, making reads more efficient.

Importing and Exporting

Like Cloud Spanner, Bigtable import and export operations are performed using Cloud Dataflow. Data can be exported to Cloud Storage and stored in either Avro format or SequenceFile format. Data can be imported from Avro and SequenceFile. Data can be imported from CSV files using a Dataflow process as well.

Cloud Firestore

Cloud Firestore is the managed document database that is replacing Cloud Datastore. Document databases are used when the structure of data can vary from one record to another. Cloud Firestore has features not previously available in Cloud Datastore, including

- Strongly consistent storage layer
- Real-time updates
- Mobile and web client libraries
- A new collection and document data model

Cloud Firestore operates in one of two modes: Native Mode and Cloud Datastore Mode. In Datastore Mode, Firestore operates like Datastore but uses the Firestore storage system. This provides for strong consistency instead of eventual consistency. In addition, Datastore had a limit of 25 entity groups, or ancestor/descendent relations, and a maximum of one write per second to an entity group. Those limits are removed. The new data model, real-time updates, and mobile and web client library features are available only in Native Mode.

Cloud Firestore Data Model

Cloud Firestore in Datastore Mode uses a data model that consists of entities, entity groups, properties, and keys.

Entities are analogous to tables in a relational database. They describe a particular type of thing, or *entity kind*. Entities have identifiers, which can be assigned automatically or specified by an application. If identifiers are randomly assigned in Cloud Datastore Mode, the identifiers are randomly generated from a uniformly distributed set of identifiers. The random distribution is important to avoid hot spotting when a large number of entities are created in a short period of time.

Entities have properties, which are name-value pairs. For example, 'color':'red' is an instance of a color property with the value red. The property of values can be different types in different entities. Properties are not strongly typed. A property can also be indexed. Note that this is a difference with the other managed NoSQL databases—Bigtable does not have secondary indexes.

Properties can have one value or multiple values. Multiple values are stored as *array properties*. For example, a news article might have a property 'topics' and values {'technology', 'business', 'finance'}.

The value of a property can be another entity. This allows for hierarchical structures. Here is an example of a hierarchical structure of an order:

```
{'order_id': 1,
  'Customer': "Margaret Smith",
  'Line_item': {
                  {'line_id': 10,
                    'description': "Blue coat",
                    'quantity': 3},
                  {'line_id': 20,
                    'description': "Green shirt",
                    'quantity': 1},
                  {'line_id': 30,
                    'description': "Black umbrella",
                    'quantity': 1}
               }
}
```

In this example, the line items are entities embedded in the order entity. The order is the parent of the line item entities. The order entity is the root identity, since it does not have a parent entity. To reference an entity within another entity, you specify a path, known as the *ancestor path*, which includes the kind-identifier from the root to the descendent entity. For example, to refer to the line item describing the blue coat line item, you would use something like the following:

```
[order:1, line_item: 10]
```

To summarize, entities have properties that can be atomic values, arrays, or entities. Atomic values include integers, floating value numbers, strings, and dates. These are used when a property can be described by a single value, such as the date an order is placed. Arrays are used for properties that have more than one value, such as topics of news articles. Child entities are entities within another entity and are used to represent complex objects that are described by properties that may be atomic values, arrays, or other entities.

An entity and all its descendent entities are known as *entity groups*.

Entities also have keys, which uniquely identify an entity. A key consists of the following:

- A namespace, which is used to support multitenancy
- The kind of entity, such as order or line item
- An identifier
- An optional ancestor path

Keys can be used to look up entities and their properties. Alternatively, entities can be retrieved using queries that specify properties and values, much like using a WHERE clause in SQL. However, to query using property values, properties need to be indexed.

Indexing and Querying

Cloud Firestore uses two kinds of indexes: built-in indexes and composite indexes. *Built-in indexes* are created by default for each property in an entity. *Composite indexes* index multiple values of an entity.

Indexes are used when querying and must exist for any property referenced in filters. For example, querying for "color" = 'red' requires an index on the color property. If that index does not exist, Cloud Firestore will not return any entities, even if there are entities with a color property and value of red. Built-in indexes can satisfy simple equality and inequality queries, but more complex queries require composite indexes.

Composite indexes are used when there are multiple filter conditions in a query. For example, the filter color = 'red' and size = 'large' requires a composite index that includes both the color and size properties.

Composite indexes are defined in a configuration file called index.yaml. You can also exclude properties from having a built-in index created using the index.yaml configuration file. You may want to exclude properties that are not used in filter conditions. This can save storage space and avoid unnecessary updating of an index that is never used.

Cloud Firestore uses a SQL-like language called GQL (GraphQL). Queries consist of an entity kind, filters, and optionally a sort order specification. Here is an example query:

```
SELECT * FROM orders
WHERE item_count > 1 AND status = 'shipping'
ORDER BY item_count DESC
```

This query will return entities from the orders collection that have a value greater than 1 for item_count and a value of 'shipping' for status. The results will be sorted in descending order by item_count. For this query to function as expected, there needs to be an index on item_count and 'shipping' and sorted in descending order.

Importing and Exporting

Entities can be imported and exported from Cloud Firestore. Exports contain entities but not indexes. Those are rebuilt during import. Exporting requires a Cloud Storage bucket to store the exported data. You can specify a filter when exporting so that only a subset of entity kinds are exported.

Exported entities can be imported into BigQuery using the bq command, but only if an entity filter was used when creating the export. There are a number of restrictions on importing Cloud Firestore exports to BigQuery:

- The Cloud Storage URI of the export file must not have a wildcard.

- Data cannot be appended to an existing table with a defined schema.

- Entities in the export have a consistent schema.

- Any property value greater than 64 KB is truncated to 64 KB on export.

Cloud Firestore in Datastore Mode is a managed document database that is well suited for applications that require semi-structured data but that do not require low-latency writes (< 10 ms). When low-latency writes are needed, Bigtable is a better option.

BigQuery

BigQuery are fully managed, petabyte-scale, low-cost analytics data warehouse databases. As with other databases, some common tasks are as follows:

- Interacting with data sets

- Importing and exporting data

- Streaming inserts

- Monitoring and logging

- Managing costs

- Optimizing tables and queries

BigQuery is an important service for the Process and Analyze stage of the data lifecycle.

BigQuery Datasets

Datasets are the basic unit of organization for sharing data in BigQuery. A dataset can have multiple tables. When you create a dataset in BigQuery, you specify the following:

- A dataset ID
- Data location
- Default table expiration

A *dataset ID* is a name of the dataset, and the *data location* is a region that supports BigQuery. The default table expiration allows you to set a time to live for the dataset. This is useful when you know that you will keep data for some period of time and then delete it. You can create tables using the BigQuery user interface or the command line. Once you have created a dataset, you can load data into it. We'll describe how to do that in the next section, but first let's describe how to use SQL to query a dataset.

Figure 2.6 shows an example BigQuery interactive interface. The query is as follows:

```
SELECT
  name, gender,
  SUM(number) AS total
FROM
  'bigquery-public-data.usa_names.usa_1910_2013'
GROUP BY
  name, gender
ORDER BY
  total DESC
LIMIT
  10
```

FIGURE 2.6   BigQuery interactive interface with sample query

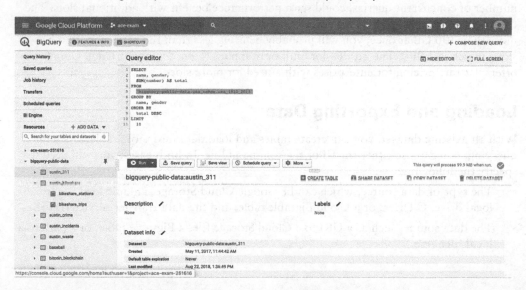

This query selects the name, gender, and number of children born with that name for each gender from a table called usa_1910_2013. That table is in a dataset named usa_names and in a project called bigquery-public-data. Note that when fully specifying a table name, the pattern is the project name, followed by the dataset name, then followed by the table name. Also note that backticks, not single quotes, are used when specifying a table name.

You could also query a dataset using the bq command line, as shown in the following example. The bodies of the SELECT statements are wrapped in single quotes, whereas the table names are wrapped in backticks.

```
bq query --nouse_legacy_sql \' SELECT
  name, gender,
  SUM(number) AS total
FROM
  'bigquery-public-data.usa_names.usa_1910_2013'
GROUP BY
  name, gender
ORDER BY
  total DESC
LIMIT
  10'
```

BigQuery supports two dialects of SQL, legacy and standard, and the bq query command takes a parameter indicating which SQL dialect to use when parsing. As the names imply, standard SQL is the preferred dialect, but both are currently supported. Standard SQL supports advanced SQL features, such as correlated subqueries, ARRAY and STRUCT data types, as well as complex join expressions.

BigQuery uses the concept of slots for allocating computing resources to execute queries. For most users, the default number of slots is sufficient, but very large queries, or a large number of concurrent queries, could see a performance benefit with additional slots. The default number of slots is shared across a project, and as long as you are not processing more than 100 GB at once, you will probably be using less than the maximum number of slots, which is 2,000. The 2,000-slot limit only applies to on-demand pricing; Google also offers flat-rate pricing for enterprises with a need for more slots.

Loading and Exporting Data

With an existing dataset, you can create tables and load data into those tables. As with querying, you can use either the UI or the command line. In both cases, you will need to specify the following:

- The type of data source, which can be Google Cloud Storage, an uploaded file from local drive, G Drive, or a Cloud Bigtable table, and the data transfer service (DTS).

- The data source, such as a URI to a Cloud Storage file, a Bigtable table, or a path to a local filename.

- File format—one of: Avro, CSV, JSON (newline delimited), ORC, or Parquet. If you are loading from Cloud Storage, you can also load Cloud Datastore and Cloud Firestore exports.

- Destination table, including project, dataset, and table name.

- Schema, which can be auto-detected, specified in text, or entered one column at a time, specifying the column name, type, and mode. Mode may be NULLABLE, REQUIRED, or REPEATED.

- Partitioning, which can be no partitioning or partitioning by ingestion time. If a table is partitioned, you can use clustering order, which optimizes the way that column data is stored and can optimize the way that queries are executed. You can also specify that any query on a partitioned table needs to specify a partition filter in the WHERE clause. This can significantly reduce cost and improve performance by limiting the amount of data scanned when executing the query.

BigQuery expects data to be encoded using UTF-8. If a CSV file is not in UTF-8, BigQuery will try to convert it. The conversion is not always correct, and there can be differences in some bytes. If your CSV file does not load correctly, specify the correct encoding. If you are loading JSON files, they need to be in UTF-8 encoding.

Avro is the preferred format for loading data because blocks of data can be read in parallel, even if the file is compressed and there are no encoding issues, such as with CSV. Parquet also stores data using a column model. Uncompressed CSV and JSON files load faster than compressed files because they can be loaded in parallel, but this can lead to higher storage costs when using Cloud Storage.

The BigQuery Data Transfer Service automates loading data from Google's software as a service (SaaS) offerings, such as Google Ad Manager, Google Ads, Google Play, and YouTube Channel Reports. It can also be used to load data from Amazon S3.

Cloud Dataflow can load directly into BigQuery.

Clustering, Partitioning, and Sharding Tables

BigQuery provides for creating clustered tables. In clustered tables, data is automatically organized based on the contents of one or more columns. Related data is collocated in a clustered table. This kind of organization can improve the performance of some queries, specifically the queries that filter rows using the columns used to cluster data. Clustered tables can be partitioned.

It is a good practice to break large tables into smaller ones or partitions to improve query efficiency. When splitting data by date or timestamp, you can use partitions, and to split data into multiple tables by other attributes, you can try *sharding*.

Partitions can be based on ingestion time or by date or timestamp in the input data. When data is partitioned by ingestion time, BigQuery creates a new partition for each day.

Shards can be based on the value in a partition column, such as customer ID. The column does not have to be a date or timestamp column. It's a best practice to use partitioning by time instead of sharding by a date. The former is more efficient with BigQuery due to the backend optimizations it creates with timestamps.

Sharding can make use of template tables, which are tables that have a schema defined in a template and that template is used to create one or more tables that have a target table name and a table suffix. The target table name is the same for all tables created with the template, but the suffix is different for each table created.

Streaming Inserts

The loading procedures just described are designed for batch loading. BigQuery also supports streaming inserts that load one row at a time. Data is generally available for analysis within a few seconds, but it may be up to 90 minutes before data is available for copy and export operations. This is not intended for transactional workloads, but rather analytical ones.

Streaming inserts provide best effort de-duplication. When inserting a row, you can include an insertID that uniquely identifies a record. BigQuery uses that identifier to detect duplicates. If no insertID is provided with a row, then BigQuery does not try to de-duplicate data. If you do provide an insertID and employ de-duplication, you are limited to 100,000 rows per second and 100 MB per second. If de-duplication is not enabled, you can insert up to 1,000,000 rows per second and 1 GB per second.

The advantage of using template tables is that you do not have to create all tables in advance. For example, if you are streaming in data from a medical device and you want to have table for each device, you could use the device identifier as the suffix, and when the first data from that device arrives, a table will be created from the template.

Standard SQL makes it easy to query across template tables by allowing wildcards in a table name. For example, if you have a set of medical device tables named 'medical_device_' + <device id>, such as 'medical_device_123', 'medical_device_124', 'medical_device_125', and so forth, you could query across those tables by using a FROM clause as follows:

```
FROM 'med_project.med_dataset.medical_device*'
```

Wildcards cannot be used with views or external tables.

Monitoring and Logging in BigQuery

Stackdriver is used for monitoring and logging in BigQuery. Stackdriver Monitoring provides performance metrics, such query counts and time to run queries. Stackdriver Logging is used to track events, such as running jobs or creating tables.

Stackdriver Monitoring collects metrics on a range of operations, including

- Number of scanned bytes
- Query time
- Slots allocated
- Slots available
- Number of tables in a dataset
- Uploaded rows

You can build dashboards in Stackdriver Monitoring to help track key performance indicators, such as top long-running queries and 95th percentile query time.

Stackdriver Logging tracks log entries that describe events. Events have resource types, which can be projects or datasets, and type-specific attributes, like a location for storage events. Events that are tracked include the following:

- Inserting, updating, patching, and deleting tables
- Inserting jobs
- Executing queries

Logs are useful for understanding who is performing actions in BigQuery, whereas monitoring is useful for understanding how your queries and jobs are performing.

BigQuery Cost Considerations

BigQuery costs are based on the amount of data stored, the amount of data streamed, and the workload required to execute queries. Since the prices of these various services can change, it is not important to know specific amounts, but it is helpful to understand the relative costs. That can help when choosing among different options.

BigQuery data is considered active if it was referenced in the last 90 days; otherwise, it is considered long-term data. Active Storage is currently billed at $0.20/GB a month, and long-term data is billed at $0.10/GB a month. The charge for long-term storage in BigQuery is currently equal to the cost of Nearline storage, so there is no cost advantage to storing long-term data in Cloud Storage unless you were to store it Coldline storage, which is currently billed at $0.07/GB a month.

Streaming inserts are billed at $0.01 per 200 MB, where each row is considered at least 1 KB.

On-demand queries are billed at $5.00 per TB scanned. Monthly flat rate billing is $10,000 per 500 slots per month. Annual flat rate billing is $8,500 a month for 500 slots.

There is no charge for loading, copying, or exporting data, but there are charges for the storage used.

There are separate charges for using BigQuery ML machine learning service (BQML), for using BigQuery's native machine learning capabilities, and for using the BigQuery Data Transfer service.

Tips for Optimizing BigQuery

One way to keep costs down is to optimize the way that you use BigQuery. Here are several ways to do this:

- Avoid using SELECT *.
- Use --dry-run to estimate the cost of a query.
- Set the maximum number of bytes billed.
- Partition by time when possible.
- Denormalize data rather than join multiple tables.

Avoid using SELECT * queries. These scan all the columns in a table or view; instead, list the specific columns that you want and limit the list only to columns that are needed. If you need to view examples of data in all columns, use the Preview option in the BigQuery GUI or run the bq head command from the command line, which functions like the Linux head command and displays the first rows of a table. Preview or bq head is a better option than running a SELECT query with a LIMIT clause because LIMIT limits the number of rows returned only, not the number of rows scanned.

If you would like to know what it would cost to run a query, you can view the query validator in the BigQuery GUI, or you can use the --dry-run option with the bq query command.

You can also set a maximum number of bytes billed for a query. If the query scans more than that number of bytes, the query fails, and you are not billed for the query. Maximum bytes billed can be specified in the GUI or in a bq query command using the --maximum_bytes_billed parameter.

Partition by time when possible. This will help reduce the amount of data that needs to be scanned. BigQuery creates a pseudo-column on partitioned tables called _PARTITIONTIME, which can be used in WHERE clauses to limit the amount of data scanned. For example, the following WHERE clause will return only rows that are in partitions holding data from January 1, 2019, to January 31, 2019.

```
WHERE _PARTITIONTIME
BETWEEN TIMESTAMP("20190101")
    AND TIMESTAMP("20190131")
```

BigQuery supports nested and repeated structures in rows. Nested data is represented in STRUCT type in SQL, and repeated types are represented in ARRAY types in SQL.

For the fastest query performance, load data into BigQuery, but if you can tolerate some longer latency, then keeping data in external data stores can minimize the amount of data loading you need to do.

BigQuery is a popular GCP service because it requires little operational overhead, supports large volumes of data, and is highly performant, especially when queries are tuned to take advantage of BigQuery's architecture.

Cloud Memorystore

Cloud Memorystore is a managed Redis service, which is commonly used for caching. Redis instances can be created using the Cloud Console or gcloud commands. There are only a small number of basic configuration parameters with Cloud Memorystore:

- Instance ID.
- Size specification.
- Region and zone.

- Redis version; currently the options are 3.2 and 4.0; 4.0 is recommended.

- Instance tier, which can be basic and is not highly available, or standard, which is includes a failover replica in a different zone.

- Memory capacity, which ranges from 1 to 300 GB.

You also have the option of specifying Redis configuration parameters, such as maximum memory policy, and an eviction policy, such as least frequently used.

Cloud Memorystore provides support for importing and exporting from Redis; this feature is in beta as of this writing. Exporting will create a backup file of the Redis cache in a Cloud Storage bucket. During export, read and write operations can occur, but administration operations, like scaling, are not allowed. Import reads export files and overwrites the contents of a Redis cache. The instance is not available for read or write operations during the import.

Redis instances in Cloud Memorystore can be scaled to use more or less memory. When scaling a Basic Tier instance, reads and writes are blocked. When the resizing is complete, all data is flushed from the cache. Standard Tier instances can scale while continuing to support read and write operations. During a scaling operation, the replica is resized first and then synchronized with the primary. The primary then fails over to the replica. Write operations are supported when scaling Standard Tier instances, but too much write load can significantly slow the resizing operation.

When the memory used by Redis exceeds 80 percent of system memory, the instance is considered under memory pressure. To avoid memory pressure, you can scale up the instance, lower the maximum memory limit, modify the eviction policy, set time-to-live (TTL) parameters on volatile keys, or manually delete data from the instance. The TTL parameter specifies how long a key should be kept in the cache before it becomes eligible for eviction. Frequently updated values should have short TTLs whereas keys with values that don't change very often can have longer TTLs. Some eviction policies target only keys with TTLs whereas other policies target all keys. If you find that you are frequently under memory pressure, your current eviction policy applies only to keys with TTLs, and there are keys without TTLs, then switching to an eviction policy that targets all keys may relieve some of that memory pressure.

Redis provides a number of eviction policies that determine which keys are removed from the cache when the maximum memory limit is reached. By default, Redis evicts the least recently used keys with TTLs set. Other options include evicting based on least frequently used keys or randomly selecting keys.

Although Cloud Memorystore is a managed service, you should still monitor the instance, particularly memory usage, duration periods of memory overload, cache-hit ratio, and the number of expirable keys.

Cloud Storage

This section first appeared in Chapter 5 of my book, *Official Google Cloud Certified Professional Cloud Architect Study Guide* (Wiley, 2019).

Google Cloud Storage is an object storage system. It is designed for persisting unstructured data, such as data files, images, videos, backup files, and any other data. It is unstructured in the sense that objects—that is, files stored in Cloud Storage—are treated as atomic. When you access a file in Cloud Storage, you access the entire file. You cannot treat it as file on a block storage device that allows for seeking and reading specific blocks in the file. There is no presumed structure within the file that Cloud Storage can exploit.

Organizing Objects in a Namespace

Also, there is minimal structure for hierarchical structures. Cloud Storage uses buckets to group objects. A *bucket* is a group of objects that share access controls at the bucket level. For example, the service account assigned to a virtual machine may have permissions to write to one bucket and read from another bucket. Individual objects within buckets can have their own access controls as well.

Google Cloud Storage uses a global namespace for bucket names, so all bucket names must have unique names. Object names do not have to be unique. A bucket is named when it is created and cannot be renamed. To simulate renaming a bucket, you will need to copy the contents of the bucket to a new bucket with the desired name and then delete the original bucket.

Google recommends the following suggestions for bucket naming:

- Do not use personally identifying information, such as names, email addresses, IP addresses, and so forth in bucket names. That kind of information could be useful to an attacker.

- Follow DNS naming conventions because bucket names can appear in a CNAME record in DNS.

- Use globally unique identifiers (GUIDs) if creating a large number of buckets.

- Do not use sequential names or timestamps if uploading files in parallel. Files with sequentially close names will likely be assigned to the same server. This can create a hotspot when writing files to Cloud Storage.

- Bucket names can also be subdomain names, such as mybucket.example.com.

To create a domain name bucket, you will have to verify that you are the owner of the domain.

The Cloud Storage service does not use a filesystem. This means that there is no ability to navigate a path through a hierarchy of directories and files. The object store does support a naming convention that allows for the naming of objects in a way that looks similar to the way that a hierarchical filesystem would structure a file path and filename. If you would like to use Google Cloud Storage as a filesystem, the Cloud Storage FUSE open source project provides a mechanism to map from object storage systems to filesystems (`https://cloud.google.com/storage/docs/gcs-fuse`).

Storage Tiers

Cloud Storage offers four tiers or types of storage. It is essential to understand the characteristics of each tier and when it should be used for the Cloud Professional Data Engineer exam. The four types of Cloud Storage are as follows:

- Regional
- Multi-regional
- Nearline
- Coldline

Regional storage stores multiple copies of an object in multiple zones in one region. All Cloud Storage options provide high durability, which means that the probability of losing an object during any particular period of time is extremely low. Cloud Storage provides 99.999999999 percent (eleven 9s) annual durability.

This level of durability is achieved by keeping redundant copies of the object. *Availability* is the ability to access an object when you want it. An object can be durably stored but unavailable. For example, a network outage in a region would prevent you from accessing an object stored in that region, although it would continue to be stored in multiple zones.

Multi-regional storage mitigates the risk of a regional outage by storing replicas of objects in multiple regions. This can also improve access time and latency by distributing copies of objects to locations that are closer to the users of those object. Consider a user in California in the western United States accessing an object stored in us-west1, which is a region located in the northwest state of Oregon in the United States. That user can expect under 5 ms latency with a user in New York, in the United States northeast, and would likely experience latencies closer to 30 ms.

For more, see Windstream Services IP Latency Statistics, `https://ipnetwork.windstream.net/`, accessed May 8, 2019.

Multi-regional storage is also known as *geo-redundant storage*. Multi-regional Cloud Storage buckets are created in one of the multi-regions—asia, eu, or us—for data centers in Asia, the European Union, and the United States, respectively.

The latencies mentioned here are based on public Internet network infrastructure. Google offers two network tiers: Standard and Premium. With the *Standard network tier*, data is routed between regions using public Internet infrastructure and is subject to network conditions and routing decisions beyond Google's control. The *Premium network tier* routes data over Google's global high-speed network. Users of Premium tier networking can expect lower latencies.

Nearline and Coldline storage are used for storing data that is not frequently accessed. Data that is accessed less than once in 30 days is a good candidate for *Nearline storage*. Data that is accessed less than once a year is a good candidate for *Coldline storage*. All storage classes have the same latency to return the first byte of data, but the costs to access data and the per-operation costs are higher than regional storage.

Multi-regional storage has a 99.95 percent availability SLA. Regional storage has a 99.9 percent availability SLA. Nearline and Coldline storage have 99.9 percent availability SLA in multi-regional locations and 99.0 percent availability in regional locations.

Cloud Storage Use Cases

Cloud Storage is used for a few broad use cases:

- Storage of data shared among multiple instances that does not need to be on persistent attached storage. For example, log files may be stored in Cloud Storage and analyzed by programs running in a Cloud Dataproc Spark cluster.

- Backup and archival storage, such as persistent disk snapshots, backups of on-premises systems, and data kept for audit and compliance requirements but not likely to be accessed.

- As a staging area for uploaded data. For example, a mobile app may allow users to upload images to a Cloud Storage bucket. When the file is created, a Cloud Function could trigger to initiate the next steps of processing.

Each of these examples fits well with Cloud Storage's treatment of objects as atomic units. If data within the file needs to be accessed and processed, that is done by another service or application, such as a Spark analytics program.

Different tiers are better suited for some use cases. For example, Coldline storage is best used for archival storage, but multi-regional storage may be the best option for uploading user data, especially if users are geographically dispersed.

Data Retention and Lifecycle Management

Data has something of a life as it moves through several stages, starting with creation, active use, infrequent access but kept online, archived, and deleted. Not all data goes through all of the stages, but it is important to consider lifecycle issues when planning storage systems.

The choice of storage system technology usually does not directly influence data lifecycles and retention policies, but it does impact how the policies are implemented. For example, Cloud Storage lifecycle policies can be used to move objects from Nearline storage to Coldline storage after some period of time. When partitioned tables are used in BigQuery, partitions can be deleted without affecting other partitions or running time-consuming jobs that scan full tables for data that should be deleted.

If you are required to store data, consider how frequently and how fast the data must be accessed:

- If submillisecond access time is needed, use a cache such as Cloud Memorystore.

- If data is frequently accessed, may need to be updated, and needs to be persistently stored, use a database. Choose between relational and NoSQL based on the structure of the data. Data with flexible schemas can use NoSQL databases.

- If data is less likely to be accessed the older it gets, store data in time-partitioned tables if the database supports partitions. Time-partitioned tables are frequently used in BigQuery, and Bigtable tables can be organized by time as well.

- If data is infrequently accessed and does not require access through a query language, consider Cloud Storage. Infrequently used data can be exported from a database, and the export files can be stored in Cloud Storage. If the data is needed, it can be imported back into the database and queried from there.

- When data is not likely to be accessed but it must still be stored, use the Coldline storage class in Cloud Storage. This is less expensive than multi-regional, regional, or Nearline classes of storage.

Cloud Storage provides object lifecycle management policies to make changes automatically to the way that objects are stored in the object datastore. These policies contain rules for manipulating objects and are assigned to buckets. The rules apply to objects in those buckets. The rules implement lifecycle actions, including deleting an object and setting the storage class. Rules can be triggered based on the age of the object, when it was created, the number of newer versions, and the storage class of the object.

Another control for data management are *retention policies*. A retention policy uses the Bucket Lock feature of Cloud Storage buckets to enforce object retention. By setting a retention policy, you ensure that any object in the bucket or future objects in the bucket are not deleted until they reach the age specified in the retention policy. This feature is particularly useful for compliance with government or industry regulations. Once a retention policy is locked, it cannot be revoked.

Unmanaged Databases

Although GCP offers a range of managed database options, there may be use cases in which you prefer to manage your own database. These are sometimes referred to as *unmanaged databases*, but self-managed is probably a better term.

When you manage your own databases, you will be responsible for an array of database and system administration tasks, including

- Updating and patching the operating system
- Updating and patching the database system
- Backing up and, if needed, recovering data

- Configuring network access
- Managing disk space
- Monitoring database performance and resource utilization
- Configuring for high availability and managing failovers
- Configuring and managing read replicas

For the purpose of the Cloud Professional Data Engineer exam, it is important to appreciate the role of Stackdriver to understanding the state of a database system. The two Stackdriver components that are used with unmanaged databases are Stackdriver Monitoring and Stackdriver Logging.

Instances have built-in monitoring and logging. Monitoring includes CPU, memory, and I/O metrics. Audit logs, which have information about who created an instance, is also available by default. If you would like insights into application performance, in this case into database performance, you should install Stackdriver Monitoring and Stackdriver Logging agents.

Once the Stackdriver Logging agent is installed, it can collect application logs, including database logs. Stackdriver Logging is configured with Fluentd, an open source data collector for logs.

Once the Stackdriver Monitoring agent is installed, it can collect application performance metrics. Monitoring a specific database may require a plug-in designed for the particular database, such as MySQL or PostgreSQL.

Exam Essentials

Cloud SQL supports MySQL, PostgreSQL, and SQL Server (beta).   Cloud SQL instances are created in a single zone by default, but they can be created for high availability and use instances in multiple zones. Use read replicas to improve read performance. Importing and exporting are implemented via the RDBMS-specific tool.

Cloud Spanner is configured as regional or multi-regional instances.   Cloud Spanner is a horizontally scalable relational database that automatically replicates data. Three types of replicas are read-write replicas, read-only replicas, and witness replicas. Avoid hotspots by not using consecutive values for primary keys.

Cloud Bigtable is a wide-column NoSQL database used for high-volume databases that require sub-10 ms latency.   Cloud Bigtable is used for IoT, time-series, finance, and similar applications. For multi-regional high availability, you can create a replicated cluster in another region. All data is replicated between clusters. Designing tables for Bigtable is fundamentally different from designing them for relational databases. Bigtable tables are denormalized, and they can have thousands of columns. There is no support for joins in Bigtable or for secondary indexes. Data is stored in Bigtable lexicographically by row-key, which is the one indexed column in a Bigtable table. Keeping related data in adjacent rows can help make reads more efficient.

Cloud Firestore is a document database that is replacing Cloud Datastore as the managed document database. The Cloud Firestore data model consists of entities, entity groups, properties, and keys. Entities have properties that can be atomic values, arrays, or entities. Keys can be used to lookup entities and their properties. Alternatively, entities can be retrieved using queries that specify properties and values, much like using a WHERE clause in SQL. However, to query using property values, properties need to be indexed.

BigQuery is an analytics database that uses SQL as a query language. Datasets are the basic unit of organization for sharing data in BigQuery. A dataset can have multiple tables. BigQuery supports two dialects of SQL: legacy and standard. Standard SQL supports advanced SQL features such as correlated subqueries, ARRAY and STRUCT data types, and complex join expressions. BigQuery uses the concepts of slots for allocating computing resources to execute queries. BigQuery also supports streaming inserts, which load one row at a time. Data is generally available for analysis within a few seconds, but it may be up to 90 minutes before data is available for copy and export operations. Streaming inserts provide for best effort de-duplication. Stackdriver is used for monitoring and logging in BigQuery. Stackdriver Monitoring provides performance metrics, such query counts and time, to run queries. Stackdriver Logging is used to track events, such as running jobs or creating tables. BigQuery costs are based on the amount of data stored, the amount of data streamed, and the workload required to execute queries.

Cloud Memorystore is a managed Redis service. Redis instances can be created using the Cloud Console or `gcloud` commands. Redis instances in Cloud Memorystore can be scaled to use more or less memory. When scaling a Basic Tier instance, reads and writes are blocked. When the resizing is complete, all data is flushed from the cache. Standard Tier instances can scale while continuing to support read and write operations. When the memory used by Redis exceeds 80 percent of system memory, the instance is considered under memory pressure. To avoid memory pressure, you can scale up the instance, lower the maximum memory limit, modify the eviction policy, set time-to-live (TTL) parameters on volatile keys, or manually delete data from the instance.

Google Cloud Storage is an object storage system. It is designed for persisting unstructured data, such as data files, images, videos, backup files, and any other data. It is unstructured in the sense that objects—that is, files stored in Cloud Storage—use buckets to group objects. A bucket is a group of objects that share access controls at the bucket level. The four storage tiers are Regional, Multi-regional, Nearline, and Coldline.

When you manage your own databases, you will be responsible for an array of database and system administration tasks. The two Stackdriver components that are used with unmanaged databases are Stackdriver Monitoring and Stackdriver Logging. Instances have built-in monitoring and logging. Monitoring includes CPU, memory, and I/O metrics. Audit logs, which have information about who created an instance, are also available by default. Once the Stackdriver Logging agent is installed, it can collect application logs, including database logs. Stackdriver Logging is configured with Fluentd, an open source data collector for logs. Once the Stackdriver Monitoring agent is installed, it can collect application performance metrics.

Review Questions

You can find the answers in the appendix.

1. A database administrator (DBA) who is new to Google Cloud has asked for your help configuring network access to a Cloud SQL PostgreSQL database. The DBA wants to ensure that traffic is encrypted while minimizing administrative tasks, such as managing SQL certificates. What would you recommend?

    A. Use the TLS protocol

    B. Use Cloud SQL Proxy

    C. Use a private IP address

    D. Configure the database instance to use auto-encryption

2. You created a Cloud SQL database that uses replication to improve read performance. Occasionally, the read replica will be unavailable. You haven't noticed a pattern, but the disruptions occur once or twice a month. No DBA operations are occurring when the incidents occur. What might be the cause of this issue?

    A. The read replica is being promoted to a standalone Cloud SQL instance.

    B. Maintenance is occurring on the read replica.

    C. A backup is being performed on the read replica.

    D. The primary Cloud SQL instance is failing over to the read replica.

3. Your department is experimenting with using Cloud Spanner for a globally accessible database. You are starting with a pilot project using a regional instance. You would like to follow Google's recommendations for the maximum sustained CPU utilization of a regional instance. What is the maximum CPU utilization that you would target?

    A. 50%

    B. 65%

    C. 75%

    D. 45%

4. A Cloud Spanner database is being deployed in us-west1 and will have to store up to 20 TB of data. What is the minimum number of nodes required?

    A. 10

    B. 20

    C. 5

    D. 40

5. A software-as-a-service (SaaS) company specializing in automobile IoT sensors collects streaming time-series data from tens of thousands of vehicles. The vehicles are owned and operated by 40 different companies, who are the primary customers of the SaaS company. The data will be stored in Bigtable using a multitenant database; that is, all customer data will be stored in the same database. The data sent from the IoT device includes a sensor ID, which is globally unique; a timestamp; and several metrics about engine efficiency. Each customer will query their own data only. Which of the following would you use as a row-key?

   A. Customer ID, timestamp, sensor ID

   B. Customer ID, sensor ID, timestamp

   C. Sensor ID, timestamp, customer ID

   D. Sensor ID, customer ID, timestamp

6. A team of game developers is using Cloud Firestore to store player data, including character description, character state, and possessions. Descriptions are up to a 60-character alphanumeric string that is set when the character is created and not updated. Character state includes health score, active time, and passive time. When they are updated, they are all updated at the same time. Possessions are updated whenever the character acquires or loses a possession. Possessions may be complex objects, such as bags of items, where each item may be a simple object or another complex object. Simple objects are described with a character string. Complex objects have multiple properties. How would you model player data in Cloud Firestore?

   A. Store description and character state as strings and possessions as entities

   B. Store description, character state, and possessions as strings

   C. Store description, character state, and possessions as entities

   D. Store description as a string; character state as an entity with properties for health score, active time, and passive time; and possessions as an entity that may have embedded entities

7. You are querying a Cloud Firestore collection of order entities searching for all orders that were created today and have a total sales amount of greater than $100. You have not excluded any indexes, and you have not created any additional indexes using index.yaml. What do you expect the results to be?

   A. A set of all orders created today with a total sales amount greater than $100

   B. A set of orders created today and any total sales amount

   C. A set of with total sales amount greater than $100 and any sales date

   D. No entities returned

8. You are running a Redis cache using Cloud Memorystore. One day, you receive an alert notification that the memory usage is exceeding 80 percent. You do not want to scale up the instance, but you need to reduce the amount of memory used. What could you try?

   A. Setting shorter TTLs and trying a different eviction policy.

   B. Switching from Basic Tier to Standard Tier.

   C. Exporting the cache.

   D. There is no other option—you must scale the instance.

9. A team of machine learning engineers are creating a repository of data for training and testing machine learning models. All of the engineers work in the same city, and they all contribute datasets to the repository. The data files will be accessed frequently, usually at least once a week. The data scientists want to minimize their storage costs. They plan to use Cloud Storage; what storage class would you recommend?

    A. Regional

    B. Multi-regional

    C. Nearline

    D. Coldline

10. Auditors have informed your company CFO that to comply with a new regulation, your company will need to ensure that financial reporting data is kept for at least three years. The CFO asks for your advice on how to comply with the regulation with the least administrative overhead. What would you recommend?

    A. Store the data on Coldline storage

    B. Store the data on multi-regional storage

    C. Define a data retention policy

    D. Define a lifecycle policy

11. As a database administrator tasked with migrating a MongoDB instance to Google Cloud, you are concerned about your ability to configure the database optimally. You want to collect metrics at both the instance level and the database server level. What would you do in addition to creating an instance and installing and configuring MongoDB to ensure that you can monitor key instances and database metrics?

    A. Install Stackdriver Logging agent.

    B. Install Stackdriver Monitoring agent.

    C. Install Stackdriver Debug agent.

    D. Nothing. By default, the database instance will send metrics to Stackdriver.

12. A group of data scientists have uploaded multiple time-series datasets to BigQuery over the last year. They have noticed that their queries—which select up to six columns, apply four SQL functions, and group by the day of a timestamp—are taking longer to run and are incurring higher BigQuery costs as they add data. They do not understand why this is the case since they typically work only with the most recent set of data loaded. What would you recommend they consider in order to reduce query latency and query costs?

    A. Sort the data by time order before loading

    B. Stop using Legacy SQL and use Standard SQL dialect

    C. Partition the table and use clustering

    D. Add more columns to the SELECT statement to use data fetched by BigQuery more efficiently

13. You are querying a BigQuery table that has been partitioned by time. You create a query and use the --dry_run flag with the bq query command. The amount of data scanned is far more than you expected. What is a possible cause of this?

   A. You did not include _PARTITIONTIME in the WHERE clause to limit the amount of data that needs to be scanned.

   B. You used CSV instead of AVRO file format when loading the data.

   C. Both active and long-term data are included in the query results.

   D. You used JSON instead of the Parquet file format when loading the data.

14. Your department is planning to expand the use of BigQuery. The CFO has asked you to investigate whether the company should invest in flat-rate billing for BigQuery. What tools and data would you use to help answer that question?

   A. Stackdriver Logging and audit log data

   B. Stackdriver Logging and CPU utilization metrics

   C. Stackdriver Monitoring and CPU utilization metrics

   D. Stackdriver Monitoring and slot utilization metrics

15. You are migrating several terabytes of historical sensor data to Google Cloud Storage. The data is organized into files with one file per sensor per day. The files are named with the date followed by the sensor ID. After loading 10 percent of the data, you realize that the data loads are not proceeding as fast as expected. What might be the cause?

   A. The filenaming convention uses dates as the first part of the file name. If the files are loaded in this order, they may be creating hotspots when writing the data to Cloud Storage.

   B. The data is in text instead of Avro or Parquet format.

   C. You are using a gcloud command-line utility instead of the REST API.

   D. The data is being written to regional instead of multi-regional storage.

Chapter

3

Designing Data Pipelines

GOOGLE CLOUD PROFESSIONAL DATA ENGINEER EXAM OBJECTIVES COVERED IN THIS CHAPTER INCLUDE THE FOLLOWING:

1. Designing data processing systems

✓ 1.2 Designing data pipelines. Considerations include:

- Data publishing and visualization (e.g., BigQuery)
- Batch and streaming data (e.g., Cloud Dataflow, Cloud Dataproc, Apache Beam, Apache Spark and Hadoop ecosystem, Cloud Pub/Sub, Apache Kafka)
- Online (interactive) vs. batch predictions
- Job automation and orchestration (e.g., Cloud Composer)

2. Building and operationalizing data processing systems

✓ 2.2 Building and operationalizing pipelines. Considerations include:

- Data cleansing
- Batch and streaming
- Transformation
- Data acquisition and import
- Integrating with new data sources

Data pipelines are sequences of operations that copy, transform, load, and analyze data. There are common high-level design patterns that you see repeatedly in batch, streaming, and machine learning pipelines. In this chapter, you will review those high-level design patterns, along with some variations on those patterns. You will also review how GCP services like Cloud Dataflow, Cloud Dataproc, Cloud Pub/Sub, and Cloud Composer are used to implement data pipelines. We'll also look at migrating data pipelines from an on-premises Hadoop cluster to GCP.

Overview of Data Pipelines

A data pipeline is an abstract concept that captures the idea that data flows from one stage of processing to another. Data pipelines are modeled as *directed acyclic graphs (DAGs)*. A *graph* is a set of nodes linked by edges. A *directed graph* has edges that flow from one node to another. Figure 3.1 shows a simple three-node graph with directed edges indicating that the flow in the graph moves from Node A to Node B and then to Node C.

FIGURE 3.1 A simple directed graph

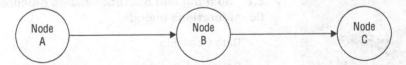

Sometimes, graphs have edges that loop back to a previous node or to the node that is the origin of the edge. Figure 3.2 shows a graph with an edge that loops from Node B back to Node A and an edge from Node C to itself. Graphs with these kinds of looping back edges are known as *cyclic graphs*, and the loops are cycles. Cycles are not allowed in data pipelines, and for that reason the graphs that model data pipelines are directed acyclic graphs.

FIGURE 3.2 A simple cyclic graph

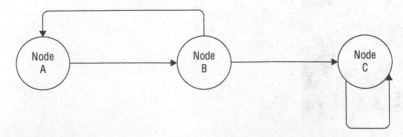

Data Pipeline Stages

The nodes in a data pipeline DAG represent processing stages in the pipeline, and edges represent the flow of data. The four types of stages in a data pipeline are as follows:

- Ingestion
- Transformation
- Storage
- Analysis

Data pipelines may have multiple nodes in each stage. For example, a data warehouse that extracts data from three different sources would have three ingestion nodes. Not all pipelines have all stages. A pipeline may ingest audit log messages, transform them, and write them to a Cloud Storage file but not analyze them. It is possible that most of those log messages will never be viewed, but they must be stored in case they are needed. Log messages that are written to storage without any reformatting or other processing would not need a transformation stage. These examples are outliers, though. In most cases, data pipelines have one or more types of each of the four stages.

Ingestion

Ingestion (see Figure 3.3) is the process of bringing data into the GCP environment. This can occur in either batch or streaming mode.

In batch mode, data sets made up of one or more files are copied to GCP. Often these files will be copied to Cloud Storage first. There are several ways to get data into Cloud Storage, including gsutil copying, Transfer Service, and Transfer Appliance.

Streaming ingestion receives data in increments, typically a single record or small batches of records, that continuously flow into an ingestion endpoint, typically a Cloud Pub/Sub topic.

FIGURE 3.3   An example ingestion stage of a data pipeline

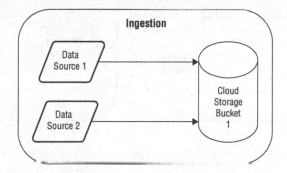

Transformation

Transformation is the process of mapping data from the structure used in the source system to the structure used in the storage and analysis stages of the data pipeline. There are many kinds of transformations, including the following:

- Converting data types, such as converting a text representation of a date to a datetime data type
- Substituting missing data with default or imputed values
- Aggregating data; for example, averaging all CPU utilization metrics for an instance over the course of one minute
- Filtering records that violate business logic rules, such as an audit log transaction with a date in the future
- Augmenting data by joining records from distinct sources, such as joining data from an employee table with data from a sales table that includes the employee identifier of the person who made the sale
- Dropping columns or attributes from a dataset when they will not be needed
- Adding columns or attributes derived from input data; for example, the average of the previous three reported sales prices of a stock might be added to a row of data about the latest price for that stock

In GCP, Cloud Dataflow and Cloud Dataproc are often used for transformation stages of both batch and streaming data. *Cloud Dataprep* is used for interactive review and preparation of data for analysis. Cloud Datafusion can be used for the same purpose, and it is more popular with enterprise customers (see Figure 3.4).

FIGURE 3.4   Data pipeline with transformations

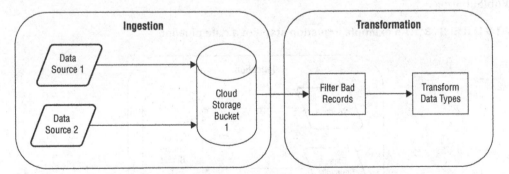

Storage

After data is ingested and transformed, it is often stored. Chapter 2, "Building and Operationalizing Storage Systems," describes GCP storage systems in detail, but key points related to data pipelines will be reviewed here as well.

Cloud Storage can be used as both the staging area for storing data immediately after ingestion and also as a long-term store for transformed data. BigQuery can treat Cloud Storage data as external tables and query them. Cloud Dataproc can use Cloud Storage as HDFS-compatible storage.

BigQuery is an analytical database that uses a columnar storage model that is highly efficient for data warehousing and analytic use cases.

Bigtable is a low-latency, wide-column NoSQL database used for time-series, IoT, and other high-volume write applications. Bigtable also supports the HBase API, making it a good storage option when migrating an on-premises HBase database on Hadoop (see Figure 3.5).

FIGURE 3.5   Example pipeline DAG with storage

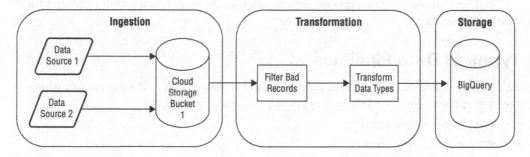

Analysis

Analysis can take on several forms, from simple SQL querying and report generation to machine learning model training and data science analysis.

Data in BigQuery, for example, is analyzed using SQL. *BigQuery ML* is a feature of the product that allows SQL developers to build machine learning models in BigQuery using SQL.

Data Studio is a GCP service used for interactive reporting tool for building reports and exploring data that is structured as dimensional models. Cloud Datalab is an interactive workbook based on the open source Jupyter Notebooks. Datalab is used for data exploration, machine learning, data science, and visualization.

Large-scale machine learning models can be built using Spark machine learning libraries running on Cloud Dataproc while accessing data in Bigtable using the HBase interface (see Figure 3.6).

FIGURE 3.6 Complete data pipeline from ingestion to analysis

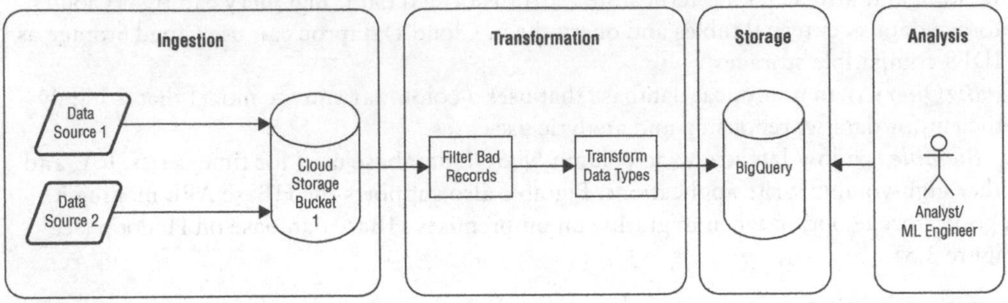

The basic four-stage data pipeline pattern can take on more specific characteristics for different kinds of pipelines.

Types of Data Pipelines

The structure and function of data pipelines will vary according to the use case to which they are applied, but three common types of pipelines are as follows:

- Data warehousing pipelines
- Stream processing pipelines
- Machine learning pipeline

Let's take a look at each in more detail.

Data Warehousing Pipelines

Data warehouses are databases for storing data from multiple data sources, typically organized in a dimensional data model. Dimensional data models are denormalized; that is, they do not adhere to the rules of normalization used in transaction processing systems. This is done intentionally because the purpose of a data warehouse is to answer analytic queries efficiently, and highly normalized data models can require complex joins and significant amounts of I/O operations. Denormalized dimensional models keep related data together in a minimal number of tables so that few joins are required.

Collecting and restructuring data from online transaction processing systems is often a multistep process. Some common patterns in data warehousing pipelines are as follows:

- Extraction, transformation, and load (ETL)
- Extraction, load, and transformation (ELT)
- Extraction and load
- Change data capture

These are often batch processing pipelines, but they can have some characteristics of streaming pipelines, especially in the case of change data capture.

Extract, Transformation, and Load

Extract, transformation, and load (ETL) pipelines begin with extracting data from one or more data sources. When multiple data sources are used, the extraction processes need to be coordinated. This is because extractions are often time based, so it is important that the extracted data cover the same time period. For example, an extraction process may run once an hour and extract data inserted or modified in the previous hour.

Consider an inventory data warehouse that extracts data once an hour from a database that tracks the number of products in each of the company's storage facilities. Products are coded using stock keeping unit (SKU) codes. A product database maintains the details on each product, such as description, suppliers, and unit costs. A data warehouse would need to extract data from the inventory database for the level of inventory information and from the products database for description information. If a new product is added to the product database and stocked in the warehouse, the data warehouse would need up-to-date data from both source databases; otherwise, there could be inventory data with no corresponding description data about the product.

In an ETL pipeline, data is transformed in the pipeline before being stored in a database. In the past, data warehouse developers may have used custom scripts to transform the data or a specialized ETL tool that allowed developers to specify transformation steps using a graphical user interface (GUI). This can work well in cases where the transformation code is already captured in scripts or when data analysts with limited programming experience are building transformations. It does, however, sometimes require developers to learn a tool in addition to SQL for manipulating data.

In GCP, transformations can be done using Cloud Dataproc or Cloud Dataflow. With Cloud Dataproc, transformations can be written in a Spark- or Hadoop-supported language. Spark uses an in-memory distributed data model for data manipulation and analysis. Spark programs can be written in Java, Scala, Python, R, and SQL. When using Cloud Dataproc, your transformations are written according to Hadoop's map reduce model or Spark's distributed tabular data structure. In addition to supporting Java for transformations, Hadoop provides *Pig*, a high-level language for data manipulation. Pig programs compile into map reduce programs that run on Hadoop.

When using Cloud Dataflow, you write transformations using the Apache Beam model, which provides a unified batch and stream processing model. Apache Beam is modeled as a pipeline and has explicit support for pipeline constructs, including the following:

Pipelines: An encapsulation of the end-to-end data processing task that executes the data operations

PCollection: A distributed dataset

PTransform: An operation on data, such as grouping by, flattening, and partitioning of data

Apache Beam programs are written in Java and Python.

For writing data to a database, Cloud Dataflow uses connectors, including Bigtable, Cloud Spanner, and BigQuery.

Cloud Dataproc is a good choice for implementing ETL processes if you are migrating existing Hadoop or Spark programs. Cloud Dataflow is the recommended tool for developing new ETL processes. Cloud Dataflow is serverless, so there is no cluster to manage and the processing model is based on data pipelines. Cloud Dataproc's Hadoop and Spark platforms are designed on big data analytics processing, so they can be used for transformations, but Cloud Dataflow model is based on data pipelines.

Extract, Load, and Transformation

Extract, load, and transformation (ELT) processes are slightly different from ETL processes. In an ELT process, data is loaded into a database before transforming the data. This process has some advantages over ETL.

When data is loaded before transformation, the database will contain the original data as extracted. This enables data warehouse developers to query the data using SQL, which can be useful for performing basic data quality checks and collecting statistics on characteristics such as the number of rows with missing data.

A second advantage is that developers can use SQL for transformation operations. This is especially helpful if developers are well versed in SQL but do not have programming experience. Developers would also be able to use SQL tools in addition to writing SQL from scratch.

Extraction and Load

Extraction and load procedures do not transform data. This type of process is appropriate when data does not require changes from the source format. Log data, for example, may be extracted and loaded without transformation. Dimensional data extracted from a data warehouse for loading into a smaller data mart also may not need transformation.

Change Data Capture

In a *change data capture* approach, each change in a source system is captured and recorded in a data store. This is helpful in cases where it is important to know all changes over time and not just the state of the database at the time of data extraction.

For example, an inventory database tracking the number of units of products available in a warehouse may have the following changes:

- Product A's inventory is set to 500 in Warehouse 1.
- Product B's inventory is set to 300 in Warehouse 1.
- Product A's inventory is reduced by 250 in Warehouse 1.
- Product A's inventory is reduced by 100 in Warehouse 1.

After these changes, Product A's inventory level is 150 and Product B's is 300. If you need to know only the final inventory level, then an ETL or ELT process is sufficient; however, if you need to know all the changes in inventory levels of products, then a change data capture approach is better.

Data warehousing pipelines are often batch oriented and run on regular schedules. When data needs to be processed continuously, a stream processing pipeline is required.

Stream Processing Pipelines

Streams are unending, continuous sources of data. Streams can be generated from many sources. Here are some examples:

- IoT devices collecting weather condition data may stream temperature, humidity, and pressure data from various locations every five minutes.

- Heart monitors in a hospital may stream cardiovascular metrics every second the monitor is in use.

- An agent collecting application performance metrics might send data every 15 seconds to a stream processing system for anomaly detection and alerting.

In the case of weather data, there may not be a need to process and analyze the data as soon as possible. This would be the case if the data is collected for long-term studies of climate change. The heart monitor example, however, may need to be analyzed as soon as possible in case the data indicates a medical condition that needs attention. Similarly, if an application has stopped reporting, then a DevOps engineer may want to be alerted immediately. In these cases, streamed data should be analyzed as soon as possible.

The kinds of analysis that you perform on streaming data is not all that different from batch processing analysis. It includes aggregating data, looking for anomalous patterns, and visualizing data in charts and graphs. The difference is in the way that you group the data. In a batch processing environment, all the data you need is available at once. This is not the case with streaming data.

Streaming data is continuous, so you need to pick subsets of the stream to work on at any one time. For example, you might average all the temperature readings from a sensor for the last hour to get an hourly average. You might calculate that average once an hour at the top of the hour. This would allow you to track how temperatures varied from hour to hour. You could also calculate the moving average of the last hours' worth of data every five minutes. This would give you a finer-grained view of how the temperatures vary. This is just one example of the different things that you should take into account when working with streaming data.

When building data pipelines for streaming data, consider several factors, including

- Event time and processing time
- Sliding and tumbling windows
- Late-arriving data and watermarks
- Missing data

There are various ways to process streaming data, and the configuration of your processing pipeline depends on these various factors.

Event Time and Processing Time

Data in time-series streams is ordered by time. If a set of data A arrives before data B, then presumably the event described by A occurred before the event described by B. There is a subtle but important issue implied in the previous sentence, which is that you are actually dealing with two points in time in stream processing:

- *Event time* is the time that something occurred at the place where the data is generated.

- *Processing time* is the time that data arrives at the endpoint where data is ingested. Processing time could be defined as some other point in the data pipeline, such as the time that transformation starts.

When working with streaming data, it is important to use one of these times consistently for ordering the streams. Event time is a good choice when the processing logic assumes that the data in the stream is in the same order as it was generated.

If data arrives at the ingestion endpoint in the same order that it was sent, then the ordering of the two times would be the same. If network congestion or some other issue causes delays, then data that was generated earlier could arrive later.

Sliding and Tumbling Windows

A *window* is a set of consecutive data points in a stream. Windows have a fixed width and a way of advancing. Windows that advance by a number of data points less than the width of the window are called *sliding windows*; windows that advance by the length of the window are *tumbling windows*.

Let's look at the example stream at the top of Figure 3.7. The stream has nine data points: 7, 9, 10, 12, 8, 9, 13, 8, and 4. The first three data points are shown in a window that is three data points wide (see Figure 3.7).

If you move the window forward one position in the stream, the window would include 9, 10, and 12. Moving the window down another position leaves the window containing 10, 12, and 8. This is how sliding windows advance through a stream of data.

If you move the window forward along the stream by the width of the window—in this case, three positions—you would have the first window include 7, 9, and 10. Advancing the window again by three positions would leave the window including 12, 8, and 9. This is how a tumbling window advances through a stream of data.

Sliding windows are used when you want to show how an aggregate—such as the average of the last three values—change over time, and you want to update that stream of averages each time a new value arrives in the stream.

Tumbling windows are used when you want to aggregate data over a fixed period of time, for example, for the last one minute. In that case, at the top of the minute you would calculate the average for the data that arrived in the last minute. The next time that you would calculate an average is at the top of the next minute. At that time, you would average the data that had arrived since the last average was calculated. There is no overlap in this case.

FIGURE 3.7   A stream with sliding and tumbling three window

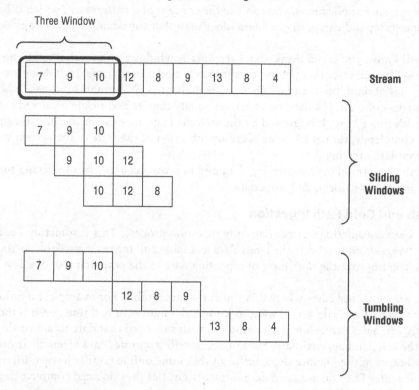

Late Arriving and Watermarks

When working with streaming data, especially time-series data, you have to decide how long you will wait for data to arrive. If you expect data to arrive about once a minute, you might be willing to wait up to three or four minutes for a late-arriving piece of data. For example, if your stream of data is from a medical device and you want to have a record of all data points whenever possible, you may be willing to wait longer than if you used the data to update a streaming chart. In that case, you may decide that after two minutes you would rather show a moving average of the last three data points instead of waiting longer.

When you wait for late-arriving data, you will have to maintain a buffer to accumulate data before performing stream processing operations. Consider a use case in which you take a stream as input and output a stream of averages for the last three minutes. If you have received data for one minute ago and three minutes ago but not two minutes ago, you will have to keep the two data points that have arrived in a buffer until you receive the two-minute data point, or until you wait as long as possible and then treat the two-minute data point as a piece of missing data.

When working with streams, you need to be able to assume at some point that no more data generated earlier than some specified time will arrive. For example, you may decide that any data that arrives 10 minutes late will not be ingested into the stream. To help stream processing applications, you can use the concept of a *watermark*, which is basically a timestamp indicating that no data older than that timestamp will ever appear in the stream.

Up until know, you could think about streams as windows of data that are finite and complete—like a dataset that you process in batch mode. In that case, windows are just small batches of data, but the reality is more complicated. Watermarks indicate a boundary on the lateness of data. If a data point arrives so late that its event time occurred before the watermark's timestamp, it is ignored by the stream. That does not mean that you should ignore it completely, though. A more accurate reflection of the state of the system would include that late-arriving data.

You can accommodate late-arriving data and improve accuracy by modifying the way that you ingest, transform, and store data.

Hot Path and Cold Path Ingestion

We have been considering a streaming-only ingestion process. This is sometimes called a *hot path ingestion*. It reflects the latest data available and makes it available as soon as possible. You improve the timeliness of reporting data at the potential risk of a loss of accuracy.

There are many use cases where this tradeoff is acceptable. For example, an online retailer having a flash sale would want to know sales figures in real time, even if they might be slightly off. Sales professionals running the flash sale need that data to adjust the parameters of the sale, and approximate, but not necessarily accurate, data meets their needs.

Accountants in the Finance department of that same online retailer have a different set of requirements. They do not need data immediately, but they do need complete data. In this case, even if the data was too late to be used in a stream processing pipeline, it could still be written to a database where it could be included in reports along with data that was included in the streaming dataset. This path from ingestion to persistent storage is called *cold path ingestion*. See Figure 3.8 for an example.

FIGURE 3.8   Data pipeline with both a hot path and a cold path

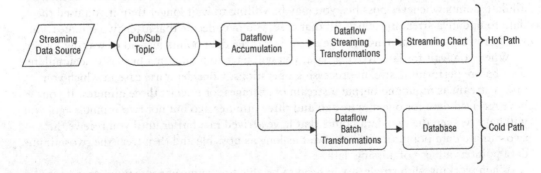

Stream and batch processing pipelines, like those described here, can meet the requirements of many use cases. The combination of the two can also meet the needs of machine

learning pipelines, but there are some machine-learning specific steps in those pipelines, so it's worth looking into those details.

Machine Learning Pipelines

Machine learning pipelines typically include some of the same steps as data warehousing pipelines but have some specific stages as well. A typical machine learning pipeline includes

- Data ingestion
- Data preprocessing, which is called *transformation* in data warehousing pipelines
- Feature engineering, which is another form of transformation
- Model training and evaluation
- Deployment

Data ingestion uses the same tools and services as data warehousing and streaming data pipelines. Cloud Storage is used for batch storage of datasets, whereas Cloud Pub/Sub can be used for the ingestion of streaming data.

Cloud Dataproc and Cloud Dataflow can be used for programmatic data preprocessing. In addition, Cloud Dataprep may be used for more ad hoc and interactive preparation of data. Cloud Dataprep is especially helpful when working with new datasets to understand the data in terms of the distribution of values of various attributes, the frequency of missing data, and for spotting other data quality problems. Ideally, once you have a good understanding of the kinds of preprocessing required by data from a particular source, you will encode that logic into a Cloud Dataflow process.

Feature engineering is a machine learning practice in which new attributes are introduced into a dataset. The new attributes are derived from one or more existing attributes. Sometimes, the new attributes are relatively simple to calculate. In the case of an IoT data stream sending weather data, you might want to calculate the ratio of temperature to pressure and of humidity to pressure and include those two ratios as new attributes or features. In other cases, the engineered features may be more complicated, like performing a fast Fourier transformation to map a stream of data into the frequency domain.

GCP Pipeline Components

GCP has several services that are commonly used components of pipelines, including the following:

- Cloud Pub/Sub
- Cloud Dataflow
- Cloud Dataproc
- Cloud Composer

Among these services, developers have a number of different processing model options.

Cloud Pub/Sub

Cloud Pub/Sub is a real-time messaging service that supports both push and pull subscription models. It is a managed service, and it requires no provisioning of servers or clusters. Cloud Pub/Sub will automatically scale and partition load as needed.

Working with Messaging Queues

Messaging queues are used in distributed systems to decouple services in a pipeline. This allows one service to produce more output than the consuming service can process without adversely affecting the consuming service. This is especially helpful when one process is subject to spikes in workload.

When working with Cloud Pub/Sub, you create a topic, which is a logical structure for organizing your messages. Once a topic is created, you create a subscription to the topic and then publish messages to the topic. Subscriptions are a logical structure for organizing the reception of messages by consuming processes.

When messaging queues receive data in a a message, it is considered a publication event. Upon publication, *push subscriptions* deliver the message to an endpoint. Some common types of endpoints are Cloud Functions, App Engine, and Cloud Run services. *Pull subscriptions* are used when you want the consuming application to control when messages are retrieved from a topic. Specifically, with pull subscriptions you send a request asking for *N* messages, and Cloud Pub/Sub responds with the next *N* or fewer messages.

Topics can be created in the console or the command line. The only required parameter is a topic ID, but you can also specify whether the topic should use a Google-managed key or a customer-managed key for encryption. The command to create a topic is gcloud pubsub topics create; for example:

```
gcloud pubsub topics create pde-topic-1
```

creates a topic called pde-exam-topic-1. Subscriptions can be created in the console, or with the gcloud pubsub subscriptions create command and specifying a topic ID and a subscription ID; for example:

```
gcloud pubsub subscriptions create --topic pde-topic-1 pde-subscripton-1
```

Messages can be written to topics using APIs and client libraries as well as a gcloud command. Processes that write messages are called *publishers* or *producers*; services that read messages are called *subscribers* or *consumers*.

Client libraries are available for a number of languages, including C#, Go, Java, Node.js, PHP, Python, and Ruby. (Additional languages may have been added by the time you read this.) Cloud Pub/Sub also supports REST APIs and gRPC APIs. The command-line tool is useful for testing your ability to publish and consume messages from a topic. For example, to publish a message with a string, you could issue the following:

```
gcloud pubsub topics publish pde-topic-1 --message "data engineer exam"
```

This command inserts or publishes the message to the pde-topic-1 topic, and the message is available to be read through a subscription. By default, when a topic is created, it is done so as a pull subscription. The `gcloud` command to read a message from a topic is `gcloud pubsub subscriptions`; for example:

```
gcloud pubsub subscriptions pull --auto-ack pde-subscripton-1
```

The `auto-ack` flag indicates that the message should be acknowledged automatically. Acknowledgments indicate to the subscription that the message has been read and processed so that it can be removed from the topic. When a message is sent but before it is acknowledged, the message is considered outstanding. While a message is outstanding to that subscriber, it will not be delivered to another subscriber on the same subscription. If the message is outstanding for a period of time greater than the time allowed for a subscriber to acknowledge the message, then it is no longer considered outstanding and will be delivered to another subscriber. The time allowed for a subscriber to acknowledge a message can be specified in the `subscription` command using the `ackDeadline` parameter. Messages can stay in a topic for up to seven days.

Pub/sub makes no guarantees that the order of message reception is the same as the publish order. In addition, messages can be delivered more than once. For these reasons, your processing logic should be idempotent; that is, the logic could be applied multiple times and still provide the same output. A trivial example is adding 0 to a number. No matter how many times you add 0 to a number, the result is always the same.

For a more interesting example, consider a process that receives a stream of messages that have identifiers and a count of the number of a particular type of event that occurred in a system in the past minute. The time is represented as the date followed by the number of minutes past midnight, so each minute of each day has a unique identifier. The stream processing system needs to keep a running cumulative total number of events for each day. If the process performing the aggregation simply added the count of each message it received to the running total, then duplicate messages would have their counts added in multiple times. This is not an idempotent operation. However, if instead the process keeps a list of all minutes for which data is received and it only adds in the counts of data points not received before, then the operation would be idempotent.

If you need guaranteed exactly once processing, use Cloud Dataflow PubsubIO, which de-duplicates based on a message ID. Cloud Dataflow can also be used to ensure that messages are processed in order.

Open Source Alternative: Kafka

One of the advantages of Cloud Pub/Sub is that it is a managed service. An open source alternative is *Apache Kafka*. Kafka is used to publish and subscribe to streams of messages and to reliably store messages in a fault-tolerant way.

Kafka runs in a cluster of one or more servers. You interact with Kafka programmatically by using one of the four APIs:

- Producer API
- Consumer API
- Streams API
- Connector API

The Producer API is used to publish messages, which are called records in Kafka parlance. The Consumer API supports subscriptions on topics. The Streams API supports stream processing operations that transform a stream of data into an output stream. The Connector API is used to enable Kafka to work with existing applications.

If you are migrating an on-premises service that uses Kafka and you want to replace self-managed Kafka with a managed service, then the Cloud Pub/Sub would meet that need. If you plan to continue to use Kafka, you can link Cloud Pub/Sub and Kafka using the CloudPubSubConnector, which is a bridge between the two messaging systems using Kafka Connect. CloudPubSubConnector is an open source tool maintained by the Cloud Pub/Sub team and is available here:

```
https://github.com/GoogleCloudPlatform/pubsub/tree/master/kafka-connector
```

Cloud Dataflow

Cloud Dataflow is a managed stream and batch processing service. It is a core component for building pipelines that collect, transform, and output data. In the past, developers would typically create a batch or stream processing pipeline—for example, the hot path and a separate batch processing pipeline; that is, the cold path. Cloud Dataflow pipelines are written using the Apache Beam API, which is a model for combined stream and batch processing. Apache Beam incorporates *Beam runners* in the data pipeline; the Cloud Dataflow runner is commonly used in GCP. Apache Flink is another commonly used Beam runner.

Cloud Dataflow does not require you to configure instances or clusters—it is a no-ops service. Cloud Dataflow pipelines are run within a region. It directly integrates with Cloud Pub/Sub, BigQuery, and the Cloud ML Engine. Cloud Dataflow integrates with Bigtable and Apache Kafka.

Much of your work with Cloud Dataflow is coding transformations in one of the languages supported by Apache Beam, which are currently Java and Python. For the purpose of the exam, it is important to understand Cloud Dataflow concepts.

Cloud Dataflow Concepts

Cloud Dataflow, and the Apache Beam model, are designed around several key concepts:

- Pipelines
- PCollection
- Transforms
- ParDo
- Pipeline I/O
- Aggregation
- User-defined functions
- Runner
- Triggers

Windowing concepts and watermarks are also important and were described earlier in the chapter.

Pipelines in Cloud Dataflow are, as you would expect, a series of computations applied to data that comes from a source. Each computation emits the results of computations, which become the input for the next computation in the pipeline. Pipelines represent a job that can be run repeatedly.

The *PCollection* abstraction is a dataset, which is the data used when a pipeline job is run. In the case of batch processing, the PCollection contains a fixed set of data. In the case of streaming data, the PCollection is unbounded.

Transforms are operations that map input data to some output data. Transforms operate on one or more PCollections as input and can produce one or more output PCollections. The operations can be mathematical calculations, data type conversions, and data grouping steps, as well as performing read and write operations.

ParDo is a parallel processing operation that runs a user-specified function on each element in a PCollection. ParDo transforms data in parallel. ParDo receives input data from a main PCollection but may also receive additional inputs from other PCollections by using a *side input*. Side inputs can be used to perform joins. Similarly, while a ParDo produces a main output PCollection, additional collections can be output using a *side output*. Side outputs are especially useful when you want to have additional processing paths. For example, a side output could be used for data that does not pass some validation check.

Pipeline I/Os are transforms for reading data into a pipeline from a source and writing data to a sink.

Aggregation is the process of computing a result from multiple input values. Aggregation can be simple, like counting the number of messages arriving in a one-minute period or averaging the values of metrics received over the past hour.

User-defined functions (UDF) are user-specified code for performing some operation, typically using a ParDo.

Runners are software that executes pipelines as jobs.

Triggers are functions that determine when to emit an aggregated result. In batch processing jobs, results are emitted when all the data has been processed. When operating on a stream, you have to specify a window over the stream to define a bounded subset, which is done by configuring the window.

Jobs and Templates

A *job* is an executing pipeline in Cloud Dataflow. There are two ways to execute jobs: the traditional method and the template method.

With the traditional method, developers create a pipeline in a development environment and run the job from that environment. The template method separates development from staging and execution. With the template method, developers still create pipelines in a development environment, but they also create a template, which is a configured job specification. The specification can have parameters that are specified when a user runs the template. Google provides a number of templates, and you can create your own as well. See Figure 3.9 for examples of templates provided by Google.

FIGURE 3.9 Creating a Cloud Dataflow job in the console using a template

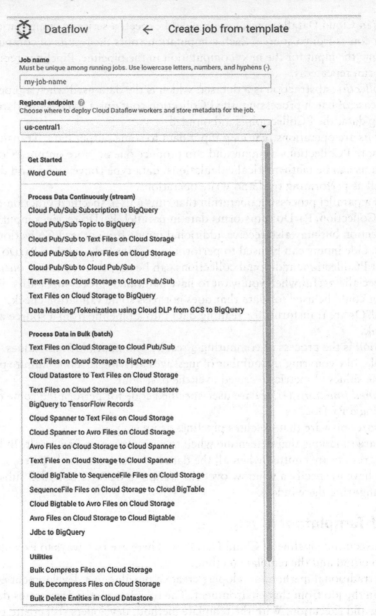

After selecting a template, you can specify parameters, such as source and sink specifications. Figure 3.10 shows the parameters and transformations used in the Word Count Template.

FIGURE 3.10   Specifying parameters for the Word Count Template

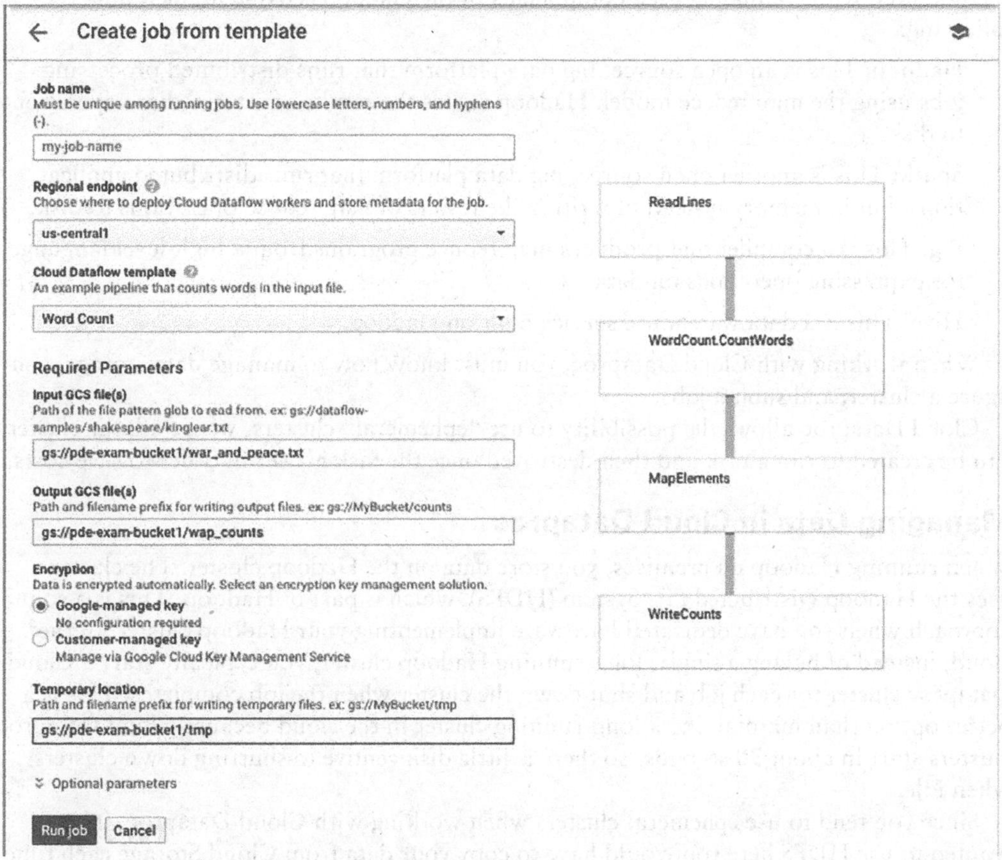

Jobs can be run from the command line and through the use of APIs as well. For example, you could use the gcloud dataflow jobs run command to start a job. An example of a complete job run command looks like this:

```
gcloud dataflow jobs run pde-job-1 \
--gcs-location gs://pde-exam-cert/templates/word-count-template
```

This command creates a job named pde-job-1 using a template file called word-count-template located in the pde-exam-cert/templates bucket.

Cloud Dataproc

Cloud Dataproc is a managed Hadoop and Spark service where a preconfigured cluster can be created with one command line or console operation. Cloud Dataproc makes it easy to migrate from on-premises Hadoop clusters to GCP. A typical Cloud Dataproc cluster is configured with commonly used components of the Hadoop ecosystem, including the following:

Hadoop: This is an open source, big data platform that runs distributed processing jobs using the map reduce model. Hadoop writes the results of intermediate operations to disk.

Spark: This is another open source, big data platform that runs distributed applications, but in memory instead of writing the results of map reduce operations to disk.

Pig: This is a compiler that produces map reduce programs from a high-level language for expressing operations on data.

Hive: This is a data warehouse service built on Hadoop.

When working with Cloud Dataproc, you must know how to manage data storage, configure a cluster, and submit jobs.

Cloud Dataproc allows the possibility to use "ephemeral" clusters, where a large cluster can be created to run a task and then destroyed once the task is over in order to save costs.

Managing Data in Cloud Dataproc

When running Hadoop on premises, you store data on the Hadoop cluster. The cluster uses the Hadoop Distributed File System (HDFS), which is part of Hadoop. This is a sound approach when you have dedicated hardware implementing your Hadoop cluster. In the cloud, instead of having a single, long-running Hadoop cluster, you typically start a Cloud Dataproc cluster for each job and shut down the cluster when the job completes. This is a better option than maintaining a long-running cluster in the cloud because Cloud Dataproc clusters start in about 90 seconds, so there is little disincentive to shutting down clusters when idle.

Since you tend to use ephemeral clusters when working with Cloud Dataproc, if you wanted to use HDFS here you would have to copy your data from Cloud Storage each time you started a cluster. A better approach is to use Cloud Storage as the data store. This saves the time and the cost of having to copy data to the cluster.

Configuring a Cloud Dataproc Cluster

Cloud Dataproc clusters consist of two types of nodes: master nodes and worker nodes. The master node is responsible for distributing and managing workload distribution. The master node runs a system called YARN, which stands for Yet Another Resource Negotiator. YARN uses data about the workload and resource availability on each worker node to determine where to run jobs.

When creating a cluster, you will specify a number of configuration parameters, including a cluster name and the region and zone to create the cluster. Clusters can run on a single node, which is a good option for development. They can also run with one master and some number of worker nodes. This is known as *standard mode*. *High availability mode* uses three master nodes and some number of workers. You can specify a machine configuration for both the master and worker nodes, and they do not have to be the same. Worker nodes can include some preemptible machines, although HDFS storage does not run on preemptible nodes, which is another reason to use Cloud Storage instead of HDFS.

Initialization scripts can be run when the cluster is created by specifying script files located in a Cloud Storage bucket.

Clusters can be created using the console or the command line. The following gcloud dataproc clusters create command, for example, will create a cluster with the default configuration:

```
gcloud dataproc clusters create pde-cluster-1
```

Once a cluster is created, it can be scaled up or down. Only the number of worker nodes can change—master nodes are fixed. You can manually scale the size of a cluster using the gcloud dataproc clusters update command, as follows:

```
gcloud dataproc clusters update pde-cluster-1 \
--num-workers 10 \
--num-preemptible-workers 20
```

This snippet will scale the cluster to run 10 regular workers and 20 preemptible worker nodes.

Cloud Dataproc also supports autoscaling by creating an autoscaling policy for a cluster. An autoscaling policy is specified in a YAML file and includes parameters such as

- maxInstances
- scaleUpFactor
- scaleDownFactor
- cooldownPeriod

Autoscaling works by checking Hadoop YARN metrics about memory use at the end of each cooldownPeriod. The number of nodes added or removed is determined by the current number and the scaling factor.

Submitting a Job

Jobs are submitted to Cloud Dataproc using an API, a gcloud command, or in the console. The gcloud dataproc jobs submit command runs a job from the command line. Here is an example command:

```
gcloud dataproc jobs submit pyspark \
--cluster pde-cluster-1 \
--region us-west-1 \
gs://pde-exam-cert/dataproc-scripts/analysis.py
```

This command submits a PySpark job to the pde-cluster-1 cluster in the us-west-1 region and runs the program in the analysis.py file in the pde-exam-cert/ dataproc-scripts Cloud Storage bucket.

In general, it is a good practice to keep clusters in the same region as the Cloud Storage buckets that will be used for storing data. You can expect to see better I/O performance when you configure nodes with larger persistent disks and that use SSDs over HDDs.

Cloud Composer

Cloud Composer is a managed service implementing Apache Airflow, which is used for scheduling and managing workflows. As pipelines become more complex and have to be resilient when errors occur, it becomes more important to have a framework for managing workflows so that you are not reinventing code for handling errors and other exceptional cases.

Cloud Composer automates the scheduling and monitoring of workflows. Workflows are defined using Python and are directed acyclic graphs. Cloud Composer has built-in integration with BigQuery, Cloud Dataflow, Cloud Dataproc, Cloud Datastore, Cloud Storage, Cloud Pub/Sub, and AI Platform.

Before you can run workflows with Cloud Composer, you will need to create an environment in GCP. Environments run on the Google Kubernetes Engine, so you will have to specify a number of nodes, location, machine type, disk size, and other node and network configuration parameters. You will need to create a Cloud Storage bucket as well.

Migrating Hadoop and Spark to GCP

When you are migrating Hadoop and Spark clusters to GCP, there are a few things for which you will need to plan:

- Migrating data
- Migrating jobs
- Migrating HBase to Bigtable

You may also have to shift your perspective on how you use clusters. On-premises clusters are typically large persistent clusters that run multiple jobs. They can be complicated to configure and manage. In GCP, it is a best practice to use an ephemeral cluster for each job. This approach leads to less complicated configurations and reduced costs, since you are not storing persistent data on the cluster and not running the cluster for extended periods of time.

Hadoop and Spark migrations can happen incrementally, especially since you will be using ephemeral clusters configured for specific jobs. The first step is to migrate some data to Cloud Storage. Then you can deploy ephemeral clusters to run jobs that use that data. It is best to start with low-risk jobs so that you can learn the details of working with Cloud Dataproc.

There may be cases where you will have to keep an on-premises cluster while migrating some jobs and data to GCP. In those cases, you will have to keep data synchronized between environments. Plan to implement workflows to keep data synchronized. You should have a way to determine which jobs and data move to the cloud and which stay on premises.

It is a good practice to migrate HBase databases to Bigtable, which provides consistent, scalable performance. When migrating to Bigtable, you will need to export HBase tables to sequence files and copy those to Cloud Storage. Next, you will have to import the sequence files using Cloud Dataflow. When the size of data to migrate is greater than 20 TB, use the Transfer Appliance. When the size is less than 20 TB and there is at least 100 Mbps of network bandwidth available, then `distcp`, a Hadoop distributed copy command, is the recommended way to copy the data. In addition, it is important to know how long it will take to transfer the data and to have a mechanism for keeping the on-premises data in sync with the data in Cloud Storage.

Exam Essentials

Understand the model of data pipelines.   A data pipeline is an abstract concept that captures the idea that data flows from one stage of processing to another. Data pipelines are modeled as directed acyclic graphs (DAGs). A graph is a set of nodes linked by edges. A directed graph has edges that flow from one node to another.

Know the four stages in a data pipeline.   *Ingestion* is the process of bringing data into the GCP environment. *Transformation* is the process of mapping data from the structure used in the source system to the structure used in the *storage* and *analysis* stages of the data pipeline. Cloud Storage can be used as both the staging area for storing data immediately after ingestion and also as a long-term store for transformed data. BigQuery and Cloud Storage treat data as external tables and query them. Cloud Dataproc can use Cloud Storage as HDFS-compatible storage. Analysis can take on several forms, from simple SQL querying and report generation to machine learning model training and data science analysis.

Know that the structure and function of data pipelines will vary according to the use case to which they are applied.   Three common types of pipelines are data warehousing pipelines, stream processing pipelines, and machine learning pipelines.

Know the common patterns in data warehousing pipelines.   Extract, transformation, and load (ETL) pipelines begin with extracting data from one or more data sources. When multiple data sources are used, the extraction processes need to be coordinated. This is because extractions are often time based, so it is important that extracts from different sources cover the same time period. Extract, load, and transformation (ELT) processes are slightly different from ETL processes. In an ELT process, data is loaded into a database before transforming the data. Extraction and load procedures do not transform data. This kind of process is appropriate when data does not require changes from the source format. In a change data capture approach, each change is a source system that is captured and recorded in a data store. This is helpful in cases where it is important to know all changes over time and not just the state of the database at the time of data extraction.

Understand the unique processing characteristics of stream processing.   This includes the difference between event time and processing time, sliding and tumbling windows, late-arriving data and watermarks, and missing data. Event time is the time that something occurred at the place where the data is generated. Processing time is the time that data arrives at the endpoint where data is ingested. Sliding windows are used when you want to show how an aggregate, such as the average of the last three values, change over time, and you want to update that stream of averages each time a new value arrives in the stream. Tumbling windows are used when you want to aggregate data over a fixed period of time—for example, for the last one minute.

Know the components of a typical machine learning pipeline.   This includes data ingestion, data preprocessing, feature engineering, model training and evaluation, and deployment. Data ingestion uses the same tools and services as data warehousing and streaming data pipelines. Cloud Storage is used for batch storage of datasets, whereas Cloud Pub/Sub can be used for the ingestion of streaming data. Feature engineering is a machine learning practice in which new attributes are introduced into a dataset. The new attributes are derived from one or more existing attributes.

Know that Cloud Pub/Sub is a managed message queue service.   Cloud Pub/Sub is a real-time messaging service that supports both push and pull subscription models. It is a managed service, and it requires no provisioning of servers or clusters. Cloud Pub/Sub will automatically scale as needed. Messaging queues are used in distributed systems to decouple services in a pipeline. This allows one service to produce more output than the consuming service can process without adversely affecting the consuming service. This is especially helpful when one process is subject to spikes.

Know that Cloud Dataflow is a managed stream and batch processing service.   Cloud Dataflow is a core component for running pipelines that collect, transform, and output data. In the past, developers would typically create a stream processing pipeline (hot path) and a separate batch processing pipeline (cold path). Cloud Dataflow is based on Apache

Beam, which is a model for combined stream and batch processing. Understand these key Cloud Dataflow concepts:

- Pipelines
- PCollection
- Transforms
- ParDo
- Pipeline I/O
- Aggregation
- User-defined functions
- Runner
- Triggers

Know that Cloud Dataproc is a managed Hadoop and Spark service. Cloud Dataproc makes it easy to create and destroy ephemeral clusters. Cloud Dataproc makes it easy to migrate from on-premises Hadoop clusters to GCP. A typical Cloud Dataproc cluster is configured with commonly used components of the Hadoop ecosystem, including Hadoop, Spark, Pig, and Hive. Cloud Dataproc clusters consist of two types of nodes: master nodes and worker nodes. The master node is responsible for distributing and managing workload distribution.

Know that Cloud Composer is a managed service implementing Apache Airflow. Cloud Composer is used for scheduling and managing workflows. As pipelines become more complex and have to be resilient when errors occur, it becomes more important to have a framework for managing workflows so that you are not reinventing code for handling errors and other exceptional cases. Cloud Composer automates the scheduling and monitoring of workflows. Before you can run workflows with Cloud Composer, you will need to create an environment in GCP.

Understand what to consider when migrating from on-premises Hadoop and Spark to GCP. Factors include migrating data, migrating jobs, and migrating HBase to Bigtable. Hadoop and Spark migrations can happen incrementally, especially since you will be using ephemeral clusters configured for specific jobs. There may be cases where you will have to keep an on-premises cluster while migrating some jobs and data to GCP. In those cases, you will have to keep data synchronized between environments. It is a good practice to migrate HBase databases to Bigtable, which provides consistent, scalable performance.

Review Questions

You can find the answers in the appendix.

1. A large enterprise using GCP has recently acquired a startup that has an IoT platform. The acquiring company wants to migrate the IoT platform from an on-premises data center to GCP and wants to use Google Cloud managed services whenever possible. What GCP service would you recommend for ingesting IoT data?

   A. Cloud Storage

   B. Cloud SQL

   C. Cloud Pub/Sub

   D. BigQuery streaming inserts

2. You are designing a data pipeline to populate a sales data mart. The sponsor of the project has had quality control problems in the past and has defined a set of rules for filtering out bad data before it gets into the data mart. At what stage of the data pipeline would you implement those rules?

   A. Ingestion

   B. Transformation

   C. Storage

   D. Analysis

3. A team of data warehouse developers is migrating a set of legacy Python scripts that have been used to transform data as part of an ETL process. They would like to use a service that allows them to use Python and requires minimal administration and operations support. Which GCP service would you recommend?

   A. Cloud Dataproc

   B. Cloud Dataflow

   C. Cloud Spanner

   D. Cloud Dataprep

4. You are using Cloud Pub/Sub to buffer records from an application that generates a stream of data based on user interactions with a website. The messages are read by another service that transforms the data and sends it to a machine learning model that will use it for training. A developer has just released some new code, and you notice that messages are sent repeatedly at 10-minute intervals. What might be the cause of this problem?

   A. The new code release changed the subscription ID.

   B. The new code release changed the topic ID.

   C. The new code disabled acknowledgments from the consumer.

   D. The new code changed the subscription from pull to push.

5. It is considered a good practice to make your processing logic idempotent when consuming messages from a Cloud Pub/Sub topic. Why is that?

    A. Messages may be delivered multiple times.

    B. Messages may be received out of order.

    C. Messages may be delivered out of order.

    D. A consumer service may need to wait extended periods of time between the delivery of messages.

6. A group of IoT sensors is sending streaming data to a Cloud Pub/Sub topic. A Cloud Dataflow service pulls messages from the topic and reorders the messages sorted by event time. A message is expected from each sensor every minute. If a message is not received from a sensor, the stream processing application should use the average of the values in the last four messages. What kind of window would you use to implement the missing data logic?

    A. Sliding window

    B. Tumbling window

    C. Extrapolation window

    D. Crossover window

7. Your department is migrating some stream processing to GCP and keeping some on premises. You are tasked with designing a way to share data from on-premises pipelines that use Kafka with GPC data pipelines that use Cloud Pub/Sub. How would you do that?

    A. Use CloudPubSubConnector and Kafka Connect

    B. Stream data to a Cloud Storage bucket and read from there

    C. Write a service to read from Kafka and write to Cloud Pub/Sub

    D. Use Cloud Pub/Sub Import Service

8. A team of developers wants to create standardized patterns for processing IoT data. Several teams will use these patterns. The developers would like to support collaboration and facilitate the use of patterns for building streaming data pipelines. What component should they use?

    A. Cloud Dataflow Python Scripts

    B. Cloud Dataproc PySpark jobs

    C. Cloud Dataflow templates

    D. Cloud Dataproc templates

9. You need to run several map reduce jobs on Hadoop along with one Pig job and four PySpark jobs. When you ran the jobs on premises, you used the department's Hadoop cluster. Now you are running the jobs in GCP. What configuration for running these jobs would you recommend?

    A. Create a single cluster and deploy Pig and Spark in the cluster.

    B. Create one persistent cluster for the Hadoop jobs, one for the Pig job and one for the PySpark jobs.

    C. Create one cluster for each job, and keep the cluster running continuously so that you do not need to start a new cluster for each job.

    D. Create one cluster for each job and shut down the cluster when the job completes.

10. You are working with a group of genetics researchers analyzing data generated by gene sequencers. The data is stored in Cloud Storage. The analysis requires running a series of six programs, each of which will output data that is used by the next process in the pipeline. The final result set is loaded into BigQuery. What tool would you recommend for orchestrating this workflow?

    A. Cloud Composer

    B. Cloud Dataflow

    C. Apache Flink

    D. Cloud Dataproc

11. An on-premises data warehouse is currently deployed using HBase on Hadoop. You want to migrate the database to GCP. You could continue to run HBase within a Cloud Dataproc cluster, but what other option would help ensure consistent performance and support the HBase API?

    A. Store the data in Cloud Storage

    B. Store the data in Cloud Bigtable

    C. Store the data in Cloud Datastore

    D. Store the data in Cloud Dataflow

12. The business owners of a data warehouse have determined that the current design of the data warehouse is not meeting their needs. In addition to having data about the state of systems at certain points in time, they need to know about all the times that data changed between those points in time. What kind of data warehousing pipeline should be used to meet this new requirement?

    A. ETL

    B. ELT

    C. Extraction and load

    D. Change data capture

Chapter

4

Designing a Data Processing Solution

GOOGLE CLOUD PROFESSIONAL DATA
ENGINEER EXAM OBJECTIVES COVERED
IN THIS CHAPTER INCLUDE THE
FOLLOWING:

1. Designing data processing systems

✓ **1.3   Designing a data processing solution. Considerations
    include:**

- Choice of infrastructure

- System availability and fault tolerance

- Use of distributed systems

- Capacity planning

- Hybrid cloud and edge computing

- Architecture options (e.g., message brokers, message
  queues, middleware, service-oriented architecture,
  serverless functions)

- At least once, in-order, and exactly once, etc., event
  processing

✓ **1.4   Migrating data warehousing and data processing.
Considerations include:**

- Awareness of current state and how to migrate a design to a
  future state

- Migrating from on-premises to cloud (Data Transfer Service,
  Transfer Appliance, Cloud Networking)

- Validating a migration

Data engineers need to understand how to design processing solutions that start with data collection and end with data exploration and visualization. In this chapter, you will learn about designing infrastructure for data engineering and machine learning, including how to do the following:

- Choose an appropriate compute service for your use case
- Design for scalability, reliability, availability, and maintainability
- Use hybrid and edge computing architecture patterns
- Design distributed processing systems and use appropriate event processing models
- Migrate a data warehouse from on-premises data centers to GCP

The discussion in this chapter further highlights the need to employ multiple GCP services together to build a comprehensive solution for common enterprise use cases.

Designing Infrastructure

Data engineers are expected to understand how to choose infrastructure appropriate for a use case; how to design for scalability, reliability, availability, and maintainability; and how to incorporate hybrid and edge computing capabilities into a design.

Choosing Infrastructure

GCP provides a range of compute infrastructure options. The best choice for your data engineering needs may depend on several factors. The four key compute options with which you should be familiar are as follows:

- Compute Engine
- Kubernetes Engine
- App Engine
- Cloud Functions

Newer services, such as Cloud Run and Anthos, are also available for use, but they are currently not included in the Professional Data Engineer exam and so will not be covered here.

Compute Engine

Compute Engine is GCP's infrastructure-as-a-service (IaaS) product. With Compute Engine, you have the greatest amount of control over your infrastructure relative to the other GCP compute services.

Compute Engine provides virtual machine (VM) instances, and users have full access to the VM's operating system. Users can choose from a large number of operating systems that are available on GCP. Once an instance is created, users are free to install and configure additional software to meet their needs.

Users also configure the machine type either by choosing a predefined machine type or by configuring a custom machine type. Machine types vary by the number of vCPUs and the amount of memory provided. Instances can be configured with more security features, such as Shielded VMs and accelerators, such as GPUs, which are often used with machine learning and other compute-intensive applications.

In addition to specifying the machine type, operating system, and optional features, you will specify a region and zone when creating a VM.

VMs can be grouped together into clusters for high availability and scalability. A managed instance group is a set of VMs with identical configurations that are managed as a single unit. Managed instance groups are configured with a minimum and a maximum number of instances. The number of instances in the group will vary to scale up or down with workload.

Compute Engine is a good option when you need maximum control over the configuration of VMs and are willing to manage instances.

Kubernetes Engine

Kubernetes is a container orchestration system, and *Kubernetes Engine* is a managed Kubernetes service. Kubernetes is an open source platform developed by Google and now widely used for deploying containerized applications. Kubernetes is deployed on a cluster of servers. You could run your own Kubernetes cluster by deploying it to VMs in Compute Engine, but then you would have to take on the responsibility for operating the cluster. With Kubernetes Engine, Google maintains the cluster and assumes responsibility for installing and configuring the Kubernetes platform on the cluster. Kubernetes Engine deploys Kubernetes on managed instance groups.

One of the advantages of Kubernetes is that users can precisely tune the allocation of cluster resources to each container. This is especially useful when applications are designed as a set of microservices. For example, a microservice might need only a small fraction of a CPU. In that case, a container running that microservice can be allocated only the amount of CPU needed. This allows for more efficient use of compute resources.

Alternatively, if the microservice were deployed on a VM with a full vCPU, the vCPU would be underutilized. This leaves developers with the choice of either tolerating inefficient utilization or running additional microservices on the same virtual machine. This approach has its own disadvantages. Unless all microservices have the same lifecycle, you may find that performing maintenance on one microservice can disrupt the operations of the other microservices.

By separating application components into microservices and running those microservices in their own containers, you can improve resource utilization and possibly make the application easier to maintain and update.

Another advantage of Kubernetes is that it can run in multiple environments, including other cloud providers and in on-premises data centers. Kubernetes can detect when containers within pods are not functioning correctly and replace them. Kubernetes can also scale up and down the number of pods to accommodate changing workloads.

Perhaps the most significant constraint of Kubernetes is that applications must be containerized to run on Kubernetes. If existing applications running on premises in VMs are migrating to the cloud, a lift-and-shift migration, in which the system architecture is not changed, to Compute Engine is likely the fastest way to get to the cloud. Once there, you can containerize your application.

 Anthos Migrate is a GCP service for migrating workloads configured to run on physical machines and virtual machines to containers. The service is currently in beta. For more information, see https://cloud.google.com/ migrate/anthos/.

App Engine

App Engine is GCP's original platform-as-a-service (PaaS) offering. App Engine is designed to allow developers to focus on application development while minimizing their need to support the infrastructure that runs their applications. App Engine has two versions: App Engine Standard and App Engine Flexible.

App Engine Standard is a platform for running applications in a language-specific serverless environment. Currently, App Engine Standard supports Go, Java, PHP, Node.js, and Python, but the set of supported languages may have changed by the time you read this. App Engine Standard is available in two forms: first generation and second generation. Second-generation services offer more memory and more runtime options.

Each application running in App Engine Standard has an instance class that determines the amount of available CPU and memory. Resources in instance classes currently run from 256 MB of memory and a 600 MHz CPU up to 2048 MB of memory and a 4.8 GHz CPU.

App Engine Flexible runs Docker containers. This allows developers to customize their runtime environments in ways not available in App Engine Standard. For example, developers can start with custom Docker images, install additional libraries and packages, and then deploy container instances based on that image. App Engine Flexible also provides health checks and automatically patches the underlying operating system.

App Engine Standard is a good option when your application is developed in one of the supported languages and needs to scale up and down based on workload. App Engine Flexible is a good option when you want to have the advantages of a PaaS as well as the ability to customize your runtime environment.

Cloud Functions

Cloud Functions is a serverless, managed compute service for running code in response to events that occur in the cloud. Events such as writing a message to a Cloud Pub/Sub topic or uploading a file to Cloud Storage can trigger the execution of a Cloud Function. Cloud Functions also respond to events in HTTP, Firebase, and Stackdriver Logging.

For each supported service, Cloud Functions respond to specific events. In Cloud Storage, a script can execute in response to uploading, deleting, and archiving files. HTTP events include GET, POST, PUT, DELETE, and OPTIONS operations.

Cloud Functions is written using JavaScript, Python 3, and Go.

Cloud Functions is a good option when you need to execute code in response to events that can occur at any time, such as uploading a file or calling a webhook. They are also useful when ingesting data using Cloud Pub/Sub, such as in an IoT ingestion pipeline.

The four main compute infrastructure options are summarized in Figure 4.1.

FIGURE 4.1   Summary of compute option features

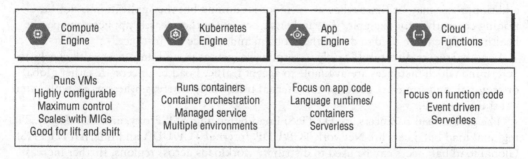

Availability, Reliability, and Scalability of Infrastructure

When we design systems, we need to consider three nonfunctional requirements: availability, reliability, and scalability.

Availability is defined as the ability of a user to access a resource at a specific time. Availability is usually measured as the percentage of time that a system is operational.

Availability is a function of *reliability*, which is defined as the probability that a system will meet service-level objectives for some duration of time. Reliability is often measured as the mean time between failures.

Scalability is the ability of a system to handle increases in workload by adding resources to the system as needed. This implies that as workload increases, resources will be available to process that workload. It also implies that as workload decreases, the amount of allocated resources will decrease to a level sufficient to meet the workload plus some marginal extra capacity.

Monitoring and logging are also essential practices to ensure infrastructure availability and reliability. Those topics will be discussed in detail in Chapter 5, "Building and Operationalizing Processing Infrastructure."

Making Compute Resources Available, Reliable, and Scalable

Highly available and scalable compute resources typically employ clusters of machines or virtual machines with load balancers and autoscalers to distribute workload and adjust the size of the cluster to meet demand.

Compute Engine

When using Compute Engine, you are responsible for ensuring high availability and scalability. This is done with managed instance groups (MIGs). MIGs are defined using a template. Templates include specifications for the machine type, boot disk image or container image, labels, and other instance properties. All members of a MIG are identical.

When an instance in a MIG fails, it is replaced with an identically configured VM. In addition, there may be times when an instance is running but the application is not functioning correctly—for example, if a fatal error occurs. In those cases, application-specific health checks can be used to detect the problem and replace the instance.

Load balancers direct traffic only to responsive instances, and they use health checks to determine which instances are available to accept traffic. Load balancers are either global or regional, and some are designed for internal traffic only whereas others work with external traffic as well.

The global load balancers are HTTP(S) Load Balancing, SSL Proxy, and TCP Proxy. The regional load balancers are Network TCP/UDP, Internal TCP/UDP, and Internal HTTP(S). Global load balancers can be used to distribute workloads across regions, further increasing the availability and reliability of applications.

Instance groups can be either zonal or regional. In zonal instance groups, all instances are created in the same zone. Regional instance groups place instances in multiple zones in the same region. The latter provides higher availability because the MIG could withstand a zone-level failure and the applications would continue to be available.

Autoscalers add and remove instances according to workload. When using autoscaling, you create a policy that specifies the criteria for adjusting the size of the group. Criteria include CPU utilization and other metrics collected by Stackdriver, load-balancing capacity, and the number of messages in a queue.

Note that when you use Compute Engine, you have the greatest level of control over your instances, but you are also responsible for configuring managed instance groups, load balancers, and autoscalers.

Kubernetes Engine

Kubernetes is designed to support high availability, reliability, and scalability for containers and applications running in a cluster. Kubernetes deploys containers in an abstraction known as a *pod*. When pods fail, they are replaced much like failed instances in a managed instance group. Nodes in Kubernetes Engine belong to a pool, and with the autorepair feature turned on, failed nodes will be reprovisioned automatically.

There are other ways Kubernetes Engine ensures high availability and reliability. When using Kubernetes Engine, you can specify whether the endpoint for accessing the cluster is zonal or regional. In the latter case, you can access the cluster even if there is a failure in a zone. Also, you can specify a high availability cluster configuration that replicates master and worker nodes across multiple zones.

App Engine and Cloud Functions

A key advantage of serverless, managed services like App Engine and Cloud Functions is that they are designed to be highly available, scalable, and reliable.

In App Engine, when the scheduler has a request, it can send it to an existing instance, add it to a queue, or start another instance, depending on how you have configured App Engine. With App Engine, you do have the option of configuring policies for scaling. This is done by specifying values for target CPU utilization, target throughput utilization, and maximum concurrent requests.

Cloud Functions are designed so that each instance of a cloud function handles one request at a time. If there is a spike in workload, additional function instances can be created. You have some control over this with the ability to set a maximum number of concurrently running instances.

Making Storage Resources Available, Reliable, and Scalable

GCP provides a range of storage systems, from in-memory caches to archival storage. Here are some examples.

Memorystore is an in-memory Redis cache. Standard Tier is automatically configured to maintain a replica in a different zone. The replica is used only for high availability, not scalability. The replica is used only when Redis detects a failure and triggers a failover to the replica.

Persistent disks are used with Compute Engine and Kubernetes Engine to provide network-based disk storage to VMs and containers. Persistent disks have built-in redundancy for high availability and reliability. Also, users can create snapshots of disks and store them in Cloud Storage for additional risk mitigation.

Cloud SQL is a managed relational database that can operate in high-availability mode by maintaining a primary instance in one zone and a standby instance in another zone within the same region. Synchronous replication keeps the data up to date in both instances. If you require multi-regional redundancy in your relational database, you should consider Cloud Spanner.

Cloud Storage stores replicas of objects within a region when using standard storage and across regions when using multi-regional storage.

Making Network Resources Available, Reliable, and Scalable

Networking resources requires advanced planning for availability, reliability, and scalability.

You have the option of using Standard Tier or Premium Tier networking. Standard Tier uses the public Internet network to transfer data between Google data centers, whereas Premium Tier routes traffic only over Google's global network. When using the Standard Tier, your data is subject to the reliability of the public Internet.

Network interconnects between on-premises data centers and Google Cloud are not rapidly scaled up or down. At the low end of the bandwidth spectrum, VPNs are used when up to 3 Gbps is sufficient. It is common practice to use two VPNs to connect an enterprise data center to the GCP for redundancy. HA VPN is an option for high-availability VPNs that uses two IP addresses and provides a 99.99 percent service availability, in contrast to the standard VPN, which has a 99.9 percent service level agreement.

For high-throughput use cases, enterprises can use Cloud Interconnect. *Cloud Interconnect* is available as a dedicated interconnect in which an enterprise directly connects to a Google endpoint and traffic flows directly between the two networks. The other option is to use a partner interconnect, in which case data flows through a third-party network but not over the Internet. Architects may choose Cloud Interconnect for better security, higher speed, and entry into protected networks. In this case, availability, reliability, and scalability are all addressed by redundancy in network infrastructure.

Another infrastructure consideration for data engineers is hybrid cloud computing.

Hybrid Cloud and Edge Computing

There are some enterprise data engineering use cases that leverage both cloud and non-cloud compute and storage resources. The analytics hybrid cloud combines on-premises transaction processing systems with cloud-based analytics platforms. In situations where connectivity may not be reliable or sufficient, a combination of cloud and edge-based computing may be used.

Analytics Hybrid Cloud

The *analytics hybrid cloud* is used when transaction processing systems continue to run on premises and data is extracted and transferred to the cloud for analytic processing. This division of computational labor works well because transaction processing systems often have predictable workloads with little variance. Analytic workloads are predictable but can be highly variable, with little or no load at given times and bursts of high demand at other times. The latter is well suited to the cloud's ability to deliver on-demand, scalable compute resources.

GCP has services that support the full lifecycle of analytics processing, including the following:

- Cloud Storage for batch storage of extracted data
- Cloud Pub/Sub for streaming data ingestion
- Cloud Dataflow and Cloud Dataproc for transformation and some analysis
- Cloud BigQuery for SQL querying and analytic operations

- Cloud Bigtable for storage of large volumes of data used for machine learning and other analytic processing
- Cloud Datalab and Cloud Data Studio for interactive analysis and visualization

Cloud Dataproc is particularly useful when migrating Hadoop and Spark jobs from an on-premises cluster to GCP. When migrating data that had been stored in an HDFS filesystem on premises, it is best to move that data to Cloud Storage. From there, Cloud Dataproc can access the data as if it were in an HDFS filesystem.

Consider how to populate a data warehouse or data lake initially in GCP. If you are migrating a large on-premises data warehouse or data lake, you may need to use the Cloud Transfer Appliance; smaller data warehouses and data marts can be migrated over the network if there is sufficient bandwidth. For additional details on how long it takes to transfer different volumes of data, see Google's helpful matrix on transfer volumes, network throughputs, and time required to transfer data at `https://cloud.google.com/products/data-transfer/`.

Edge Cloud

A variation of hybrid clouds is an *edge cloud,* which uses local computation resources in addition to cloud platforms (see Figure 4.2). This architecture pattern is used when a network may not be reliable or have sufficient bandwidth to transfer data to the cloud. It is also used when low-latency processing is required.

FIGURE 4.2   Edge computing brings some computation outside the cloud and closer to where the results of computation are applied.

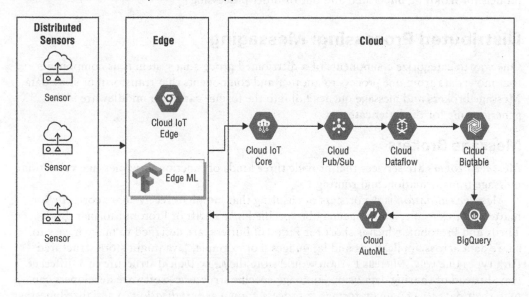

For example, an IoT system monitoring a manufacturing device may employ machine learning models to detect anomalies in the device's functioning. If an anomaly is detected, the IoT sensor must decide quickly if the machine should be shut down. Rather than sending data to the machine learning model running in the cloud, the model could be run near the monitored machine using an Edge TPU, which is a tensor processing unit (TPU) designed for inference at the edge. (For details, see `https://cloud.google.com/edge-tpu/`.)

When using an edge cloud, you will need to have a continuous integration/continuous deployment (CI/CD) process to ensure consistency across edge devices. When full applications are run at the edge, consider using containers. This approach will help with consistency as well.

Designing infrastructure for data engineering services requires that you understand compute service options in GCP; know how to design for availability, reliability, and scalability; and know how to apply hybrid cloud design patterns as needed.

Designing for Distributed Processing

Distributed processing presents challenges not found when processing is performed on a single server. For starters, you need mechanisms for sharing data across servers. These include message brokers and message queues, collectively known as *middleware*. There is more than one way to do distributed processing. Some common architecture patterns are service-oriented architectures, microservices, and serverless functions. Distributed systems also have to contend with the possibility of duplicated processing and data arriving out of order. Depending on requirements, distributed processing can use different event processing models for handling duplicated and out-of-order processing.

Distributed Processing: Messaging

One way to categorize components of a distributed processing system is as components that move data from one process to another and components that transform or store data. Message brokers and message queues fall into the former category; middleware is the generic name for the latter category.

Message Brokers

Message brokers are services that provide three kinds of functionality: message validation, message transformation, and routing.

Message validation is the process of ensuring that messages received are correctly formatted. For example, a message may be specified in a Thrift or Protobuf format. Both Thrift and Protobuf, which is short for Protocol Buffers, are designed to make it easy to share data across applications and languages. For example, Java might store structured data types one way, whereas Python would store the same logical structure in a different way. Instead of sharing data using language-specific structures, software developers can map their data to a common format, a process known as *serialization*. A serialized message can then be placed on a message broker and routed to another service that can read the message without having to have information about the language or data structure used in the source system.

Message transformation is the process of mapping data to structures that can be used by other services. This is especially important when source and consumer services can change independently. For example, an accounting system may change the definition of a sales order. Other systems, like data warehouses, which use sales order data, would need to update ETL processes each time the source system changes unless the message broker between the accounting system and data warehouse implemented necessary transformations. The advantage of applying these transformations in the message broker is that other systems in addition to the data warehouse can use the transformed data without having to implement their own transformation.

Message brokers can receive a message and use data in the message to determine where the message should be sent. *Routing* is used when hub-and-spoke message brokers are used. With a *hub-and-spoke model*, messages are sent to a central processing node and from there routed to the correct destination node. See Figure 4.3 for an example of a hub-and-spoke model.

FIGURE 4.3   A hub-and-spoke message broker pattern

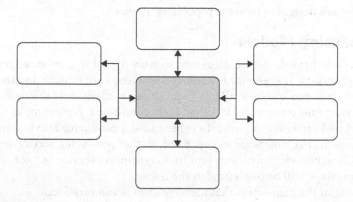

Message Queues

Message queues are used to enable asynchronous communications between processes. In the simplest case, one process writes a message to a message queue, and another process reads that message and removes it from the queue. In some cases, a message may be read by multiple processes. This kind of processing model is well suited to the publish and subscribe model.

In the *publish and subscribe model*, one or more processes write messages to a queue. For example, an IoT sensor could write a message to a message queue in the cloud. In addition, other sensors of the same type can write to the same queue. The data in the message queue may be consumed by one or more processes. For example, Sensor 1 may write to a message queue called Monitoring Queue, and Instance A of the processing service reads the message and processes the data. Next, Sensor 2 writes a message to Monitoring Queue, and that message is read by Instance B of the consuming process. See Figure 4.4 for an example of asynchronous message processing.

FIGURE 4.4   Simple asynchronous message processing

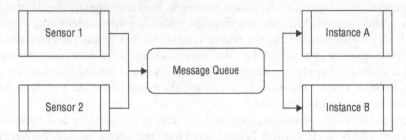

When the receiving processes are stateless—that is, they do not need to track information over time and across messages—then messages can be consumed by an instance of the receiving process. If the consumers need to maintain state information, such as maintaining the average value of the last 10 readings from a sensor, then all the data from a sensor must be processed by the same instance. The need to maintain state is one of the key considerations when you are designing message processing services.

Event Processing Models

Message queues can provide different guarantees with regard to how messages are provided to consuming processes. It is assumed that message queues are reliable and that a message that is written to a queue will be available to processes reading from the queue. Distributed systems also have to function under less than ideal conditions. For example, some messages may be delayed and arrive out of order. In other cases, a producing service may not receive an acknowledgment that a message was received, so that producing service sends the message again. If the acknowledgment was sent by a consuming service but not received by the producer, the message will be duplicated in the queue.

Here are some of the guarantees that message queues can provide:

At Least Once Delivery   In this case, all messages are delivered at least once to a consuming service, though messages may be delivered more than once either to the same consuming service or to different consuming services.

At Least Once, in Order Delivery   This is like at least once delivery, but it also adds a guarantee that messages will be ordered by time. This kind of guarantee can lead to some delay in processing because the message queue may buffer messages while waiting for late-arriving data to appear so that it can be sent in the correct order.

Exactly Once   This model guarantees that a message is processed exactly once. This is an important guarantee if operations on messages are not idempotent. For example, if a message includes the number of products sold in an order and that number is used to decrement inventory levels, then duplicate messages can leave the inventory database in an incorrect state since the number of products sold will be decremented more than once.

Message queues and consuming processes must deal with late and missing data. In the case of late data, a message queue could be configured to drop data that is later than some threshold period. This is known as a *watermark*. Watermarks are widely used in stream processing to help bound the amount of time processes wait before performing operations, such as aggregating data for a particular time period.

Distributed Processing: Services

Messaging components, such as message queues, are responsible for moving data between services. The services that operate on that data may be organized around one of a few service models. Three such models are service-oriented architectures (SOAs), microservices, and serverless functions.

Service-Oriented Architectures

A *service-oriented architecture (SOA)* is a distributed architecture that is driven by business operations and delivering business value. Typically, an SOA system serves a discrete business activity. SOAs are self-contained sets of services. Services are independent and do not need to know anything about other services except enough to pass messages. Some other characteristics of SOA systems are components are loosely coupled, long-lived, and autonomous. SOA systems have been designed using the Simple Object Access Protocol (SOAP) and Common Object Request Broker Architecture (CORBA), but Representational State Transfer (REST) is more widely used today.

Microservices

Microservices are a distributed systems architecture. Like other distributed systems, microservice architectures use multiple, independent components and common communication protocols to provide higher-level business services. Microservices are often used with Agile software development practices, including frequent deployments. Microservices are designed to implement a single function. This allows services to be updated independently of one another. Microservices can be readily deployed in containers as well. The combination of independencies and container-based deployments makes microservices well suited to teams and organizations that practice Agile development.

Serverless Functions

Serverless functions extend the principles of microservices by removing concerns for containers and managing runtime environments. With serverless functions, code that implements a single function can be deployed on a PaaS, such as Google Cloud Functions, without having to configure containers. Serverless functions can still use message queues and common messaging protocols so that they provide more support for DevOps teams who want to focus on coding application functionality more than systems administration.

Migrating a Data Warehouse

In the strictest sense, *data warehouses* are repositories of enterprise data organized for business intelligence reporting and analysis. For the purpose of our discussions, data warehouses include extraction, transformation, and load scripts; views and embedded user-defined functions; as well as reporting and visualization tools. Identity management information and access control policies used to protect the confidentiality, integrity, and availability of a data warehouse are also included for our purposes.

At a high level, the process of migrating a data warehouse involves four stages:

- Assessing the current state of the data warehouse
- Designing the future state
- Migrating data, jobs, and access controls to the cloud
- Validating the cloud data warehouse

All data warehouse migrations should follow this basic pattern, but it is important to note that there are different kinds of migrations.

An *off-loading data warehouse migration* involves copying data and schema from the on-premises data warehouse to the cloud to get a solution up and running in the cloud as fast as possible. This is a reasonable choice when the business needs the extra storage and compute capacity of the cloud, or if you want end users to have access to cloud-based reporting and analysis tools as fast as possible.

A *full data warehouse migration* includes all the steps in the scope of an off-loading migration plus moving data pipelines so that data can be loaded directly into the data warehouse from source systems. This approach allows you to take advantage of cloud tools for extraction, transformation, and load.

Both off-loading and full migration should follow the four-stage process outlined here.

Assessing the Current State of a Data Warehouse

The initial assessment stage includes work to identify both technical requirements of existing use cases as well as detailing the business benefits of migrating from an on-premises solution to a cloud data warehouse.

Technical Requirements

One of the first things to do in a data warehouse migration is to identify existing use cases, including information about the data needed, such as its source, frequency of updating, ETL jobs used with the data, and access controls applied in the use case. Gathering technical requirements should include the following:

- A *list of data sources*, including metadata about data sources, such as the frequency at which the data source is updated
- A *data catalog*, which includes both attributes collected from source systems and derived attributes, such as summaries by time and location

- A *data model*, including schemas, tables, views, indexes, and stored procedures
- A *list of ETL scripts and their purposes*
- A *list of reports and visualization* generated from the data in the data warehouse
- A *list of roles and associated access controls*, including administrators, developers, and end users

These items should be fairly well defined. You should also include some less well-defined details about the existing data warehouse, such as limitations in the data or reporting tools that limit analysis; constraints, such as when data is available from sources and when it has to be available for querying from the data warehouse; and any unmet technical requirements, like sufficiently fine-grained adequate access controls.

Business Benefits

The business benefits of a data warehouse migration should be assessed in the early stages of a migration project. Business value can be derived from cost savings, reduction in backlog of ETL and reporting work, and increased agility and ability to deliver insights under changing conditions.

The total cost of ownership should be considered when assessing a data warehouse migration. This includes the cost of software licensing, hardware infrastructure, developer and system administrator's time, along with any third-party support or consulting costs.

If legacy software and limitations of an existing data warehouse implementation are leading to a backlog of reporting and data ETL work in an enterprise, that enterprise is incurring an opportunity cost. The cost of insights that are not available to business decision-makers are not readily quantifiable, but it is still a factor that should be considered along with other business benefit topics.

Designing the Future State of a Data Warehouse

Once it is determined that it makes business sense to migrate a data warehouse to GCP, it is time to plan the future state of the data warehouse. The use cases identified in the initial stages should provide the broad boundaries of what will be deployed in the cloud. You will also need to define the key performance indicators (KPIs) that are used to measure how well the migration process is meeting objectives. KPIs may include the amount of data migrated, the number of reports now available in the cloud warehouse, and the number of workloads completely migrated.

As part of designing for the future state, you should consider how you can take advantage of BigQuery features for data warehousing, including the following:

- There is no need to plan for storage and query resources since BigQuery is a serverless, managed service.
- BigQuery uses the columnar format, which supports nested and repeated fields, which can help denormalize data models, thus reducing the need for joins.
- Data is stored on the Colossus filesystem, which stores redundant blocks of data on multiple physical disks so that you do not have to manage redundant copies of data to ensure availability and durability.

- Federated storage is used to query data stored in Cloud Storage, Bigtable, or Google Drive.
- BigQuery maintains a seven-day history of changes so that you can query a point-in-time snapshot of data.

BigQuery has some differences from other data warehouse databases. In BigQuery, tables are grouped into datasets. Identity and access management (IAM)–based access controls are applied at the dataset level, not the table level. For this reason, if you need to grant someone permission to view data in one table in a dataset, they will have permission to view data in any table in that dataset. You can restrict access, however, by creating views over the data to which you would like users to have access. Those views can be placed in another dataset, and users can be granted roles that allow them to access data through the view. Users do not need access to the datasets that provide the underlying data to the views.

Migrating Data, Jobs, and Access Controls

After assessing and planning, data and job migration begins. There is no one best way to migrate data and jobs. A few ways to prioritize are as follows:

- Exploiting current opportunities
- Migrating analytical workloads first
- Focusing on the user experience first
- Prioritizing low-risk use cases first

Exploiting current opportunities focuses on use cases that demonstrate clear business value. This could be a long backlog request that can be delivered now that you have access to the improved query-processing capabilities of BigQuery.

Online transaction processing systems are typically the source of data for data warehouses; however, data warehouses can also be the source of information for transaction-processing systems. For example, sales KPIs can be calculated in the data warehouse and sent back to a sales management system, where the data is used to calculate sales bonuses. In cases like this, the transaction-processing system may have more dependencies and may not be easily moved to the cloud. In that case, the analytical workload can be migrated to the cloud while the online transaction processing systems stay in on-premises systems.

Another option is to deliver data and reporting tools that can be leveraged by analysts or other users who can start generating insights immediately. Also, customers may find it useful to have aggregated data about their accounts. For example, small to midsize businesses may want to know how much they are spending on different categories of goods, and a weekly email with summary data can help address that need.

When a team of data warehouse developers is new to GCP and BigQuery, it may be best to start with low-risk use cases. These would be use cases that do not have other systems depending on them, and they are not needed for high-priority business processes that have to be available and reliable.

Regardless of which approach you use, you should approach migrations as an iterative process. This strategy allows you to learn about your requirements, data characteristics, and GCP functional characteristics in one iteration and apply that knowledge in later iterations.

Validating the Data Warehouse

The last step of migrating a data warehouse is to validate the migration. This includes testing and verifying that

- Schemas are defined correctly and completely
- All data expected to be in the data warehouse is actually loaded
- Transformations are applied correctly and data quality checks pass
- Queries, reports, and visualizations run as expected
- Access control policies are in place
- Other governance practices are in place

It is a good practice to validate each iterative phase of the migration and document your findings. In large enterprises, there may be multiple teams migrating different workloads, and each of those teams could learn valuable lessons from the other teams.

Exam Essentials

Know the four main compute GCP products.   Compute Engine is GCP's infrastructure-as-a-service (IaaS) product.

- With Compute Engine, you have the greatest amount of control over your infrastructure relative to the other GCP compute services.

- Kubernetes is a container orchestration system, and Kubernetes Engine is a managed Kubernetes service. With Kubernetes Engine, Google maintains the cluster and assumes responsibility for installing and configuring the Kubernetes platform on the cluster. Kubernetes Engine deploys Kubernetes on managed instance groups.

- App Engine is GCP's original platform-as-a-service (PaaS) offering. App Engine is designed to allow developers to focus on application development while minimizing their need to support the infrastructure that runs their applications. App Engine has two versions: App Engine Standard and App Engine Flexible.

- Cloud Functions is a serverless, managed compute service for running code in response to events that occur in the cloud. Events are supported for Cloud Pub/Sub, Cloud Storage, HTTP events, Firebase, and Stackdriver Logging.

Understand the definitions of availability, reliability, and scalability.   Availability is defined as the ability of a user to access a resource at a specific time. Availability is usually measured as the percentage of time a system is operational. Reliability is defined as the probability that a system will meet service-level objectives for some duration of time. Reliability is often measured as the mean time between failures. Scalability is the ability of a system to meet the demands of workloads as they vary over time.

Know when to use hybrid clouds and edge computing.   The analytics hybrid cloud is used when transaction processing systems continue to run on premises and data is extracted and transferred to the cloud for analytic processing. A variation of hybrid clouds is an edge cloud, which uses local computation resources in addition to cloud platforms. This architecture pattern is used when a network may not be reliable or have sufficient bandwidth to transfer data to the cloud. It is also used when low-latency processing is required.

Understand messaging.   Message brokers are services that provide three kinds of functionality: message validation, message transformation, and routing. Message validation is the process of ensuring that messages received are correctly formatted. Message transformation is the process of mapping data to structures that can be used by other services. Message brokers can receive a message and use data in the message to determine where the message should be sent. Routing is used when hub-and-spoke message brokers are used.

Know distributed processing architectures.   SOA is a distributed architecture that is driven by business operations and delivering business value. Typically, an SOA system serves a discrete business activity. SOAs are self-contained sets of services. Microservices are a variation on SOA architecture. Like other SOA systems, microservice architectures use multiple, independent components and common communication protocols to provide higher-level business services. Serverless functions extend the principles of microservices by removing concerns for containers and managing runtime environments.

Know the steps to migrate a data warehouse.   At a high level, the process of migrating a data warehouse involves four stages:

- Assessing the current state of the data warehouse
- Designing the future state
- Migrating data, jobs, and access controls to the cloud
- Validating the cloud data warehouse

Review Questions

You can find the answers in the appendix.

1. A startup is designing a data processing pipeline for its IoT platform. Data from sensors will stream into a pipeline running in GCP. As soon as data arrives, a validation process, written in Python, is run to verify data integrity. If the data passes the validation, it is ingested; otherwise, it is discarded. What services would you use to implement the validation check and ingestion?

    A. Cloud Storage and Cloud Pub/Sub

    B. Cloud Functions and Cloud Pub/Sub

    C. Cloud Functions and BigQuery

    D. Cloud Storage and BigQuery

2. Your finance department is migrating a third-party application from an on-premises physical server. The system was written in C, but only the executable binary is available. After the migration, data will be extracted from the application database, transformed, and stored in a BigQuery data warehouse. The application is no longer actively supported by the original developer, and it must run on an Ubuntu 14.04 operating system that has been configured with several required packages. Which compute platform would you use?

    A. Compute Engine

    B. Kubernetes Engine

    C. App Engine Standard

    D. Cloud Functions

3. A team of developers has been tasked with rewriting the ETL process that populates an enterprise data warehouse. They plan to use a microservices architecture. Each microservice will run in its own Docker container. The amount of data processed during a run can vary, but the ETL process must always finish within one hour of starting. You want to minimize the amount of DevOps tasks the team needs to perform, but you do not want to sacrifice efficient utilization of compute resources. What GCP compute service would you recommend?

    A. Compute Engine

    B. Kubernetes Engine

    C. App Engine Standard

    D. Cloud Functions

4. Your consulting company is contracted to help an enterprise customer negotiate a contract with a SaaS provider. Your client wants to ensure that they will have access to the SaaS service and it will be functioning correctly with only minimal downtime. What metric would you use when negotiating with the SaaS provider to ensure that your client's reliability requirements are met?

    A. Average CPU utilization

    B. A combination of CPU and memory utilization

    C. Mean time between failure

    D. Mean time to recovery

5. To ensure high availability of a mission-critical application, your team has determined that it needs to run the application in multiple regions. If the application becomes unavailable in one region, traffic from that region should be routed to another region. Since you are designing a solution for this set of requirements, what would you expect to include?

   A. Cloud Storage bucket

   B. Cloud Pub/Sub topic

   C. Global load balancer

   D. HA VPN

6. A startup is creating a business service for the hotel industry. The service will allow hotels to sell unoccupied rooms on short notice using the startup's platform. The startup wants to make it as easy as possible for hotels to share data with the platform, so it uses a message queue to collect data about rooms that are available for rent. Hotels send a message for each room that is available and the days that it is available. Room identifier and dates are the keys that uniquely identify a listing. If a listing exists and a message is received with the same room identifier and dates, the message is discarded. What are the minimal guarantees that you would want from the message queue?

   A. Route randomly to any instance that is building a machine learning model

   B. Route based on the sensor identifier so identifiers in close proximity are used in the same model

   C. Route based on machine type so only data from one machine type is used for each model

   D. Route based on timestamp so metrics close in time to each other are used in the same model

7. Sensors on manufacturing machines send performance metrics to a cloud-based service that uses the data to build models that predict when a machine will break down. Metrics are sent in messages. Messages include a sensor identifier, a timestamp, a machine type, and a set of measurements. Different machine types have different characteristics related to failures, and machine learning engineers have determined that for highest accuracy, each machine type should have its own model. Once messages are written to a message broker, how should they be routed to instances of a machine learning service?

   A. Route randomly to any instance that is building a machine learning model

   B. Route based on the sensor identifier so that identifiers in close proximity are used in the same model

   C. Route based on machine type so that only data from one machine type is used for each model

   D. Route based on timestamp so that metrics close in time to one another are used in the same model

8. As part of a cloud migration effort, you are tasked with compiling an inventory of existing applications that will move to the cloud. One of the attributes that you need to track for each application is a description of its architecture. An application used by the finance department is written in Java, deployed on virtual machines, has several distinct services, and uses the SOAP protocol for exchanging messages. How would you categorize this architecture?

   A. Monolithic

   B. Service-oriented architecture (SOA)

C. Microservice

D. Serverless functions

9. As part of a migration to the cloud, your department wants to restructure a distributed application that currently runs several services on a cluster of virtual machines. Each service implements several functions, and it is difficult to update one function without disrupting operations of the others. Some of the services require third-party libraries to be installed. Your company has standardized on Docker containers for deploying new services. What kind of architecture would you recommend?

A. Monolithic

B. Hub-and-spoke

C. Microservices

D. Pipeline architecture

10. The CTO of your company is concerned about the rising costs of maintaining your company's enterprise data warehouse. Some members of your team are advocating to migrate to a cloud-based data warehouse such as BigQuery. What is the first step for migrating from the on-premises data warehouse to a cloud-based data warehouse?

A. Assessing the current state of the data warehouse

B. Designing the future state of the data warehouse

C. Migrating data, jobs, and access controls to the cloud

D. Validating the cloud data warehouse

11. When gathering requirements for a data warehouse migration, which of the following would you include in a listing of technical requirements?

A. Data sources, data model, and ETL scripts

B. Data sources, data model, and business sponsor roles

C. Data sources only

D. Data model, data catalog, ETL scripts, and business sponsor roles

12. In addition to concerns about the rising costs of maintaining an on-premises data warehouse, the CTO of your company has complained that new features and reporting are not being rolled out fast enough. The lack of adequate business intelligence has been blamed for a drop in sales in the last quarter. Your organization is incurring what kind of cost because of the backlog?

A. Capital

B. Operating

C. Opportunity

D. Fiscal

13. The data modelers who built your company's enterprise data warehouse are asking for your guidance to migrate the data warehouse to BigQuery. They understand that BigQuery is an analytical database that uses SQL as a query language. They also know that BigQuery supports joins, but reports currently run on the data warehouse are consuming significant amounts of CPU because of the number and scale of joins. What feature of BigQuery would you suggest they consider in order to reduce the number of joins required?

    A. Colossus filesystem

    B. Columnar data storage

    C. Nested and repeated fields

    D. Federated storage

14. While the CTO is interested in having your enterprise data warehouse migrated to the cloud as quickly as possible, the CTO is particularly risk averse because of errors in reporting in the past. Which prioritization strategy would you recommend?

    A. Exploiting current opportunities

    B. Migrating analytical workloads first

    C. Focusing on the user experience first

    D. Prioritizing low-risk use cases first

15. The enterprise data warehouse has been migrated to BigQuery. The CTO wants to shut down the on-premises data warehouse but first wants to verify that the new cloud-based data warehouse is functioning correctly. What should you include in the verification process?

    A. Verify that schemas are correct and that data is loaded

    B. Verify schemas, data loads, transformations, and queries

    C. Verify that schemas are correct, data is loaded, and the backlog of feature requests is prioritized

    D. Verify schemas, data loads, transformations, queries, and that the backlog of feature requests is prioritized

Chapter 5

Building and Operationalizing Processing Infrastructure

GOOGLE CLOUD PROFESSIONAL DATA ENGINEER EXAM OBJECTIVES COVERED IN THIS CHAPTER INCLUDE THE FOLLOWING:

✓ **2.3 Building and operationalizing processing infrastructure. Considerations include:**

- Provisioning resources
- Monitoring pipelines
- Adjusting pipelines
- Testing and quality control

Data engineering depends heavily on computing, or processing, resources. In this chapter, you will learn how to provision and adjust processing resources, including Compute Engine, Kubernetes Engine, Cloud Bigtable, and Cloud Dataproc. You will also learn about configuring managed, serverless processing resources, including those offered by App Engine, Cloud Functions, and Cloud Dataflow. The chapter also includes a discussion of how to use Stackdriver Metrics, Stackdriver Logging, and Stackdriver Trace to monitor processing infrastructure.

Provisioning and Adjusting Processing Resources

GCP has a variety of processing resources. For the purpose of the Professional Data Engineer exam, let's categorize them into server-based and serverless resources. *Server-based resources* are those that require you to specify virtual machines (VMs) or clusters; *serverless resources* do not require you to specify VMs or clusters but do still require some configuration.

The server-based services described here include the following:

- Compute Engine
- Kubernetes Engine
- Cloud Bigtable
- Cloud Dataproc
- Cloud Dataflow

Compute Engine can be configured using individual VMs or instance groups. The others are configured as clusters of VMs, sometimes with VMs taking on different roles within the cluster.

The serverless GCP services covered here include the following:

- App Engine
- Cloud Functions

Although you do not need to specify machine types or cluster configurations, you can specify some parameters to adjust these services to meet the requirements of different use cases.

Provisioning and Adjusting Compute Engine

Compute Engine supports provisioning single instances or groups of instances, known as *instance groups*. Instance groups are either managed or unmanaged. *Managed instance groups (MIGs)* consist of identically configured VMs; unmanaged instance groups allow for heterogeneous VMs, but you should prefer managed instance groups unless you have a need for heterogeneous VMs. The configuration of a VM in a managed instance group is specified in a template, known as an *instance template*.

Provisioning Single VM Instances

The basic unit of provisioning in Compute Engine is a virtual machine. VMs are provisioned using the cloud console, the command-line SDK, or the REST API. Regardless of the method used to provision a VM, you can specify a wide range of parameters, including the following:

- Machine type, which specifies the number of vCPUs and the amount of memory
- Region and zone to create the VM
- Boot disk parameters
- Network configuration details
- Disk image
- Service account for the VM
- Metadata and tags

In addition, you can specify optional features, such as Shielded VMs for additional security or GPUs and tensor processing units (TPUs) for additional processing resources.

Compute Engine instances are created in the cloud console using a form like the one shown in Figure 5.1.

Instances can be provisioned from the command line using the gcloud compute instances create command. For example, consider the following command:

```
gcloud compute instances create instance-1 --zone=us-central1-a
          --machine-type=n1-standard-1 --subnet=default --network-tier=PREMIUM
          --image=debian-9-stretch-v20191115 --image-project=debian-cloud
          --boot-disk-size=10GB --boot-disk-type=pd-standard
```

This command creates a VM of n1-standard type in the us-centerall-a zone using the Premium network tier and the specified Debian operating system. The boot disk would be a 10 GB standard disk—in other words, not an SSD.

Once a VM instance is created, if the instance is stopped, you can adjust some configuration parameters. For example, you can detach and reattach a boot disk if it is in need of repair. You can also add or remove GPUs from stopped instances.

FIGURE 5.1   A basic VM instance provisioning form in the cloud console

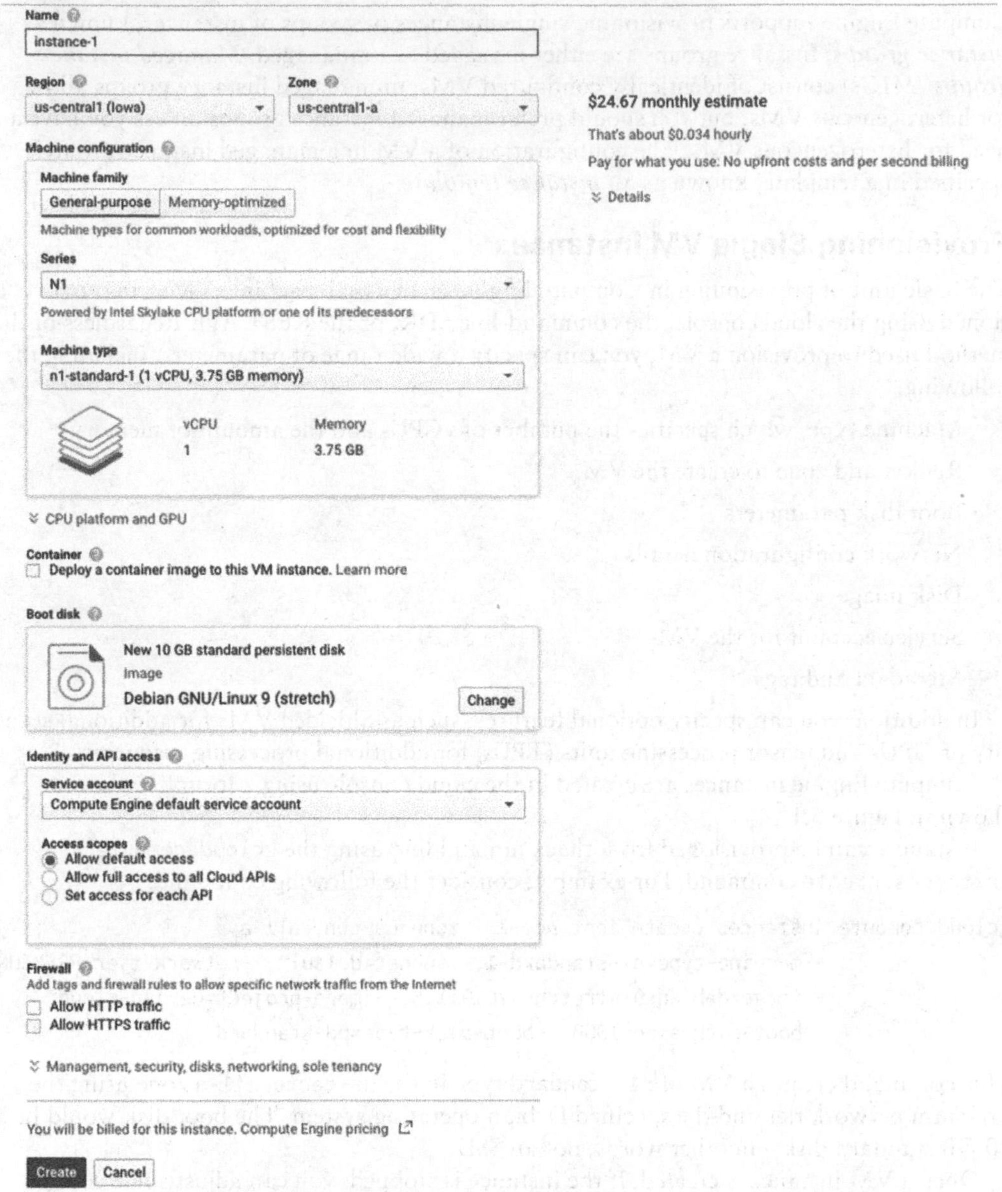

Name ⓘ

instance-1

Region ⓘ   Zone ⓘ

us-central1 (Iowa)   ▾   us-central1-a   ▾

Machine configuration ⓘ

Machine family

| General-purpose | Memory-optimized |

Machine types for common workloads, optimized for cost and flexibility

Series

N1   ▾

Powered by Intel Skylake CPU platform or one of its predecessors

Machine type

n1-standard-1 (1 vCPU, 3.75 GB memory)   ▾

vCPU   Memory
1   3.75 GB

⌄ CPU platform and GPU

Container ⓘ
☐ Deploy a container image to this VM instance. Learn more

Boot disk ⓘ

New 10 GB standard persistent disk
Image
Debian GNU/Linux 9 (stretch) | Change |

Identity and API access ⓘ

Service account ⓘ
Compute Engine default service account   ▾

Access scopes ⓘ
◉ Allow default access
○ Allow full access to all Cloud APIs
○ Set access for each API

Firewall ⓘ
Add tags and firewall rules to allow specific network traffic from the Internet
☐ Allow HTTP traffic
☐ Allow HTTPS traffic

⌄ Management, security, disks, networking, sole tenancy

You will be billed for this instance. Compute Engine pricing ↗

| Create | Cancel

$24.67 monthly estimate

That's about $0.034 hourly

Pay for what you use: No upfront costs and per second billing

⌄ Details

Provisioning Managed Instance Groups

Managed instance groups are managed as a single logical resource. MIGs have several useful properties, including:

- Autohealing based on application-specific health checks, which replaces nonfunctioning instances
- Support for multizone groups that provide for availability in spite of zone-level failures
- Load balancing to distribute workload across all instances in the group
- Autoscaling, which adds or removes instances in the group to accommodate increases and decreases in workloads
- Automatic, incremental updates to reduce disruptions to workload processing

The specifications for a MIG are defined in an instance template, which is a file with VM specifications. A template can be created using the `gcloud compute instances-templates create` command. For example, here is a command to create a template that specifies `n1-standard-4` machine types, the Debian 9 operating system, and a 250 GB boot disk:

```
gcloud compute instance-templates create pde-exam-template-custom \
    --machine-type n1-standard-4 \
    --image-family debian-9 \
    --image-project debian-cloud \
    --boot-disk-size 250GB
```

To create an instance from this template, you can use the `gcloud compute instances create` command seen earlier and include the `source-instance-template` parameter. For example, the following command will create an instance using the instance template just created:

```
gcloud compute instances create pde-exam-instance
            --source-instance-template=pde-exam-template-custom
```

You can also create an instance template using the cloud console. Figure 5.2 shows a typical form. Note that it is similar to the form used for creating an individual instance.

FIGURE 5.2 Form for creating an instance template

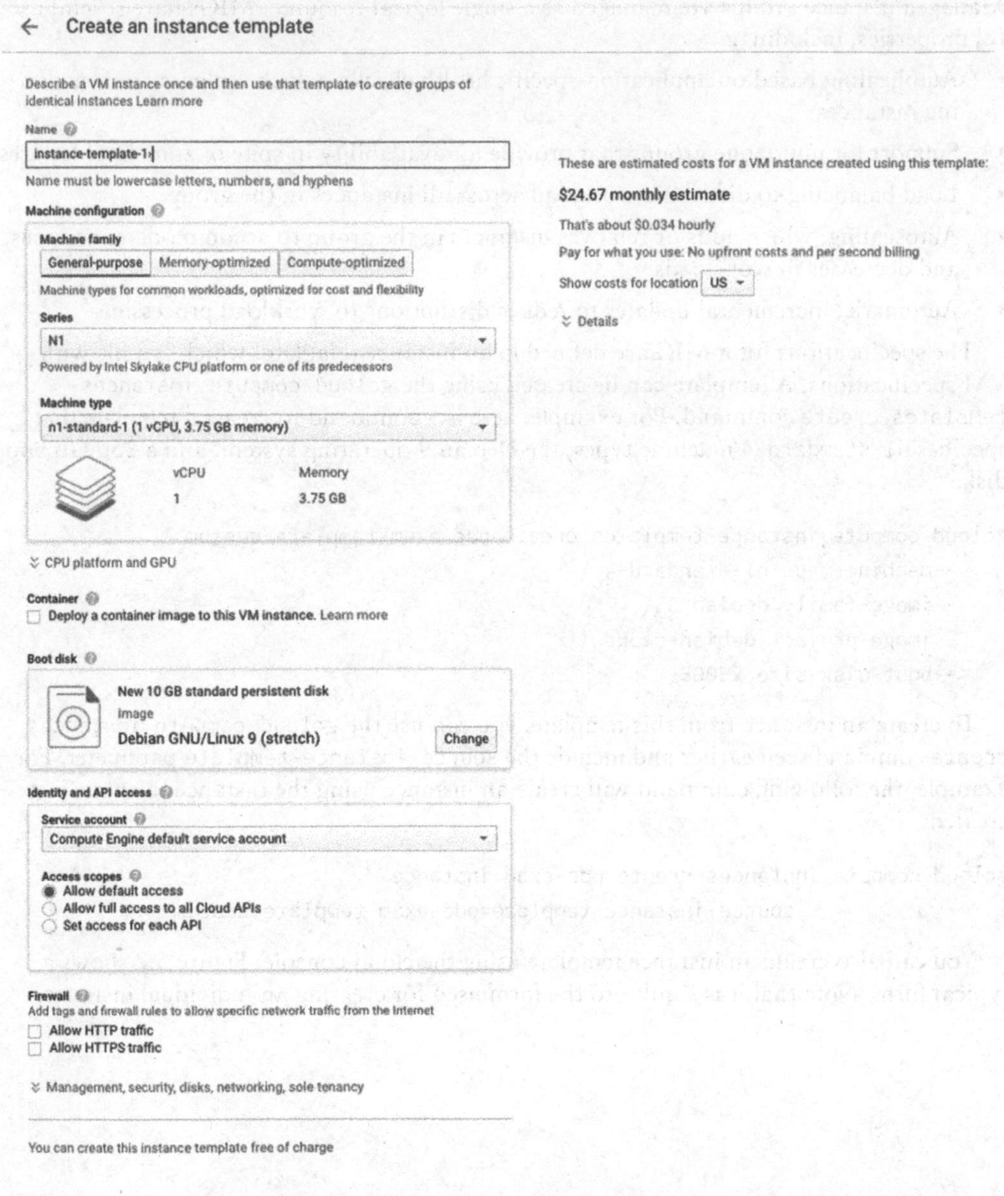

← Create an instance template

Describe a VM instance once and then use that template to create groups of
identical instances Learn more

Name ⓘ

`instance-template-1`

Name must be lowercase letters, numbers, and hyphens

Machine configuration ⓘ

Machine family

| General-purpose | Memory-optimized | Compute-optimized |

Machine types for common workloads, optimized for cost and flexibility

Series

N1 ▾

Powered by Intel Skylake CPU platform or one of its predecessors

Machine type

n1-standard-1 (1 vCPU, 3.75 GB memory) ▾

	vCPU	Memory
	1	3.75 GB

⌄ CPU platform and GPU

Container ⓘ
☐ Deploy a container image to this VM instance. Learn more

Boot disk ⓘ

New 10 GB standard persistent disk
Image
Debian GNU/Linux 9 (stretch)   [Change]

Identity and API access ⓘ

Service account ⓘ

Compute Engine default service account ▾

Access scopes ⓘ
◉ Allow default access
◯ Allow full access to all Cloud APIs
◯ Set access for each API

Firewall ⓘ
Add tags and firewall rules to allow specific network traffic from the Internet
☐ Allow HTTP traffic
☐ Allow HTTPS traffic

⌄ Management, security, disks, networking, sole tenancy

You can create this instance template free of charge

These are estimated costs for a VM instance created using this template:

$24.67 monthly estimate

That's about $0.034 hourly

Pay for what you use: No upfront costs and per second billing

Show costs for location US ▾

⌄ Details

Once an instance template is created, you can create an instance group using the console
as well, as shown in Figure 5.3.

FIGURE 5.3   Form for creating a managed instance group

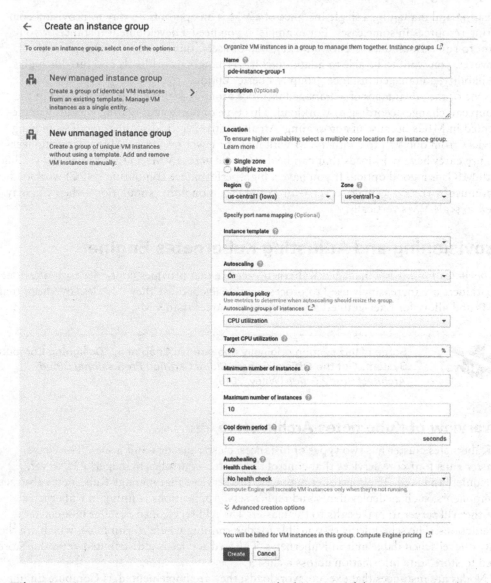

When creating an instance group, you can specify the name of the instance template along with a target CPU utilization that will trigger adding instances to the group up to the maximum number of instances allowed. You can also specify a minimum number of instances. You can also adjust the default cooldown period, which is the amount of time GCP will wait before collecting performance statistics from the instance. This gives the instance time to complete startup before its performance is considered for adjusting the instance group.

Adjusting Compute Engine Resources to Meet Demand

Creating and managing a single instance of a VM is an appropriate way to provision computing resources in some cases. For example, if you need a development instance or you want to run a small database for a local group of users, this is a reasonable approach. If, however, you want to be able to adapt quickly to changing workloads and provide high availability, a managed instance group is a better option.

One of the advantages of a managed instance group is that the number of VMs in the group can change according to workload. This type of horizontal scaling is readily implemented in MIGs because of autoscaling. An alternative, vertical scaling, requires moving services from one VM to another VM with more or fewer resources. Many data engineering use cases have workloads that can be distributed across VMs so that horizontal scaling with MIGs is a good option. If you have a high-performance computing (HPC) workload that must be run on a single server—for example, a monolithic simulation—then you may need to scale VMs vertically.

Provisioning and Adjusting Kubernetes Engine

Kubernetes Engine is a managed Kubernetes service that provides container orchestration. Containers are increasingly used to process workloads because they have less overhead than VMs and allow for finer-grained allocation of resources than VMs.

 Some of this section originally appeared in Chapter 4, "Designing Compute Systems," of the *Official Google Cloud Certified Professional Cloud Architect Study Guide* (Wiley, 2019).

Overview of Kubernetes Architecture

A Kubernetes cluster has two types of instances: cluster masters and nodes. The *cluster master* runs four core services that control the cluster: controller manager, API server, scheduler, and etcd. The controller manager runs services that manage Kubernetes abstract components, such as deployments and replica sets. Applications running in Kubernetes use the API server to make calls to the master. The API server also handles intercluster interactions. The scheduler is responsible for determining where to run *pods*, which are the lowest-level schedulable unit in Kubernetes. The etcd service is a distributed key-value store used to store state information across a cluster.

Nodes are instances that execute workloads; they are implemented as Compute Engine VMs that are run within MIGs. They communicate with the cluster master through an agent called *kubelet*.

Kubernetes introduces abstractions that facilitate the management of containers, applications, and storage services. Some of the most important are as follows:

▪ Pods

▪ Services

- ReplicaSets
- Deployments
- PersistentVolumes
- StatefulSets
- Ingress

Pods are the smallest computation unit managed by Kubernetes. Pods contain one or more containers. Usually, pods have just one container, but if the services provided by two containers are tightly coupled, then they may be deployed in the same pod. For example, a pod may include a container running an extraction, transformation, and load process, as well as a container running ancillary services for decompressing and reformatting data. Multiple containers should be in the same pod only if they are functionally related and have similar scaling and lifecycle characteristics.

Pods are deployed to nodes by the scheduler. They are usually deployed in groups or replicas. This provides for high availability, which is especially needed with pods. Pods are ephemeral and may be terminated if they are not functioning properly. One of the advantages of Kubernetes is that it monitors the health of the pods and replaces them if they are not functioning properly. Since multiple replicas of pods are run, pods can be destroyed without completely disrupting a service. Pods also support scalability. As load increase or decreases, the number of pods deployed for an application can increase or decrease.

Since pods are ephemeral, other services that depend on them need a way to discover them when needed. Kubernetes uses the service abstraction for this. A *service* is an abstraction with a stable API endpoint and stable IP address. Applications that need to use a service communicate with the API endpoints. A service keeps track of its associated pods so that it can always route calls to a functioning pod.

A *ReplicaSet* is a controller that manages the number of pods running for a deployment. A *deployment* is a higher-level concept that manages ReplicaSets and provides declarative updates. Each pod in a deployment is created using the same template, which defines how to run a pod. The definition is called a *pod specification*.

Kubernetes deployments are configured with a desired number of pods. If the actual number of pods varies from the desired state—for example, if a pod is terminated for being unhealthy—then the ReplicaSet will add or remove pods until the desired state is reached.

Pods may need access to persistent storage, but since pods are ephemeral, it is a good idea to decouple pods that are responsible for computation from persistent storage, which should continue to exist even after a pod terminates. *PersistentVolumes* is Kubernetes's way of representing storage allocated or provisioned for use by a pod. Pods acquire access to persistent volumes by creating a *PersistentVolumeClaim*, which is a logical way to link a pod to persistent storage.

Pods as described so far work well for stateless applications, but when state is managed in an application, pods are not functionally interchangeable. Kubernetes uses the StatefulSets abstraction, which is used to designate pods as stateful and assign a unique identifier to them. Kubernetes uses these to track which clients are using which pods and to keep them paired.

An *Ingress* is an object that controls external access to services running in a Kubernetes cluster. An Ingress Controller must be running in a cluster for an Ingress to function.

Provisioning a Kubernetes Engine Cluster

When you use Kubernetes Engine, you start by provisioning a cluster using either the cloud console, the command line, or the REST API. Figure 5.4 shows an example of the cloud console form for creating a Kubernetes cluster.

FIGURE 5.4   Cloud console user interface for creating a Kubernetes cluster

When creating a cluster, you will need to specify a cluster name, indicate whether the cluster will run in a single zone or in multiple zones within a region, and specify a version of GKE and a set of node pools.

To create a Kubernetes cluster from the command line, you can use the `gcloud container clusters create` command. For example, consider the following command:

```
gcloud container clusters create "standard-cluster-1" --zone "us-central1-a"
                --cluster-version "1.13.11-gke.14" --machine-type "n1-standard-1"
                --image-type "COS" --disk-type "pd-standard" --disk-size "100"
                --num-nodes "5" --enable-autoupgrade --enable-autorepair
```

This command starts with `gcloud container clusters create`. Kubernetes Engine was originally called Container Engine, hence the use of `gcloud container` instead of `gcloud kubernetes`. The zone, cluster versions, machine type, disk configuration, and number of nodes in the cluster are also specified. The `autoupgrade` and `autorepair` options are also specified.

Node pools are collections of VMs running in managed instance groups. Since node pools are implemented as MIGs, all machines in the same node pool have the same configuration. Clusters have a default node pool, but you can add custom node pools as well. This is useful when some loads have specialized needs, such as more memory or higher I/O performance. They are also useful if you want to have a pool of preemptible VMs to help keep costs down.

When jobs are submitted to Kubernetes, a scheduler determines which nodes are available to run the job. Jobs create pods and ensure that at least some of them successfully terminate. Once the specified number of pods successfully complete, the job is considered complete. Jobs include a specification of how much CPU and memory are required to run the job. If a node has sufficient available resources, the scheduler can run the job on that node. You can control where jobs are run using the Kubernetes abstractions known as *taints*. By assigning taints to node pools and tolerances for taints to pods, you can control when pods are run.

Adjusting Kubernetes Engine Resources to Meet Demand

In Kubernetes Engine, two important ways to adjust resources is by scaling applications running in clusters and scaling clusters themselves.

Autoscaling Applications in Kubernetes Engine

When you run an application in Kubernetes, you specify how many replicas of that application should run. When demand for a service increases, more replicas can be added, and as demand drops, replicas can be removed.

To adjust the number of replicas manually, you can use `kubectl`, which is the command-line utility for interacting with Kubernetes clusters. Note that this is not a `gcloud container` command; `kubectl` is used to control Kubernetes components. The `gcloud container` commands are used for interacting with Kubernetes Engine.

Let's take a look at an example `kubectl` command to adjust the number of replicas for a deployment named pde-example-application:

```
kubectl scale deployment pde-example-application --replicas 6
```

This command will set the number of desired replicas for the `pde-example-application` deployment to 6. There may be times when Kubernetes cannot provide all the desired replicas. To see how many replicas are actually running, you can use the `kubectl get deployments` command to list the name of deployments, the desired number of replicas, the current number of replicas, the number of replicas available to users, and the amount of time the application has been running in the cluster.

Alternatively, you can configure deployments to autoscale using the `kubectl autoscale` command. For example, consider the following:

```
kubectl autoscale deployment pde-example-application --min 2 --max 8 --cpu-percent 65
```

This command will autoscale the number of replicas of the `pde-example-application` between two and eight replicas depending on CPU utilization. In this case, if CPU utilization across all pods is greater than 65 percent, replicas will be added up to the maximum number specified.

Autoscaling Clusters in Kubernetes Engine

Kubernetes Engine provides the ability to autoscale the number of nodes in a node pool. (Remember, nodes are implemented as Compute Engine VMs, and node pools are implemented using managed instance groups.)

Cluster autoscaling is done at the node pool level. When you create a node pool, you can specify a minimum and maximum number of nodes in the pool. The autoscaler adjusts the number of nodes in the pool based on resource requests, not actual utilization. If pods are unscheduled because there is not a sufficient number of nodes in the node pool to run those pods, then more nodes will be added up to the maximum number of nodes specified for that node pool. If nodes are underutilized, the autoscaler will remove nodes from the node pool down to the minimum number of nodes in the pool.

By default, GKE assumes that all pods can be restarted on other nodes. If the application is not tolerant of brief disruptions, it is recommended that you not use cluster autoscaling for that application.

Also, if a cluster is running in multiple zones and the node pool contains multiple instance groups of the same instance type, the autoscaler tries to keep them balanced when scaling up.

You can specify autoscaling parameters when creating a cluster. Here is an example:

```
gcloud container clusters create pde-example-cluster \
          --zone us-central1-a \
          --node-locations us-central1-a,us-central1-b,us-central1-f \
          --num-nodes 2 --enable-autoscaling --min-nodes 1 --max-nodes 4
```

This command creates a cluster called `pde-example-cluster` in the `us-central1-a` zone, with nodes in three zones and a starting set of two nodes per node pool. Autoscaling is enabled with a minimum of one node and a maximum of four nodes.

Kubernetes YAML Configurations

As with any other GCP service, we can use the command line, cloud console, and REST APIs to configure GKE resources. Kubernetes makes extensive use of declarative specifications using YAML files. These files contain information needed to configure a resource, such as a cluster or a deployment. Here, for example, is a deployment YAML specification for a deployment of an Nginx server using three replicas:

```
apiVersion: "apps/v1"
kind: "Deployment"
metadata:
  name: "nginx-1"
  namespace: "default"
  labels:
    app: "nginx-1"
spec:
  replicas: 3
  selector:
    matchLabels:
      app: "nginx-1"
  template:
    metadata:
      labels:
        app: "nginx-1"
    spec:
      containers:
      - name: "nginx"
        image: "nginx:latest"
---
apiVersion: "autoscaling/v2beta1"
kind: "HorizontalPodAutoscaler"
metadata:
  name: "nginx-1-hpa"
  namespace: "default"
  labels:
    app: "nginx-1"
spec:
  scaleTargetRef:
    kind: "Deployment"
    name: "nginx-1"
    apiVersion: "apps/v1"
  minReplicas: 1
```

```
maxReplicas: 5
metrics:
- type: "Resource"
  resource:
    name: "cpu"
    targetAverageUtilization: 80
```

One of the advantages of using a managed Kubernetes service like GKE is that configuration files like this are generated for you when using command-line and cloud console commands.

Provisioning and Adjusting Cloud Bigtable

Cloud Bigtable is a managed wide-column NoSQL database used for applications that require high-volume, low-latency random reads and writes, such as IoT applications, and for analytic use cases, such as storing large volumes of data used to train machine learning models. Bigtable has an HBase interface, so it is also a good alternative to using Hadoop HBase on a Hadoop cluster.

Provisioning Bigtable Instances

Bigtable instance can be provisioned using the cloud console, command-line SDK, and REST API. When creating an instance, you provide an instance name, an instance ID, an instance type, a storage type, and cluster specifications. Figure 5.5 shows an example cloud console form for creating a Bigtable instance.

The instance type can be either production or development. Production instances have clusters with a minimum of three nodes; development instances have a single node and do not provide for high availability.

Storage types are SSD and HDD. SSDs are used when low-latency I/O is a priority. Instances using SSDs can support faster reads and are recommended for real-time applications. HDD instances have higher read latency but are less expensive and performant enough for scanning, making them a good choice for batch analytical use cases. HDD-configured instances cost less than SSD instances.

Clusters are sets of nodes in a specific region and zone. You specify a name, the location, and the number of nodes when creating a cluster. You can create multiple, replicated clusters in a Bigtable instance.

FIGURE 5.5   Form to create a Bigtable instance

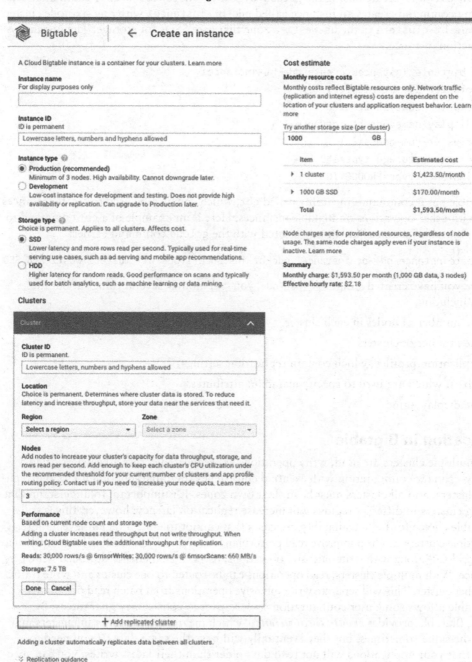

Instances can be created using the `gcloud bigtable instances create` command. The following command creates an instance called `pde-bt-instance1` with one six-node cluster called `pde-bt-cluster1` in the `us-west1-a` zone that uses SSDs for storage. The instance is a production instance.

```
gcloud bigtable instances create pde-bt-instance1
    --cluster=pde-bt-cluster1 \
    --cluster-zone=us-west1-a
    --display-name=pdc-bt-instance-1 \
    --cluster-num-nodes=6 \
    --cluster-storage-type=SSD \
    --instance-type=PRODUCTION
```

Bigtable has a command-line utility called `cbt`, which can also be used to create instances along with other operations on Bigtable instances. Here is an example of a `cbt` command to create a Bigtable instance like the one created with the `gcloud` command earlier:

```
cbt createinstance pde-bt-instance1 pdc-bt-instance-1 pde-bt-cluster1 west1-a 6 SSD
```

Once you have created a Bigtable instance, you can modify several things about the cluster, including:

- The number of nodes in each cluster
- The number of clusters
- Application profiles, which contain replication settings
- Labels, which are used to specify metadata attributes
- The display name

Replication in Bigtable

When multiple clusters are used, write operations are replicated across all clusters using a primary-primary configuration with eventual consistency. Bigtable supports up to four replicated clusters, and all clusters must be in their own zones. It is important to understand that running clusters in different regions will increase replication latency; however, this is still a reasonable choice for high-availability use cases that cannot tolerate a region-level failure.

Multiple clusters can help improve read performance as well. When running large batch analytic workloads along with write-intensive operations, users can experience degraded write performance. With multiple clusters, read operations can be routed to one cluster and write traffic to another cluster. This will separate write-intensive operations from batch read operations.

Bigtable allows some user configuration with respect to consistency guarantees. By default, Bigtable provides *eventual consistency*, which means that the data in clusters may not be the same sometimes, but they eventually will have the same data. If you need to ensure that your applications will not read data older than their latest writes, you can specify *read-your-writes consistency*. When all users must have a consistent view of data, you can specify *strong consistency*. That configuration will route all traffic to the same cluster, which will be configured with read-your-writes consistency. This configuration uses the other cluster only for failover.

Provisioning and Adjusting Cloud Dataproc

Cloud Dataproc is a managed Hadoop and Spark service. When provisioning Cloud Dataproc resources, you will specify the configuration of a cluster using the cloud console, the command-line SDK, or the REST API. When you create a cluster, you will specify a name, a region, a zone, a cluster mode, machine types, and an autoscaling policy. Figure 5.6 shows an example cloud console for creating a cluster.

FIGURE 5.6   A cloud console form for creating a Cloud Dataproc cluster

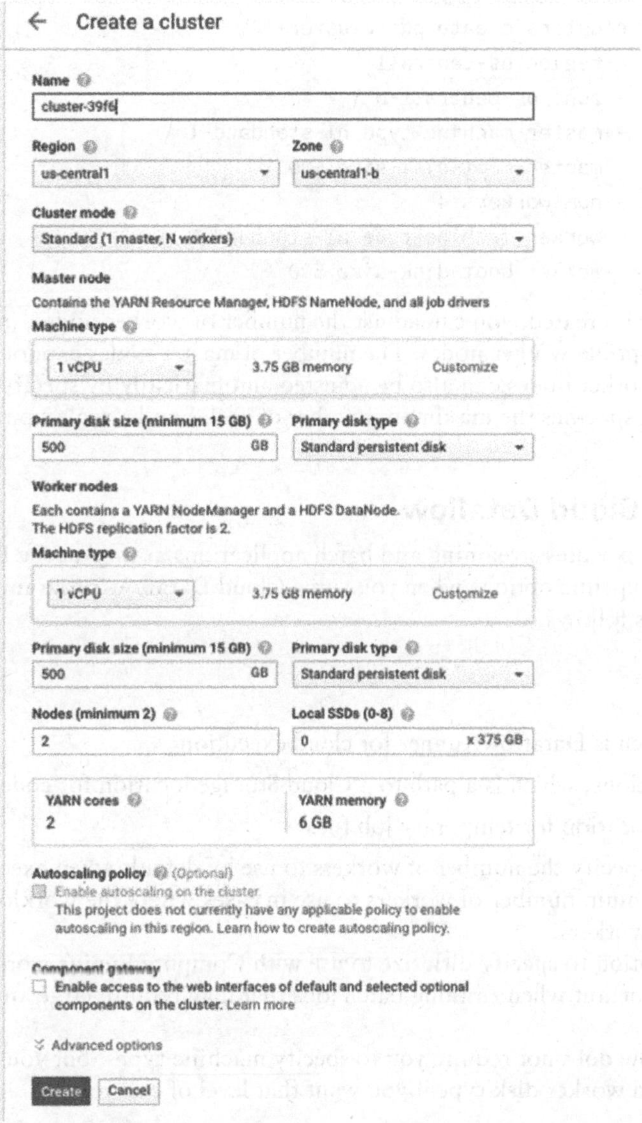

The cluster mode determines the number of master nodes and possible worker nodes. The standard mode has one master and some number of workers. The single mode has one master and no workers. The high availability mode has three master nodes and some number of worker nodes. Master nodes and worker nodes are configured separately. For each type of node, you can specify a machine type, disk size, and disk type. For worker nodes, you can specify machine type, disk size and type, a minimum number of nodes, and optional local SSDs.

The gcloud dataproc clusters create command is used to create a cluster from the command line. Here is an example:

```
gcloud dataproc clusters create pde-cluster-1 \
                --region us-central1 \
                --zone us-central1-b \
                --master-machine-type n1-standard-1 \
                --master-boot-disk-size 500 \
                --num-workers 4
                --worker-machine-type n1-standard-1 \
                --worker-boot-disk-size 500
```

After a cluster is created, you can adjust the number of worker nodes, including the number of preemptible worker nodes. The number of master nodes cannot be modified. The number of worker nodes can also be adjusted automatically by specifying an autoscaling policy, which specifies the maximum number of nodes and a scale-up rate and a scale-down rate.

Configuring Cloud Dataflow

Cloud Dataflow executes streaming and batch applications as an Apache Beam runner. You can specify pipeline options when you run a Cloud Dataflow program. Required parameters are as follows:

- Job name
- Project ID
- Runner, which is DataflowRunner for cloud execution
- Staging locations, which is a path to a Cloud Storage location for code packages
- Temporary location for temporary job files

You can also specify the number of workers to use by default when executing a pipeline as well as a maximum number of workers to use in cases where the workload would benefit from additional workers.

There is an option to specify disk size to use with Compute Engine worker instances. This may be important when running batch jobs that may require large amounts of space on the boot disk.

Cloud Dataflow does not require you to specify machine types, but you can specify machine type and worker disk type if you want that level of control.

Configuring Managed Serverless Processing Services

Several processing services in GCP are serverless, so there is no need to provision instances or clusters. You can, however, configure some parameters in each of the services. For the purposes of the Cloud Professional Data Engineer exam, we will review configuring the following:

- App Engine
- Cloud Functions

Configuring App Engine

App Engine is a serverless platform-as-a-service (PaaS) that is organized around the concept of a service, which is an application that you run in the App Engine environment. You can configure your service as well as supporting services by specifying three files:

- `app.yaml`
- `cron.yaml`
- `dispatch.yaml`

There is an app.yaml file associated with each version of a service. Usually, you create a directory for each version of a service and keep the app.yaml file and other configuration files there.

The app.yaml file has three required parameters: runtime, handlers, and threadsafe. runtime specifies the runtime environment, such as Python 3.

 Support for Python 2 by the Python community was officially deprecated on January 1, 2020.

handlers is a set of URL patterns that specify what code is run in response to invoking a URL.

cron.yaml is used to configure scheduled tasks for an application. Parameters include a schedule of when to run the task and a URL to be invoked when the task is run.

The dispatch.yaml file is a place for specifying routing rules to send incoming requests to a specific service based on the URL.

Configuring Cloud Functions

Cloud Functions is another serverless processing service. This service runs code in response to events in Google Cloud. In addition to specifying the code to run, you have the option of configuring several parameters, including:

- memory
- timeout
- region
- max-instances

The amount of memory allocated to a function ranges from 128 MB to 2 GB.

timeout is the maximum time that the function is allowed to run before completing. If the function does not finish by the end of the timeout period, it is terminated. The default is 1 minute, but it can be set to as high as 9 minutes.

region is the geographical region in which the function will execute.

max-instances is the number of Cloud Function instances that will exist at any one time.

Monitoring Processing Resources

Once processing resources are provisioned and applications are running, it is important to monitor both the resources and the application performance. GCP includes *Stackdriver*, a set of monitoring tools that includes infrastructure and application monitoring, logging, and distributed tracing.

Stackdriver Monitoring

Stackdriver Monitoring collects metrics on the performance of infrastructure resources and applications. Resources can be in GCP as well as the Amazon Web Services cloud.

Stackdriver Monitoring collects data on more than 1,000 metrics, which vary by service type. For example:

- App Engine has metrics about the utilization of all VMs serving an application, the number of current active connections, and the total number of reserved cores.
- Compute Engine Autoscalers have metrics related to capacity and current utilization.
- BigQuery has metrics about query counts, execution times, scanned bytes, and table count.
- Cloud Bigtable collects data on CPU load, disk load, node count, bytes used, and storage capacity.
- Cloud Functions collects data on active instances, execution count, and execution times.

As you can see from the list, metrics are captured information about all the important characteristics of a service.

The data collected by Stackdriver Monitoring can be viewed on Stackdriver Monitoring dashboards and used for alerting.

Alerting allows you to specify a condition using metrics to identify when a resource is unhealthy or otherwise needs intervention. In Stackdriver Monitoring, alerts are created using an alerting policy. Alerting polices include conditions, such as CPU utilization exceeding 70 percent for three minutes, a notification channel, and optional documentation for those responding to the alert.

Stackdriver Logging

Stackdriver Logging is a service used for storing and searching log data about events in infrastructure and applications. Stackdriver Logging is able to collect data from more than 150 common applications.

Stackdriver Monitoring collects metrics, whereas Stackdriver Logging collects log entries. A *log entry* is a record about some event. These records may be created by an application, an operating system, middleware, or other service. A *log* is a collection of log entries.

Logs are maintained in Stackdriver for a specific period of time known as the *retention period*. If you want to keep them longer, you will need to export the logs before the end of the retention period. The retention period varies by log type. Admin activity audit logs, system event audit logs, and access transparency logs are kept for 400 days. Data access audit logs and other logs not related to auditing are kept 30 days.

Logs can be searched using a query language that supports pattern matching and Boolean expressions. You can use the query language to create filters that can be run from the Stackdriver Logging interface, as shown in Figure 5.7.

FIGURE 5.7   A example log listing in Stackdriver Logging

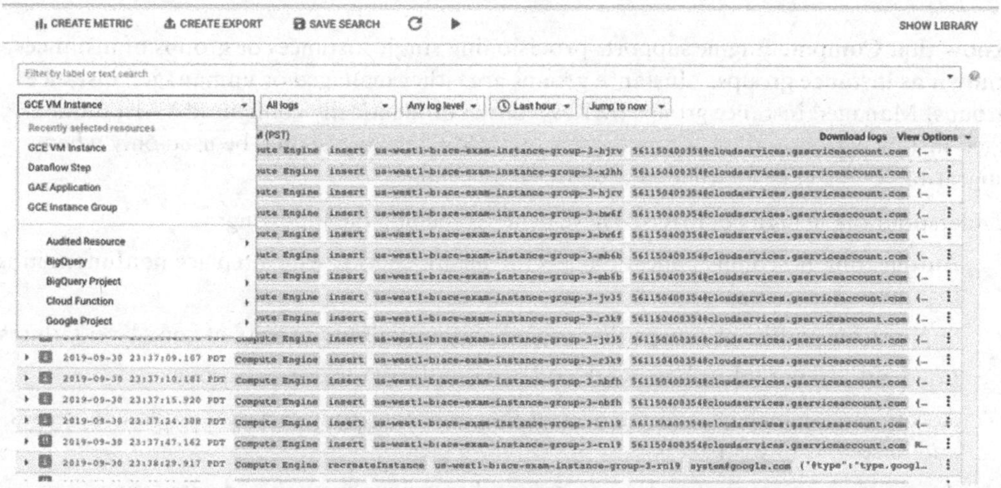

The query language can be used to specify log entries to export out of Stackdriver Logging. When you export log entries, they are written to a destination or sink, which could be Cloud Storage, BigQuery, or Cloud Pub/Sub. When a new log entry is written to a log, it is compared to export filters, and if there is a match, a copy of the log entry is written to the sink. Note that since only new log entries are written to the sink, this process cannot export log entries that already exist.

Stackdriver Trace

Stackdriver Trace is a distributed tracing system designed to collect data on how long it takes to process requests to services. This is especially useful when you're using microservices architectures. Stackdriver Trace is available in Compute Engine, Kubernetes Engine, and App Engine.

Stackdriver Trace has two main components: a tracing client and a tracing user interface. The tracing client collects data and sends it to GCP. The tracing interface is used to view and analyze that trace data. The interface provides a curated experience that includes

- Performance insights
- Recent traces and times
- Most frequent URIs
- Daily analysis reports

Stackdriver Trace also provides a trace list interface that allows you to view traces in detail.

Exam Essentials

Know that Compute Engine supports provisioning single instances or groups of instances, known as instance groups.   Instance groups are either managed or unmanaged instance groups. Managed instance groups (MIGs) consist of identically configured VMs; unmanaged instance groups allow for heterogeneous VMs, but they should be used only when migrating legacy clusters from on-premises data centers.

Understand the benefits of MIGs. These benefits include the following:

- Autohealing based on application-specific health checks, which replace nonfunctioning instances
- Support for multizone groups that provide for availability in spite of zone-level failures
- Load balancing to distribute workload across all instances in the group
- Autoscaling, which adds or removes instances in the group to accommodate increases and decreases in workloads
- Automatic, incremental updates to reduce disruptions to workload processing

Know that Kubernetes Engine is a managed Kubernetes service that provides container orchestration.   Containers are increasingly used to process workloads because they have less overhead than VMs and allow for finer-grained allocation of resources than VMs. A Kubernetes cluster has two types of instances: cluster masters and nodes.

Understand Kubernetes abstractions.   Pods are the smallest computation unit managed by Kubernetes. Pods contain one or more containers. A ReplicaSet is a controller that manages the number of pods running for a deployment. A deployment is a higher-level concept that manages ReplicaSets and provides declarative updates. PersistentVolumes is Kubernetes' way of representing storage allocated or provisioned for use by a pod. Pods acquire access to persistent volumes by creating a PersistentVolumeClaim, which is a logical way to link a pod to persistent storage. StatefulSets are used to designate pods as stateful and assign a unique identifier to them. Kubernetes uses them to track which clients are using which pods and to keep them paired. An Ingress is an object that controls external access to services running in a Kubernetes cluster.

Know how to provision Bigtable instances.   Cloud Bigtable is a managed wide-column NoSQL database used for applications that require high-volume, low-latency writes. Bigtable has an HBase interface, so it is also a good alternative to using Hadoop HBase on a Hadoop cluster. Bigtable instances can be provisioned using the cloud console, the command-line SDK, and the REST API. When creating an instance, you provide an instance name, an instance ID, an instance type, a storage type, and cluster specifications.

Know how to provision Cloud Dataproc.   When provisioning Cloud Dataproc resources, you will specify the configuration of a cluster using the cloud console, the command-line SDK, or the REST API. When you create a cluster, you will specify a name, a region, a zone, a cluster mode, machine types, and an autoscaling policy. The cluster mode determines the number of master nodes and possible worker nodes. Master nodes and worker nodes are configured separately. For each type of node, you can specify a machine type, disk size, and disk type.

Understand that serverless services do not require conventional infrastructure provisioning but can be configured.   You can configure App Engine using the app.yaml, cron.yaml, distpatch.yaml, or queue.yaml file. Cloud Functions can be configured using parameters to specify memory, region, timeout, and max instances. Cloud Dataflow parameters include job name, project ID, running, staging location, and the default and maximum number of worker nodes.

Understand the purpose of Stackdriver Monitoring, Stackdriver Logging, and Stackdriver Trace.   Stackdriver Metrics collect metrics on the performance of infrastructure resources and applications. Stackdriver Logging is a service for storing and searching log data about events in infrastructure and applications. Stackdriver Trace is a distributed tracing system designed to collect data on how long it takes to process requests to services.

Review Questions

You can find the answers in the appendix.

1. A group of data scientists wants to preprocess a large dataset that will be delivered in batches. The data will be written to Cloud Storage and processed by custom applications running on Compute Engine instances. They want to process the data as quickly as possible when it arrives and are willing to pay the cost of running up to 10 instances at a time. When a batch is finished, they'd like to reduce the number of instances to 1 until the next batch arrives. The batches do not arrive on a known schedule. How would you recommend that they provision Compute Engine instances?

   A. Use a Cloud Function to monitor Stackdriver metrics, add instances when CPU utilization peaks, and remove them when demand drops.

   B. Use a script running on one dedicated instance to monitor Stackdriver metrics, add instances when CPU utilization peaks, and remove them when demand drops.

   C. Use managed instance groups with a minimum of 1 instance and a maximum of 10.

   D. Use Cloud Dataproc with an autoscaling policy set to have a minimum of 1 instance and a maximum of 10.

2. You are running a high-performance computing application in a managed instance group. You notice that the throughput of one instance is significantly lower than that for other instances. The poorly performing instance is terminated, and another instance is created to replace it. What feature of managed instance groups is at work here?

   A. Autoscaling

   B. Autohealing

   C. Redundancy

   D. Eventual consistency

3. A new engineer in your group asks for your help with creating a managed instance group. The engineer knows the configuration and the minimum and maximum number of instances in the MIG. What is the next thing the engineer should do to create the desired MIG?

   A. Create each of the initial members of the instance group using `gcloud compute instance create` commands

   B. Create each of the initial members of the instance group using the cloud console

   C. Create an instance template using the `gcloud compute instance-templates create` command

   D. Create an instance template using the `cbt create instance-template` command

4. Your team is migrating applications from running on bare-metal servers and virtual machines to running in containers. You would like to use Kubernetes Engine to run those containers. One member of the team is unfamiliar with Kubernetes and does not understand why they cannot find a command to deploy a container. How would you describe the reason why there is no deploy container command?

    A. Kubernetes uses pods as the smallest deployable unit, and pods have usually one but possibly multiple containers that are deployed as a unit.

    B. Kubernetes uses deployments as the smallest deployable unit, and pods have usually one but possibly multiple containers that are deployed as a unit.

    C. Kubernetes uses replicas as the smallest deployable unit, and pods have usually one but possibly multiple containers that are deployed as a unit.

    D. Kubernetes calls containers "pods," and the command to deploy is
`kubectl deploy pod`.

5. A Kubernetes administrator wants to improve the performance of an application running in Kubernetes. They have determined that the four replicas currently running are not enough to meet demand and want to increase the total number of replicas to six. The name of the deployment is `my-app-123`. What command should they use?

    A. `kubectl scale deployment my-app-123 --replicas 6`

    B. `kubectl scale deployment my-app-123 --replicas 2`

    C. `gcloud containers scale deployment my-app-123 --replicas 6`

    D. `gcloud containers scale deployment my-app-123 --replicas 2`

6. A Cloud Bigtable instance with one cluster is not performing as expected. The instance was created for analytics. Data is continuously streamed from thousands of sensors, and statistical analysis programs run continually in a batch. What would you recommend to improve performance?

    A. Use a write-optimized operating system on the nodes

    B. Use a read-optimized operating system on the nodes

    C. Add a cluster, run batch processing on one cluster, and have writes routed to the other cluster

    D. Add another node pool to the cluster in each zone that already has a node pool or that cluster

7. A Cloud Dataproc cluster is running with a single master node. You have determined that the cluster needs to be highly available. How would you increase the number of master nodes to 3?

    A. Use the gcloud dataproc clusters update command with parameter --num-masters 3

    B. Use the gcloud dataproc clusters update command with parameter --add-masters 2

    C. Use the cbt dataproc clusters update command with parameter --add-masters 2

    D. The number of master nodes cannot be changed. A new cluster would have to be deployed with three master nodes.

8. You have provisioned a Kubernetes Engine cluster and deployed an application. The application load varies during the day, and you have configured autoscaling to add replicas when CPU utilization exceeds 60 percent. How is that CPU utilization calculated?

    A. Based on all CPUs used by the deployment

    B. Based on all CPUs in the cluster

    C. Based on all CPU utilization of the most CPU-intensive pod

    D. Based on the CPU utilization of the least CPU-intensive pod

9. A team of data scientists wants to run a Python application in a Docker container. They want to minimize operational overhead, so they decide to use App Engine. They want to run the application in a Python 3.4 environment. Which configuration file would they modify to specify that runtime?

    A. app.yaml

    B. queue.yaml

    C. dispatch.yaml

    D. cron.yaml

10. Your team is experimenting with Cloud Functions to build a pipeline to process images uploaded to Cloud Storage. During the development stage, you want to avoid sudden spikes in Cloud Functions use because of errors in other parts of the pipeline, particularly the test code that uploads test images to Cloud Storage. How would you reduce the risk of running large numbers of Cloud Functions at one time?

    A. Use the --limit parameter when deploying the function

    B. Use the --max-instances parameter when deploying the function

    C. Set a label with the key max-instances and the value of the maximum number of instances

    D. Set a language-specific parameter in the function to limit the number of instances

11. Audit control requirements at your company require that all logs be kept for at least 365 days. You prefer to keep logs and log entries in Stackdriver logging, but you understand that logs with predefined retention periods of less than 1 year will require you to set up an export to another storage system, such as Cloud Storage. Which of the following logs would you need to set up exports for to meet the audit requirement?

    A. Admin activity audit logs

    B. System event audit logs

    C. Access transparency logs

    D. Data access audit logs

12. You would like to collect data on the memory utilization of instances running in a particular managed instance group. What Stackdriver service would you use?

    A. Stackdriver Debugger

    B. Stackdriver Logging

    C. Stackdriver Monitoring

    D. Stackdriver Trace

13. You would like to view information recorded by an application about events prior to the application crashing. What Stackdriver service would you use?

    A. Stackdriver Debugger

    B. Stackdriver Logging

    C. Stackdriver Monitoring

    D. Stackdriver Trace

14. Customers are complaining of long waits while your e-commerce site processes orders. There are many microservices in your order processing system. You would like to view information about the time each microservice takes to run. What Stackdriver service would you use?

    A. Stackdriver Debugger

    B. Stackdriver Logging

    C. Stackdriver Monitoring

    D. Stackdriver Trace

15. You have created a test environment for a group of business analysts to run several Cloud Dataflow pipelines. You want to limit the processing resources any pipeline can consume. What execution parameter would you specify to limit processing resources?

    A. numWorkers

    B. maxNumWorkers

    C. streaming

    D. maxResources

Chapter

6

Designing for Security and Compliance

GOOGLE CLOUD PROFESSIONAL DATA ENGINEER EXAM OBJECTIVES COVERED IN THIS CHAPTER INCLUDE THE FOLLOWING:

✓ **4.1 Designing for security and compliance. Considerations include:**

- Identity and access management (e.g., Cloud IAM)

- Data security (encryption, key management)

- Ensuring privacy (e.g., Data Loss Prevention API)

- Legal compliance (e.g., Health Insurance Portability and Accountability Act (HIPAA), Children's Online Privacy Protection Act (COPPA),FedRAMP, General Data Protection Regulation (GDPR))

Since data engineers work with diverse sets of data, they will likely need to use a variety of data stores that use access controls. They also should be prepared to work with sensitive data that needs additional protections. This chapter introduces several key topics of security and compliance, including

- Identity and access management
- Data security, including encryption and key management
- Data loss prevention
- Compliance

We'll begin with identity and access management, because it is fundamental to many security practices.

Identity and Access Management with Cloud IAM

Cloud IAM is Google Cloud's fine-grained identity and access management service that is used to control which users can perform operations on resources within GCP. Cloud IAM uses the concept of *roles*, which are collections of permissions that can be assigned to identities. Permissions are granted to roles, and then individuals can be assigned multiple roles to gain these permissions. Cloud IAM provides a large number of roles tuned to common use cases, such as server administrators or database operators.

Along with roles, additional attributes about resources or identities, such as IP address and date and time, can be considered when making access control decisions; this is known as *context-aware access*.

Cloud IAM maintains an audit log of changes to permissions, including authorizing, removing, and delegating permissions.

This chapter describes key aspects of Cloud IAM that you should understand when taking the Professional Data Engineer exam, including

- Predefined roles
- Custom roles

- Using roles with service accounts
- Access controls with policies

Together, these constitute the ways that you can control access to resources in GCP.

In GCP, users, groups, service accounts, and G Suite domains are authorized to access resources by granting those identities roles. As noted earlier, roles are collections of permissions. When a role is granted to an identity, that identity is granted all the permissions in that role. You do not directly assign permissions to an identity; identities get permissions only via roles.

GCP uses three types of roles:

- Primitive roles
- Predefined roles
- Custom roles

Primitive roles include the Owner, Editor, and Viewer, which existed prior to the introduction of Cloud IAM. These roles apply at the project level and so are considered coursegrained access controls.

- The *Viewer role* grants read-only access resources.
- The *Editor role* includes all Viewer permissions plus the ability to modify the state of a resource.
- The *Owner role* includes all Editor role permissions and permissions to manage roles and permissions, along with setting up billing for a project.

In general, you should not use primitive roles except in cases where coarse-grained access controls are acceptable. For example, you could use primitive roles to grant access to developers in a development environment, since the developers would be responsible for administering the development environment.

Predefined Roles

Predefined roles are generally associated with a GCP service, such as App Engine or BigQuery, and a set of related activities, such as editing data in a database or deploying an application to App Engine.

The naming convention for roles is to start the role name with roles/ followed by a string that identifies the service, such as appengine; followed by the type of entity to which the role applies, such as instance or table; followed by an operation, such as get, list, or create.

Let's look at a couple of examples. The roles/appengine.deployer role grants readonly access to all application and configuration settings and write access to create new versions. This role does not provide permission to modify existing applications except for deleting versions that are no longer receiving traffic. The permissions included in this role are as follows:

- `appengine.applications.get`
- `appengine.instances.get`
- `appengine.instances.list`
- `appengine.operations.*`
- `appengine.services.get`
- `appengine.services.list`
- `appengine.versions.create`
- `appengine.versions.delete`
- `appengine.versions.get`
- `appengine.versions.list`
- `resourcemanager.projects.get`
- `resourcemanager.projects.list`

As you can see, the naming convention for permissions is the name of the service followed by a resource type specific to that service and an action on resources of that type. The asterisk in this example indicates all types of actions applicable to the operation's resource, such as `get`, `list`, and `create`.

As a second example, BigQuery has a user role called `roles/bigquery.user` that grants permissions to run queries and other jobs within a project. Users can list their own jobs and datasets as well as create new datasets.

- `bigquery.config.get`
- `bigquery.datasets.create`
- `bigquery.datasets.get`
- `bigquery.datasets.getIamPolicy`
- `bigquery.jobs.create`
- `bigquery.jobs.list`
- `bigquery.models.list`
- `bigquery.readsessions.*`
- `bigquery.routines.list`
- `bigquery.savedqueries.get`
- `bigquery.savedqueries.list`
- `bigquery.tables.list`

- `bigquery.transfers.get`
- `resourcemanager.projects.get`
- `resourcemanager.projects.list`

Many services have similar sets of roles having a similar set of permissions, often including admins, viewers, and some kind of worker roles. For example, the roles available with the following GCP services include

Cloud Dataproc: `roles/dataproc.editor`, `roles/dataproc.viewer`, `roles/dataproce.admin`, and `roles/dataproc.worker`

Cloud Dataflow: `roles/dataflow.admin`, `roles/dataflow.developer`, `roles/dataflow.viewer`, and `roles/dataflow.worker`

Cloud Bigtable: `roles/bigtable.admin`, `roles/bigtable.user`, `roles/bigtable.viewer`, and `roles/bigtable.reader`

BigQuery: `roles/biguery.admin`, `roles/biguery.connectionAdmin`, `roles/biguery.connectionUser`, `roles/biguery.dataEditor`, `roles/biguery.dataOwner`, `roles/biguery.dataViewer`, `roles/biguery.jobUser`, `roles/biguery.metadataViewer`, `roles/biguery.readSessionUser`, and `roles/biguery.user`

Note that BigQuery uses fine-grained permissions on BigQuery resources, such as connections, metadata, and sessions.

Custom Roles

In addition to primitive and predefined roles, GCP allows for the use of custom-defined roles. With *custom roles*, you can assign one or more permissions to a role and then assign that role to a user, group, or service account.

Custom roles are especially important when implementing the *principle of least privilege*, which states that users should be granted the minimal set of permissions needed for them to perform their jobs. Because of this, you may want to grant someone a different subset/combination of permissions than what is available in the predefined roles.

Users must have the `iam.roles.create` permission to be able to create a custom role.

Figure 6.1 shows an example of the Create Role form in the IAM console. In addition to typical name, description, and identifier parameters, you can also specify a role launch stage, which can be alpha, beta, general availability, or deprecated. Custom roles usually start in the alpha stage and are then promoted to the beta or general availability stage after sufficient testing. The deprecation stage is used to indicate to users that the role should not be used.

FIGURE 6.1   Create Role form in the cloud console

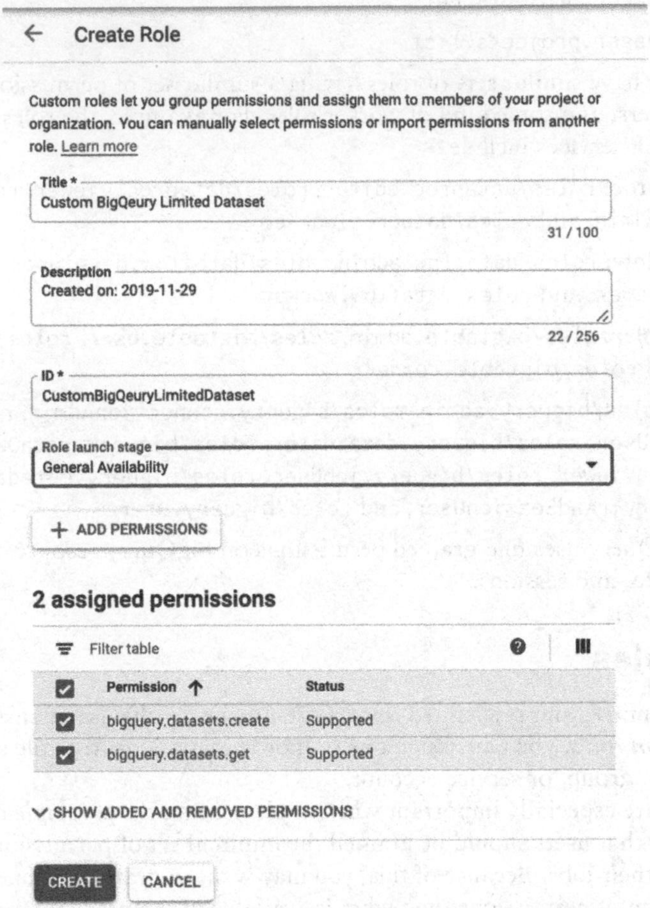

When creating a custom role, you can select from permissions assigned to predefined roles. This is helpful if you want someone to have a more limited version of a predefined role, in which case you can start with the list of permissions in a predefined role and select only the permissions that you would like to grant (see Figure 6.2).

FIGURE 6.2 Selecting permissions from predefined roles

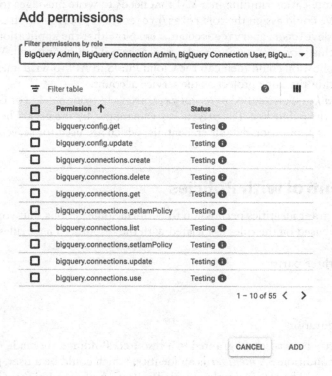

Using Roles with Service Accounts

Service accounts are a type of identity often used with VM instances and applications, which are able to make API calls authorized by roles assigned to the service account. A service account is identified by a unique email address. The email address name varies by the type of service account. For example:

App Engine service account: Uses <PROJECT-ID> followed by @appspot-gserviceaccount.com, such as pde-exam-project-98765@appspot .gserviceaccount.com

Compute Engine service account: Uses <PROJECT-NUMBER> followed by -compute@developer.gerviceaccount.com, such as 601440987865@developer .gserviceaccount.com

User-defined service accounts, such as pde-exam-service-account@601440987865@iam.gserviceaccount.com

Service accounts do not have passwords and cannot be used to log in interactively via a browser. These accounts are authenticated by a pair of public/private keys.

Consider an application running in a VM that needs to write messages to a Cloud Pub/Sub topic. We could assign the role `roles/projects.topics.publish` to `pde-exam-project-98765@developer.gserviceaccount.com`. Note that the application or VM is the entity using this service account in order to get the publish permission. With that role assigned, the application could then call the Cloud Pub/Sub API to write messages to a topic created within the same project as the service account.

User-managed keys, also called *external keys*, are used from outside of Google Cloud. GCP stores only the public key. The private key is managed by the user. These keys are usually used as application default credentials, which are used for server-to-server authentication.

Access Control with Policies

You use roles to grant identities permission to perform some actions, but you can also access resources based on the rules associated with the resource. These rules are called *policies*.

A policy has three parts:

- Bindings
- Metadata
- Audit configuration

Bindings specify how access is granted to a resource. Bindings are made up of members, roles, and conditions. A *member* is an identity, which could be a user, group, service account, or domain. The *role* is simply a named collection of permissions. *Conditions* are logic expressions for describing context-based restrictions.

The *metadata* of a policy includes an attribute called `etag`, which is used for concurrency control when updating policies. This is needed because multiple applications can write to a policy at the same time. When retrieving a policy, you also retrieve the `etag`, and when writing the policy, you compare the `etag` that you retrieved with the current `etag` of the policy. If the two `etags` are different, then another application wrote to the policy after you retrieved it. In those cases, you should retry the entire update operation. Metadata also includes a version to indicate the iteration of the schema used in the policy.

Here is an example of a binding that binds the user `data-enginer@example.com` to the role `roles/resourcemanager.projectCreator`:

```
{
  "bindings": [
    {
      "members": [
        "user:data-engineer@example.com"
      ],
```

```
      "role": "roles/resourcemanager.projectCreator"
    },
  ],
  "etag": "adjfadURHlad",
  "version": 1
}
```

Audit configurations describe which permission types are logged and which identities are exempt from logging. For example, the following audit configuration enables logging on reads and writes and exempts the user data-engineer@example.com from logging read operations.

```
{
  "auditLogConfigs": [
    {
      "logType": "DATA_READ",
      "exemptedMembers": ["user:data-engineer@example.com"]
    },
    {
      "logType": "DATA_WRITE",
    }
  ]
}
```

Policies can be defined at different levels of the resource hierarchy, including organizations, folders, projects, and individual resources. Only one policy at a time can be assigned to an organization, folder, project, or individual resource.

Policies are inherited through the resource hierarchy. Folders inherit the policies of the organization. If a folder is created within another folder, it inherits the policies of the encapsulating folder. Projects inherit the policies of the organization and any higher-level folders. Resources inherit the policies of the organization, folders, and projects above them in the hierarchy. The combination of policies directly assigned to a resource, and the policies inherited from ancestors in the resource hierarchy, is called the *effective policy*.

It is important to remember that IAM is additive only. You can't revoke, for example, permissions at a project level that were granted at the folder level.

Cloud IAM is a comprehensive service that provides for fine-grained access controls through the use of roles and policies. Predefined roles are available in Cloud IAM and are designed to group permissions needed for common use cases, such as administration of a database. Custom rules can be created when the predefined roles do not meet your specific needs, especially with respect to the principle of least privilege. Roles can also be used with service accounts to provide authorizations to VMs and applications. Also, access control policies can be used to control access to resources.

Using IAM with Storage and Processing Services

The previous section described IAM in general. Now let's take a look at some specific examples of how IAM predefined roles can be used with the following GCP services:

- Cloud Storage
- Cloud Bigtable
- BigQuery
- Cloud Dataflow

Of course, there are other relevant services, but once you understand these, you should be able generalize to other services as well.

Cloud Storage and IAM

There are several ways to control access to Cloud Storage resources, including buckets and objects in those buckets.

- Cloud IAM is the preferred way to control access to buckets and objects.
- For complex access control logic or when you need to control access to individual objects, you may need to use access control lists (ACLs).
- Signed URLs is another option for granting access. These URLs are generated by you and shared with someone to whom you want to grant access but only for a short period of time.
- If you want to control what can be uploaded to a bucket, you can use a signed policy document.

In this section, we will focus on the use of Cloud IAM with Cloud Storage.

Cloud Storage permissions are organized around resources, such as buckets, objects, and Hash-based Message Authentication Code (HMAC) keys. The bucket permissions allow users to create, delete, and list buckets. There are also permissions for getting and updating metadata as well as setting and getting IAM policies.

Object permissions also have `create`, `delete`, and `list` permissions as well as metadata and IAM policy permissions.

HMAC keys are used to authenticate access to Cloud Storage. The permissions for HMAC keys include creating, deleting, and listing keys as well as getting and updating metadata.

Five standard roles are used with Cloud Storage:

roles/storage.objectCreator: Allows a user to create an object

roles/storage.objectViewer: Allows a user to view an object and its metadata, but not ACLs. Users with this permission can also list the contents of a bucket

roles/storage.objectAdmin: Gives a user full control over objects, including creating, deleting, viewing, and listing

roles/storage.hmacKeyAdmin: Gives a user full control over HMAC keys within the project

roles/storage.admin: Gives a user full control over buckets and objects, but when applied to a single bucket, it gives the user full control over only that bucket

If primitive roles are used in a project, they grant viewer, editor, and owner access to objects in Cloud Storage.

Cloud Bigtable and IAM

The access controls for Cloud Bigtable can be configured at the project, instance, or table level.

At the project level, you can do the following:

- Allow a user to read from any table in any instance of the project but not write to those tables
- Allow a user to read from and write to any table in any instance of the project
- Allow a user to manage any instance within the project

At the instance level, you can do the following:

- Restrict a user to be able to read from development but not production instances
- Allow a user to read and write to development instances and read from production instances
- Allow a user to manage development instances but not production instances

At the table level, you can do the following:

- Allow a user to read from a table but not write to the table
- Allow a user to write to a table but not read from the table

Cloud Bigtable has permissions that allow access to resources, such as instances, application profiles, clusters, and tables.

The predefined roles for Cloud Bigtable include Admin, User, Reader, and Viewer. Anyone with the roles/bigtable.admin role will be able to administer any instance in a project, including creating new instances. The roles/bigtable.user role allows for read and write access to tables. The roles/bigtable.reader role allows for read-only access to data in tables. Someone with the roles/bigtable.viewer role is restricted to accessing the GCP console for Bigtable.

BigQuery and IAM

BigQuery provides a large number of permissions. This is understandable since BigQuery has many resources, such as tables, datasets, jobs, connections, saved queries, and more.

Most of the permissions allow for creating, deleting, updating, and listing components. Some components, like tables, have permissions for other operations, such as exporting data.

The BigQuery roles are as follows:

roles/BigQuery.admin: Gives a user permission to manage all BigQuery resources in a project.

roles/BigQuery.dataEditor: When applied to a dataset, this gives a user permission to list tables and read metadata as well as create, update, get, and delete tables in a dataset; if this role is applied at the organization or project level, then the user can also create datasets.

roles/BigQuery.dataOwner: When applied to a dataset, this gives a user permission to read, update, and delete the dataset as well as create, update, get, and delete the datasets tables; if this role is applied at the organization or project level, then the user can also create datasets.

roles/BigQuery.dataViewer: When applied to a dataset, this gives a user permission to read dataset metadata, list tables in the dataset, and read table metadata; when applied at the organization or project level, the user can list all datasets in a project.

roles/BigQuey.jobUser: Gives permission to run jobs, including queries; list jobs; and cancel the user's jobs.

roles/BigQuery.metadataViewer: At the organization and project levels, this role allows a user to list all datasets and read metadata for all datasets in a project as well as list all tables and views and read metadata for all tables and views in project.

roles/BigQuery.user: Gives permission to run jobs, enumerate and cancel the user's jobs, and enumerate datasets in a project. Users can also create new datasets, which grants roles/Bigquery.dataOwner to the user for the newly created table.

Note that this list includes non-beta roles, and the list may have changed by the time you read this.

Cloud Dataflow and IAM

IAM includes permissions and roles to control access to Cloud Dataflow resources, including jobs, messages, and metrics.

The permissions for Cloud Dataflow include creating, listing, updating, and canceling jobs. There are also permissions to list messages and get metrics.

Since Cloud Dataflow is a stream and batch processing system, there are some differences in roles from the storage services. The IAM roles for Cloud Dataflow are as follows:

roles/dataflow.admin: Gives permissions to create and manage jobs

roles/dataflow.developer: Gives permissions to execute and modify jobs

roles/dataflow.viewer: Gives permissions for read-only access to all Cloud Dataflow resources

roles/dataflow.worker: Gives permissions to a Compute Engine service account to execute work units of a pipeline

The roles outlined here are predefined roles. If you find that a role has more permissions than you want to grant to a user, you can create a custom role with fewer permissions. You could also add more permissions in case a predefined role is too restrictive but the others are not restrictive enough.

Data Security

 The following section originally appeared in *Official Google Cloud Certified Professional Cloud Architect Study Guide* (Wiley, 2019).

GCP provides multiple mechanisms for securing data in addition to IAM policies, which control access to data. Two essential services are encryption and key management.

Encryption

Encryption is the process of encoding data in such a way that it yields a coded version of the data that cannot be practically converted back to the original form without additional information. That additional information is a key that was used to encrypt the data. We typically distinguish between encryption at rest and encryption in transit.

Encryption at Rest

Google encrypts data at rest by default. You do not have to configure any policy to enable this feature. This applies to all Google data storage services, such as Cloud Storage, Cloud SQL, and Cloud Bigtable. *Encryption at rest* actually occurs at multiple levels:

- At the *platform level*, database and file data is protected using AES256 and AES128 encryption.
- At the *infrastructure level*, data is grouped into data chunks in the storage system, and each chunk is encrypted using AES256 encryption.
- At the *hardware level*, storage devices apply AES256 or AES128 encryption.

At the platform level, distributed filesystems and databases encrypt data. The granularity of encryption can vary across services. For example, Cloud SQL encrypts all data in a database instance with the same key, whereas Cloud Spanner, Bigtable, and Cloud Firestore encrypt data using the infrastructure encryption mechanism.

When Google Cloud stores data in the storage system, it stores it in subfile chunks that can be up to several gigabytes in size. Each chunk is encrypted with its own key, known as a *data encryption key (DEK)*. If a chunk is updated, a new key is used. Keys are not used for more than one chunk. Also, each chunk has a unique identifier that is referenced by access control lists (ACLs) to limit access to the chunks, which are stored in different locations to make it even more difficult for a malicious actor to piece them together.

In addition to encrypting data that is in chunks, Google encrypts the data encryption keys using a second key. This is known as *envelope encryption*. The key used to encrypt a DEK is known as a *key encryption key (KEK)*.

In addition to the chunk-level encryption that occurs at the infrastructure level, when blocks of data are written to persistent storage, the storage device encrypts those blocks using either AES128 or AES256. Older devices use AES128, but new storage devices use AES256.

To summarize encryption at rest:

- Data at rest is encrypted by default in Google Cloud Platform.
- Data is encrypted at multiple levels, including the application, infrastructure, and device levels.
- Data is encrypted in chunks. Each chunk has its own encryption key, which is called a *data encryption key*.
- Data encryption keys are themselves encrypted using a *key encryption key*.

Google Cloud manages much of the encryption process, including managing keys. This is helpful for users who want Google Cloud to manage all aspects of encryption. In cases where organizations need to manage their own keys, they will have to use one of two key management methods described in the "Key Management" section.

Before delving into key management, let's look at encryption in transit.

Encryption in Transit

Encryption in transit, also called *encryption in motion*, is used to protect the confidentiality and integrity of data in the event that the data is intercepted in transit. GCP uses a combination of authenticating sources and encryption to protect data in transit.

Google distinguishes data in transit on the Google network and data in transit on the public Internet. Data within the boundaries of the Google network is authenticated but may not be encrypted. Data moving into and out of the physical boundaries of the Google network is encrypted.

Users of applications running in Google Cloud communicate with the application over the Internet. Traffic incoming from users to the Google Cloud is routed to the Google Front End (GFE), a globally distributed proxy service. The *Google Front End* terminates HTTP and HTTPS traffic and routes it over the Google network to servers running the application. The GFE provides other security services, such as protecting against distributed denial-of-service (DDoS) attacks. GFE also implements global load balancers.

All traffic to Google Cloud services is encrypted by default. Google Cloud and the client negotiate how to encrypt data using either *Transport Layer Security (TLS)* or the Google-developed protocol QUIC. (In the past, the term stood for Quick UDP Internet Connections [QUIC], but now the name of the protocol is simply QUIC.)

Within the Google Cloud infrastructure, Google uses *Application Layer Transport Security (ALTS)* for authentication and encryption. This is done at Layer 7 of the OSI network model.

GCP offers encryption at rest and encryption in transit by default. Cloud users do not have to do anything in order to ensure that encryption is applied to their data. Users of GCP services can, however, determine how encryption keys are managed.

Key Management

There are many data encryption and key encryption keys in use for encryption at rest at any time in the Google Cloud.

Default Key Management

Google manages these encryption keys by default for users. Data encryption keys are stored near the data chunks that they encrypt. There is a separate data encryption key for each data chunk, but one key encryption key can be used to encrypt multiple data encryption keys. The key encryption keys are stored in a centralized key management service.

The data encryption keys are generated by the storage service that is storing the data chunk using a common cryptographic library. The data encryption keys are then sent to the centralized key management service where they are themselves encrypted using the storage systems key encryption key. When the storage system needs to retrieve data, it sends the data encryption key to the key management service, where the calling service is authenticated and the data key is decrypted and sent back to the storage system.

Customer-Managed Encryption Keys

Cloud KMS is a hosted key management service in Google Cloud. It enables customers to generate and store keys in GCP. It is used when customers want control over key management but do not need keys to reside on their own key management infrastructure. Note that customer-managed encryption keys (CMEKs) are often used to refer to KMS-based keys.

Cloud KMS supports a variety of *cryptographic keys*, including AES256, RSA 2048, RSA 3072, RSA 4096, EC P256, and EC P384. It also provides functionality for automatically rotating keys and encrypting data encryption keys with key encryption keys. Cloud KMS keys can be destroyed, but there is a 24-hour delay before the key is actually destroyed in case someone accidentally deletes a key or in the event of a malicious act.

Cloud KMS keys can be used for application-level encryption in GCP services, including Compute Engine, BigQuery, Cloud Storage, and Cloud Dataproc.

Customer-Supplied Encryption Keys

A third alternative for key management is *customer-supplied encryption keys (CSEKs)*. Customer-supplied keys are used when an organization needs complete control over key management, including storage. CSEK is often used to refer to customer-supplied keys.

In this model, keys are generated and kept on premises and used by GCP services to encrypt the customer's data. These keys are passed with other arguments to API function calls. When the keys are sent to GCP, they are stored in memory while being used.

Customer-supplied keys are not written to storage. They cannot be restored from GCP—the customer is the only one with persistent copies of the keys.

Encryption and key management are essential components of a comprehensive security regime. Data at rest and data in transit are encrypted by default. Keys are managed by default by GCP but can also be managed by cloud users. Users have two options. One is CMEK using Cloud KMS, which is a hosted managed key service that generates and stores keys in the cloud on behalf of a user. The other option is customer-supplied keys, which are managed on premises and sent to Google as part of API calls. Customer-supplied keys provide customers with the greatest amount of control, but they also require infrastructure and management procedures that are not needed when using default encryption.

Ensuring Privacy with the Data Loss Prevention API

The *Data Loss Prevention API* is a service that can detect sensitive information in text and images, redact or mask sensitive information, and perform risk analysis. This service operates as a job that applies pattern detection techniques to text or images. *Patterns* are defined as information types or InfoType detectors.

Detecting Sensitive Data

Google provides hundreds of InfoType detectors to identify known types of sensitive information, including

- Credit card numbers
- Dates of birth
- Email addresses
- Passport number
- Authentication tokens
- Passwords

There are also country-specific InfoType detectors, such as

- U.S. Social Security numbers
- Indian GST identification number (GSTIN)
- Japanese bank account numbers
- Spanish national identity numbers
- Paraguay civil identity card numbers

You specify InfoType detectors and data to inspect when creating an inspection job. The API works with text or base64-encoded images.

When an InfoType detector matches a string in a text, the API returns the InfoType detector that matched, a likelihood score, and a location specified by byte range or by record location if the text is structured. When an InfoType detector matches something in an image, the API returns the InfoType that matched, a likelihood score, and a location specified in pixel locations.

In addition to detecting patterns, the Data Loss Prevention API can redact the sensitive information. For example, if you were to scan the following text for email addresses:

"And my email address is djohnson@example.com"

the API could return an obfuscated version such as:

"And my email address is [EMAIL_ADDRESS]"

Similarly, when sensitive information is found in images, the section of the image containing it is blocked out, as shown in Figure 6.3.

FIGURE 6.3   An example of a redacted image generated by the Data Loss Prevention API

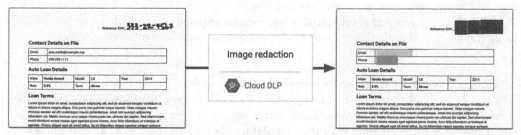

Image source: https://cloud.google.com/dlp/docs/redacting-sensitive-data-images

Running Data Loss Prevention Jobs

There are two types of Data Loss Prevention jobs: inspection jobs and risk analysis jobs. *Inspection jobs* scan content for sensitive information using InfoTypes that you specify and generate reports on the location and type of sensitive information found. *Risk analysis jobs* calculate the likelihood that data could be re-identified.

Jobs are scheduled by creating *job triggers*. Job triggers start a scan on some Google Cloud storage service, including Cloud Storage and BigQuery.

After a job completes, you can automatically perform an action. There are two types of actions. The results of a scan job can be saved to BigQuery using a table that you specify. The other action is to publish the results of the scan job to a Cloud Pub/Sub topic.

Inspection Best Practices

Google has identified several best practices for using the Data Loss Prevention API.

First, you should inventory and prioritize the content you wish to scan. This is especially true if you have a large backlog of content that needs to be scanned. The data that is most at risk should be scanned first.

Make sure that the Cloud DLP service account has all the correct roles to access your storage services.

Start by sampling data and using simple matching criteria. This will help you identify which InfoType detectors you should use. You may find that your scans generate more false positives than are acceptable. In that case, you can create exclusion rules to reduce false positives.

Schedule scans using job triggers. Scans can be configured to inspect only data that has changed since the last scan.

Legal Compliance

 Some of the material in this section originally appeared in *Official Google Cloud Certified Professional Cloud Architect Study Guide* (Wiley, 2019).

Google is regularly reviewed by independent organizations for verification of security, privacy, and compliance controls. Google Cloud's security, certifications and legal commitments can help support your compliance with a variety of regulations, but ultimately you are responsible for evaluating your own regulatory compliance. Some of the best-known regulations are listed below.

Health Insurance Portability and Accountability Act (HIPAA)

The *Health Insurance Portability and Accountability Act (HIPAA)* is a federal law in the United States that protects individuals' healthcare information. It was enacted in 1996 and updated in 2003 and 2005. HIPAA is a broad piece of legislation, but from a security perspective, the most important parts are the HIPAA Privacy Rule and the HIPAA Security Rule.

The *HIPAA Privacy Rule* is a set of rules established to protect patient's healthcare information. It sets limits on data that can be shared by healthcare providers, insurers, and others with access to protected information. This rule also grants patients the right to review information in their records and request information. For further details on this rule, see www.hhs.gov/hipaa/for-professionals/privacy/index.html.

The *HIPAA Security Rule* defines standards for protecting electronic records containing personal healthcare information. The rule requires organizations that hold electronic healthcare data to ensure the confidentiality, integrity, and availability of healthcare information; protect against expected threats; and prevent unauthorized disclosures. In practice, this requires security management practices, access control practices, incident response procedures, contingency planning, and evaluation of security measures. For more information on the HIPAA Security Rule, see www.hhs.gov/hipaa/for-professionals/ security/index.html.

The *Health Information Technology for Economic and Clinical Health (HITECH) Act* was enacted in 2009, and it includes rules governing the transmission of health information. HITECH extended the application of HIPAA to business associates of healthcare providers and insurers. Business associates that provide services to healthcare and insurance providers must follow HIPAA regulations as well.

Google Cloud Platform can support your HIPAA compliance within the scope of a Business Associate Agreement (BAA). If you use Google Cloud for data and processes covered by HIPAA and enter into a BAA with Google Cloud, you should know that all of the Google Cloud infrastructure is covered under Google's Cloud's BAA and that many GCP services are as well, including Compute Engine, App Engine, Kubernetes Engine, BigQuery, Cloud SQL, and many other products. For a complete list, see https://cloud.google.com/ security/compliance/hipaa/.

For more on HITECH, see:

www.hhs.gov/hipaa/for-professionals/special-topics/hitech-act-enforcement-interim-final-rule/index.html

Children's Online Privacy Protection Act

The *Children's Online Privacy Protection Act (COPPA)* is a U.S. federal law passed in 1998 that requires the U.S. Federal Trade Commission to define and enforce regulations regarding children's online privacy. This legislation is primarily focused on children under the age of 13, and it applies to websites and online services that collect information about children.

The rules require online service operators to do the following:

- Post clear and comprehensive privacy policies
- Provide direct notice to parents before collecting a child's personal information
- Give parents a choice about how a child's data is used
- Give parents access to data collected about a child
- Give parents the opportunity to block collection of a child's data
- Keep a child's data only as long as needed to fulfill the purpose for which it was created
- In general, maintain the confidentiality, integrity, and availability of collected data

Personal information covered by this rule includes name, address, online contact information, telephone number, geolocation data, and photographs.

For more information on COPPA, see:

www.ftc.gov/tips-advice/business-center/guidance/complying-coppa-frequently-asked-questions

FedRAMP

The *Federal Risk and Authorization Management Program (FedRAMP)* is a U.S. federal government program that promotes a standard approach to assessment, authorization, and monitoring of cloud resources. The program is designed to ensure that cloud systems used by governments are adequately secure, reduce duplication of effort, and reduce risk management costs.

The FedRAMP framework includes four broad areas:

Document: Includes categorizing systems, selecting security controls, and implementing and documenting controls

Assess: The use of a third-party assessor to ensure that the controls in place are sufficient and effective

Authorize: Involves analysis of risks, plans of action and milestones, and submission of a security package for authorizations

Monitoring: A continuous process of monitoring systems once FedRAMP certifications are awarded

FedRAMP is required for U.S. federal agency cloud deployments. For more details on FedRAMP, see www.fedramp.gov.

General Data Protection Regulation

The European Union's (EU) *General Data Protection Regulation (GDPR)* was passed in 2016, and enforcement of the GDPR began in 2018. The purpose of this regulation is to standardize privacy protections across the EU, grant controls to individuals over their private information, and specify security practices required for organizations holding private information of EU citizens.

GDPR distinguishes controllers and processors. A *controller* is a person or organization that determines the purpose and means of processing personal data. A *processor* is a person or organization that processes data on behalf of a controller. Controllers are responsible for gaining and managing the consent of individuals whose data is collected. Controllers direct processors on implementing the wishes of individuals who request access or changes to data. Processors are responsible for securing data and conducting audits in order to ensure that security practices are functioning as expected.

In the event of a data breach, data processors must notify the controller. Controllers in turn must notify the supervising authority, which varies by country, as well as the individuals whose data was compromised.

For more information on GDPR, see https://gdpr-info.eu/.

Exam Essentials

Understand the components of Cloud IAM.   Cloud IAM provides fine-grained identity and access management for resources within GCP. Cloud IAM uses the concept of roles, which are collections of permissions that can be assigned to identities. Cloud IAM provides a large number of roles tuned to common use cases, such as server administrators or database operators. Additional attributes about resources or identities, such as IP address and date and time, can be considered when making access control decisions. Cloud IAM maintains an audit log of changes to permissions, including authorizing, removing, and delegating permissions.

Know the three types of roles.   Primitive roles existed prior to Cloud IAM and include Owner, Editor, and Viewer roles. Predefined roles are generally associated with a GCP service, such as App Engine or BigQuery, and a set of related activities, such as editing data in a database or deploying an application to App Engine. With custom roles, you can assign one or more permissions to a role and then assign that role to a user, group, or service account. Custom roles are especially important when implementing the principle of least privilege, which states that users should be granted the minimal set of permissions needed for them to perform their jobs.

Understand the purpose of service accounts.   Service accounts are a type of identity that are used with VM instances and applications, which are able to make API calls authorized by roles assigned to the service account. A service account is identified by a unique email address. These accounts are authenticated by two sets of public/private keys. One set is managed by Google, and the other set is managed by users. Public keys are provided to API calls to authenticate the service account.

Understand the structure and function of policies.   A policy consists of binding, metadata, and an audit configuration. Bindings specify how access is granted to a resource. Bindings are made up of members, roles, and conditions. The metadata of a policy includes an attribute called etag and versions. Audit configurations describe which permission types are logged and which identities are exempt from logging. Policies can be defined at different levels of the resource hierarchy, including organizations, folders, projects, and individual resources. Only one policy at a time can be assigned to an organization, folder, project, or individual resource.

Understand data-at-rest encryption.   Encryption is the process of encoding data in a way that yields a coded version of data that cannot be practically converted back to the original form without additional information. Data at rest is encrypted by default on Google Cloud Platform. Data is encrypted at multiple levels, including the application, infrastructure, and device levels. Data is encrypted in chunks. Each chunk has its own encryption key, which is called a data encryption key. Data encryption keys are themselves encrypted using a key encryption key.

Understand data-in-transit encryption.   All traffic to Google Cloud services is encrypted by default. Google Cloud and the client negotiate how to encrypt data using either Transport Layer Security (TLS) or the Google-developed protocol QUICC.

Understand key management.   Cloud KMS is a hosted key management service in the Google Cloud. It enables customers to generate and store keys in GCP. It is used when customers want control over key management. Customer-supplied keys are used when an organization needs complete control over key management, including storage.

Know the basic requirements of major regulations.   The Health Insurance Portability and Accountability Act (HIPAA) is a federal law in the United States that protects individuals' healthcare information. The Children's Online Privacy Protection Act (COPPA) is primarily focused on children under the age of 13, and it applies to websites and online services that collect information about children. The Federal Risk and Authorization Management Program (FedRAMP) is a U.S. federal government program that promotes a standard approach to assessment, authorization, and monitoring of cloud resources. The European Union's (EU) General Data Protection Regulation (GDPR) is designed to standardize privacy protections across the EU, grant controls to individuals over their private information, and specify security practices required for organizations holding private information of EU citizens.

Review Questions

You can find the answers in the appendix.

1. You have been tasked with creating a pilot project in GCP to demonstrate the feasibility of migrating workloads from an on-premises Hadoop cluster to Cloud Dataproc. Three other engineers will work with you. None of the data that you will use contains sensitive information. You want to minimize the amount of time that you spend on administering the development environment. What would you use to control access to resources in the development environment?

    A. Predefined roles

    B. Custom roles

    C. Primitive roles

    D. Access control lists

2. The auditors for your company have determined that several employees have more permissions than needed to carry out their job responsibilities. All the employees have users accounts on GCP that have been assigned predefined roles. You have concluded that the optimal way to meet the auditors' recommendations is by using custom roles. What permission is needed to create a custom role?

    A. iam.roles.create

    B. iam.custom.roles

    C. roles/iam.custom.create

    D. roles/iam.create.custom

3. You have created a managed instance group in Compute Engine to run a high-performance computing application. The application will read source data from a Cloud Storage bucket and write results to another bucket. The application will run whenever new data is uploaded to Cloud Storage via a Cloud Function that invokes the script to start the job. You will need to assign the role roles/storage.objectCreator to an identity so that the application can write the output data to Cloud Storage. To what kind of identity would you assign the roles?

    A. User.

    B. Group.

    C. Service account.

    D. You wouldn't. The role would be assigned to the bucket.

4. Your company has implemented an organizational hierarchy consisting of two layers of folders and tens of projects. The top layer of folders corresponds to a department, and the second layer of folders are working groups within a department. Each working group has one or more projects in the resource hierarchy. You have to ensure that all projects comply with regulations, so you have created several policies. Policy A applies to all departments.

Policies B, C, D, and E are department specific. At what level of the resource hierarchy would you assign each policy?

A. Assign policies A, B, C, D, and E to each folder

B. Assign policy A to the organizational hierarchy and policies B, C, D, and E to each department's corresponding folder

C. Assign policy A to the organizational hierarchy and policies B, C, D, and E to each department's corresponding projects

D. Assign policy A to each department's folder and policies B, C, D, and E to each project

5. Your startup is developing a mobile app that takes an image as input and produces a list of names of objects in the image. The image file is uploaded from the mobile device to a Cloud Storage bucket. A service account is associated with the server-side application that will retrieve the image. The application will not perform any other operation on the file or the bucket. Following the principle of least privilege, what role would you assign to the service account?

A. roles/storage.objectViewer

B. roles/storage.objectAdmin

C. roles/storage.objectCreator

D. roles/storage.objectViewer and roles/storage.objectCreator

6. A data analyst asks for your help on a problem that users are having that involves BigQuery. The data analyst has been granted permissions to read the tables in a particular dataset. However, when the analyst runs a query, an error message is returned. What role would you think is missing from the users' assigned roles?

A. roles/BigQuery.admin

B. roles/BigQuery.jobUser

C. roles/BigQuery.metadataViewer

D. roles/BigQuery.queryRunner

7. Your company is subject to financial industry regulations that require all customer data to be encrypted when persistently stored. Your CTO has tasked you with assessing options for encrypting the data. What must you do to ensure that applications processing protected data encrypt it when it is stored on disk or SSD?

A. Configure a database to use database encryption.

B. Configure persistent disks to use disk encryption.

C. Configure the application to use application encryption.

D. Nothing. Data is encrypted at rest by default.

8. Data can be encrypted at multiple levels, such as at the platform, infrastructure, and device levels. At the device level, how is data encrypted in the Google Cloud Platform?

A. AES256 or AES128 encryption

B. Elliptic curve cryptography

C. Data Encryption Standard (DES)

D. Blowfish

9. In GCP, each data chunk written to a storage system is encrypted with a data encryption key. How does GCP protect the data encryption key so that an attacker who gained access to the storage system storing the key could not use it to decrypt the data chunk?

    A. GCP writes the data encryption key to a hidden location on disk.

    B. GCP encrypts the data encryption key with a key encryption key.

    C. GCP stores the data encryption key in a secure Cloud SQL database.

    D. GCP applies an elliptic curve encryption algorithm for each data encryption key.

10. The CTO has asked you to participate in a prototype project to provide better privacy controls. The CTO asks you to run a risk analysis job on a text file that has been inspected by the Data Loss Prevention API. What is the CTO interested in knowing?

    A. The number of times sensitive information is redacted

    B. The percentage of text that is redacted

    C. The likelihood that the data can be re-identified

    D. What InfoType patterns were detected

11. Your company is about to start a huge project to analyze a large number of documents to redact sensitive information. You would like to follow Google-recommended best practices. What would you do first?

    A. Identify InfoTypes to use

    B. Prioritize the order of scanning, starting with the most at-risk data

    C. Run a risk analysis job first

    D. Extract a sample of data and apply all InfoTypes to it

12. Your startup is creating an app to help students with math homework. The app will track assignments, how long the student takes to answer a question, the number of incorrect answers, and so on. The app will be used by students ages 9 to 14. You expect to market the app in the United States. With which of the following regulations must you comply?

    A. HIPAA

    B. GDPR

    C. COPPA

    D. FedRAMP

Chapter 7

Designing Databases for Reliability, Scalability, and Availability

GOOGLE CLOUD PROFESSIONAL DATA ENGINEER EXAM OBJECTIVES COVERED IN THIS CHAPTER INCLUDE THE FOLLOWING:

4. Ensuring solution quality

✓ **4.2   Ensuring scalability and efficiency. Considerations include:**

- Building and running test suites

- Assessing, troubleshooting, and improving data representations and data processing infrastructure

- Resizing and autoscaling resources

✓ **4.3   Ensuring reliability and fidelity. Considerations include:**

- Performing data preparation and quality control (e.g., Cloud Dataprep)

- Verification and monitoring

- Planning, executing, and stress testing data recovery (fault tolerance, rerunning failed jobs, performing retrospective re-analysis)

A significant amount of a data engineer's time can go into working with databases. Chapter 2, "Building and Operationalizing Storage Systems," introduced the GCP databases and highlighted their features and some use cases. In this chapter, we will delve into more detail about designing for reliability, scalability, and availability of three GCP databases:

- Cloud Bigtable
- Cloud Spanner
- Cloud BigQuery

A fourth database, Cloud SQL, could be used as well, but it does not scale beyond the region level. If you do need a multi-regional relational database, you should use Cloud Spanner.

By the end of this chapter, you should have an understanding of how to apply best practices for designing schemas, querying data, and taking advantage of the physical design properties of each database.

Designing Cloud Bigtable Databases for Scalability and Reliability

Cloud Bigtable is a nonrelational database based on a sparse three-dimensional map. The three dimensions are rows, columns, and cells. By understanding this 3D map structure, you will be able to figure out the best way to design Cloud Bigtable schemas and tables to meet scalability, availability, and reliability requirements. In particular, we will consider the following:

- Data modeling with Cloud Bigtable
- Designing row-keys
- Designing for time-series data
- Using replication to improve scalability and availability

Data Modeling with Cloud Bigtable

The 3D map structure of Cloud Bigtable lends itself to distributed implementations. Cloud Bigtable databases are deployed on a set of resources known as an *instance*. (This is not the same thing as a virtual machine (VM) instance in Compute Engine.) An *instance* consists of a set of nodes, which are virtual machines, as well as a set of sorted string tables and log data that is stored in Google's Colossus filesystem. Figure 7.1 shows the basic architecture of Cloud Bigtable.

FIGURE 7.1   Cloud Bigtable uses a cluster of VMs and the Colossus filesystem for storing, accessing, and managing data.

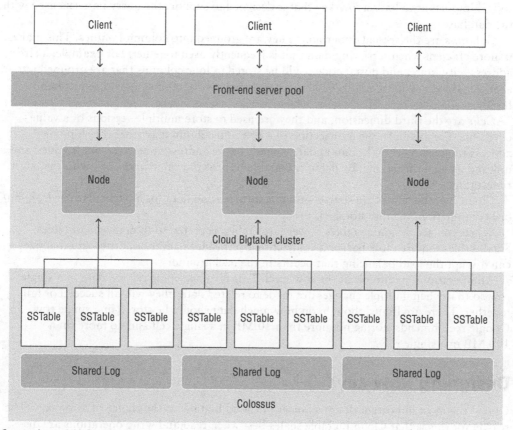

Source: https://cloud.google.com/bigtable/docs/overview

When you create a Cloud Bigtable instance, you specify a number of nodes. These nodes manage the metadata about the data stored in the Cloud Bigtable database, whereas the actual data is stored outside of the nodes on the Colossus filesystem. Within the Colossus filesystem, data is organized into sorted string tables, or SSTables, which are known as tablets in GCP terminology. As the name implies, data is stored in a sorted order. SSTables are also immutable.

Separating metadata from data has several advantages, including the following:

- Fast rebalancing of tablets from one node to another
- The ability to recover a failed node by migrating metadata only
- The scalability, reliability, and availability of the Colossus filesystem for data

A master process balances workloads in a cluster, including splitting and merging tablets.

In Cloud Bigtable, *rows* are indexed by a *row-key*, which is analogous to a primary key in a relational database. Data is stored in a lexicographically sorted order by row-key. Data is retrieved from Bigtable by using a row-key to specify a particular row or a range of row-keys to specify a set of contiguous rows. There are no secondary indexes in Cloud Bigtable, so it is important to have a row-key that is designed to support the query patterns used with the database.

Columns are the second dimension. They are grouped into column families. This makes it more efficient when retrieving data that is frequently used together. For example, a street address, city, state, and postal code could be stored in four columns that are grouped into a single address column family. Columns are sorted lexicographically within a column family.

Cells are the third dimension, and they are used to store multiple versions of a value over time. For example, the intersection of a row and column may store the shipping address of a customer. When an update is made to the address, a new version is added and indexed using a timestamp. By default, Bigtable returns the value in the cell with the latest timestamp.

Cloud Bigtable tables are sparse—that is, if there is no data for a particular row/column/cell combination, then no storage is used.

When you are designing tables, fewer large tables is preferred to many small tables. Small tables require more backend connection overhead. In addition, different table sizes can disrupt the load balancing that occurs in the background.

All operations are atomic at the row level. This favors keeping related data in a single row so that when multiple changes are made to related data, they will all succeed or fail together. There are limits, though, on how much data should be stored in a single row. Google recommends storing no more than 10 MB in a single cell and no more than 100 MB in a single row.

Designing Row-keys

One of the most important design choices in Cloud Bigtable is the choice of a row-key. The reason for this is that Cloud Bigtable scales best when read and write operations are distributed across nodes and tablets. If read and write operations are concentrated in a small number of nodes and tablets, the overall performance is limited to the performance of those few resources.

Row-key Design Best Practices

In general, it is best to avoid monotonically increasing values or lexicographically close strings at the beginning of keys because this can cause hotspots. Google notably makes an exception to this rule and suggests using reverse domain names as a row-key when the entity can be represented as a domain name and there are many domain names. For example, the domain mysubdomain.groupsubdomain.example.com can be reversed to create a row-key called com.example.groupsubdomain.domain. This is helpful if there is some data that is repeated across rows. In that case, Cloud Bigtable can compress the repeated data efficiently. Reverse domain names should not be used as row-keys if there are not enough distinct domains to distribute data adequately across nodes.

Also, when a using a multitenant Cloud Bigtable database, it is a good practice to use a tenant prefix in the row-key. This will ensure that all of a customer's data is kept together and not intermingled with other customers' data. In this situation, the first part of the row-key could be a customer ID or other customer-specific code.

String identifiers, such as a customer ID or a sensor ID, are good candidates for a row-key. *Timestamps* may be used as part of a row-key, but they should not be the entire row-key or the start of the row-key. This is especially helpful when you need to perform range scans based on time. The first part of a row-key that includes a timestamp should be a high-cardinality—that is, a large number of possible values—attribute, such as a sensor ID. For example, 1873838#1577569258 is a sensor ID concatenated with a timestamp in seconds past the epoch. This ordering will work as long as the sensors report in a fairly random order.

Moving timestamps from the front of a row-key so that another attribute is the first part of the row-key is an example of *field promotion*. In general, it is a good practice to promote, or move toward the front of the key, values that are highly varied.

Another way to avoid hotspots is to use *salting*, which is the process of adding a derived value to the key to make writes noncontiguous. For example, you could use the hash of a timestamp divided by the number of nodes in a cluster. This approach would evenly distribute the write load across all nodes. Of course, this simple salting function depends on the number of nodes in the cluster, which can change over time.

Antipatterns for Row-key Design

In addition to employing best practices for designing row-keys, you need to avoid some antipatterns. Specifically, avoid the following:

- Domain names
- Sequential numeric IDs
- Frequently updated identifiers
- Hashed values

In the case of the domain names and sequential IDs, you can create hotspots for read and write operations. Frequently updated identifiers should not be used because the update operations can overload the tablet that stores the row that is often updated.

Key Visualizer

Key Visualizer is a Cloud Bigtable tool for understanding usage patterns in a Cloud Bigtable database. This tool helps you identify the following:

- Where hotspots exist
- Rows that may contain too much data
- The distribution of workload across all rows in a table

Key Visualizer generates hourly and daily scans of tables that have at least 30 GB of data at some point in time and for which there was an average of at least 10,000 reads and writes per second over the previous 24 hours. Data from Key Visualizer is displayed in a heatmap in which dark areas have low activity and bright areas have heavy activity (see Figure 7.2 for an example).

FIGURE 7.2   An example heatmap generated by Cloud Bigtable Key Visualizer

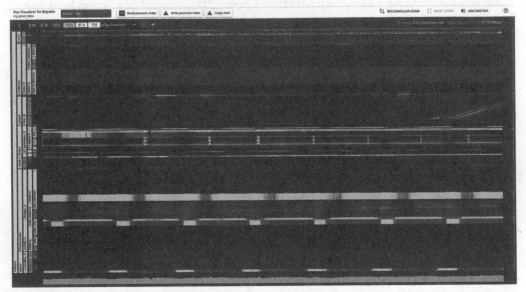

Source: https://cloud.google.com/bigtable/docs/keyvis-overview

Designing for Time Series

Time-series data, such as financial data and IoT data streams, is well suited to Cloud Bigtable. The managed database provides low-latency writes, and it is highly scalable, which is needed for large-volume time-series data. Time-series data is a natural fit for tables with many rows and few columns. These are known as tall and narrow. Also, time-series data is often queried using time ranges as filters. Data that is likely to be queried together— for example, data from an IoT device that was generated within the same hour, day, and so on—can be stored together in Cloud Bigtable. This storage pattern can help reduce the volume of data scanned to answer a query.

Google has several recommendations for designing for time-series data:

Keep names short.   This reduces the size of metadata since names are stored along with data values.

Favor tables with many rows and few columns ("tall and narrow" tables).   Within each row, store few events—ideally only one event per row. This makes querying easier. Also, storing multiple events increases the chance of exceeding maximum recommended row sizes.

Using tall and narrow tables typically leads to one table per modeled entity. For example, consider two IoT sensors: one is an environmental sensor that measures temperature, humidity, and pressure, and the other is a sensor that counts the number of vehicles passing the sensor. Both devices collect data at the same location and at the same frequency. Although the two types of sensors may be part of the same application, the data from each should be stored in their own tables.

Design row-keys for looking up a single value or a range of values.   Range scans are common in time-series analysis. Keep in mind that there is only one index on Cloud Bigtable tables. If you need to look up or range scan data in different orders, then you will need to denormalize the data and create another table with a different ordering. For example, if you have an IoT application that groups data by sensor type and by monitored device type, you could create one table with the sensor type in the row-key and another table with the monitored device type in the row-key. To minimize storage, only the data that is needed to answer queries should be stored in the additional table.

Use Replication for Availability and Scalability

Cloud Bigtable replication allows you to keep multiple copies of your data in multiple regions or multiple zones. This approach can improve availability and durability. You can also take advantage of replicated data to distribute workloads across multiple clusters.

When creating a Cloud Bigtable instance, you can create multiple clusters, as highlighted in Figure 7.3.

Cloud Bigtable supports up to four replicated clusters. Clusters can be regional or multi-regional. When a change is made to one of the clusters, it is replicated in the others. This includes the following:

- Updating data in tables
- Adding and deleting tables
- Adding and deleting column families
- Configuring garbage collection

Note that there is no single primary cluster. All replicated clusters can perform read and write operations. Cloud Bigtable is eventually consistent, so all replicas should be updated within a few seconds or minutes in most cases. Performing large updates or replicating clusters that are far apart can take longer.

If you want to ensure that a cluster will never read data that is older than its most recent writes, you can specify read-your-writes consistency by stipulating single-cluster routing in an app profile. *App profiles* are configurations that specify how to handle client requests. If you want strong consistency, you would have to specify single-cluster routing in the app configuration, and you must not use the other clusters except for failover. If you want Cloud Bigtable to fail over automatically to one region if your application cannot reach another region, you should use multicluster routing.

FIGURE 7.3   Specifying multiple clusters when creating a Cloud Bigtable instance

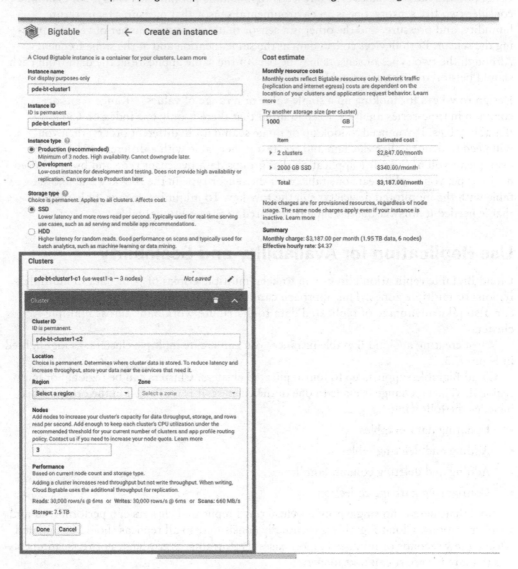

Designing Cloud Spanner Databases for Scalability and Reliability

Cloud Spanner is a globally scalable relational database that offers many of the scalability benefits once limited to NoSQL databases. It does so while maintaining key features of relational databases, such as support for normalized data models and transaction support.

Data engineers need to understand factors that influence the performance of Cloud Spanner databases in order to avoid design choices that can limit performance and scalability.

For the purposes of the Cloud Professional Data Engineer exam, it is important to understand several aspects of Cloud Spanner, including

- Relational database features
- Interleaved tables
- Primary keys and hotspots
- Database splits
- Secondary indexes
- Query best practices

Relational Database Features

Many of Cloud Spanner features are common to other relational databases. The data model is centered around tables, which are composed of columns that represent attributes and rows that are collections of values for attributes about a single entity. For example, an e-commerce application may have tables about customers, orders, and inventory, with rows representing a single customer, order, and inventory item, respectively. The customer table may have columns such as customer name, address, and credit limit, whereas the order table may have an order ID, date of order, customer ID, and total value of the order. An inventory table could have columns with product names, quantity, and location of the item in a warehouse.

Relational databases are strongly typed. Cloud Spanner supports the following types:

Array: An ordered list of zero or more elements of a non-array type

Bool: Boolean TRUE or FALSE

Bytes: Variable-length binary data

Date: A calendar date

Float64: Approximate numeric values with fractional components

INT64: Numeric values without fractional components

String: Variable-length characters

Struct: Container of ordered typed fields

Timestamp: A point in time with nanosecond precision

Cloud Spanner supports both primary and secondary indexes. The *primary index* is an index automatically created on the primary key of a table. Other columns or combinations of columns can be indexed as well using secondary indexes. Note that this is different from Cloud Bigtable, which does not support secondary indexes. This reduces the need to denormalize and duplicate data to support multiple query patterns. Whereas in Cloud Bigtable you would need to duplicate data to query the data efficiently without referencing the primary key, in Cloud Spanner you can create secondary indexes that support different query patterns.

Interleaved Tables

Another important performance feature of Cloud Spanner is its ability to interleave data from related tables. This is done through a parent-child relationship in which parent data, such as a row from the order table, is stored with child data, such as order line items. This makes retrieving data simultaneously from both tables more efficient than if the data were stored separately and is especially helpful when performing joins. Since the data from both tables is co-located, the database has to perform fewer seeks to get all the needed data.

Cloud Spanner supports up to seven layers of interleaved tables. Tables are interleaved using the INTERLEAVE IN PARENT clause in a CREATE TABLE statement. For example, to interleave orders with the customers who placed the order, you could use the following commands:

```
CREATE TABLE Customers (
  CustomerId   INT64 NOT NULL,
  FirstName   STRING(1024),
  LastName    STRING(1024),
  AddressLine STRING(1024),
  City STRING(1024),
  State STRING(1024),
  PostalCode STRING(10),
) PRIMARY KEY (CustomerId);

CREATE TABLE Orders (
  CustomerId      INT64 NOT NULL,
  OrderId        INT64 NOT NULL,
  OrderDescription   STRING(MAX),
) PRIMARY KEY (CustomerId, OrderId),
  INTERLEAVE IN PARENT Customers ON DELETE CASCADE;
```

Interleaving is used when tables are frequently joined. By storing the related data together, joins can be performed with fewer I/O operations than if they were stored independently.

Primary Keys and Hotspots

Cloud Spanner is horizontally scalable, so it should be no surprise that it shares some characteristics with Cloud Bigtable, another horizontally scalable database. Cloud Spanner uses multiple servers, and it divides data among servers by key range. This creates the potential for hotspots just as in Cloud Bigtable. Monotonically increasing keys, for example, can cause read and write operations to happen in a few servers at once instead of being evenly distributed across all servers.

As with Cloud Bigtable, there are several recommended ways of defining primary keys to avoid hotspots. These include the following:

Using a Hash of the Natural Key   Note that using a hash of the natural key is not recommended with Cloud Bigtable, but meaningless keys are regularly used in relational databases.

Swapping the Order of Columns in Keys to Promote Higher-Cardinality Attributes   Doing so makes the start of the keys more likely to be nonsequential.

Using a Universally Unique Identifier (UUID), Specifically Version 4 or Later   Some older UUIDs store timestamps in the high-order bits, and that can lead to hotspotting.

Using Bit-Reverse Sequential Values   Bit-reverse sequential values can be used when the best candidate primary key is monotonically increasing. By reversing the value, you can eliminate the potential for hotspots because the start of the reversed value will vary from one value to the next.

Also, like Cloud Bigtable, Cloud Spanner has to manage breaking down datasets into manageable-sized units that can be distributed across servers.

Database Splits

Cloud Spanner breaks data into chunks known as *splits*. Splits are up to about 4 GB in size and move independently of one another. A split is a range of rows in a top-level table—that is, a table that is not an interleaved part of another table. Rows in a split are ordered by primary key, and the first and last keys are known as the *split boundaries*.

Rows that are interleaved are kept with their parent row. For example, if there is a customer table with an interleaved order table and below that an interleaved order line item table, then all order and order line item rows are kept in the same split as the corresponding customer row. Here it is important to keep splits and split limits in mind when creating interleaved tables. Defining a parent-child relationship collocates data, and that could cause more than 4 GB of data to be interleaved. Four GB is the split limit, and exceeding it can lead to degraded performance.

Cloud Spanner creates splits to alleviate hotspots. If Cloud Spanner detects a large number of read/write operations on a split, it will divide the rows into two splits so that they can be placed on different servers. Figure 7.4 shows a Cloud Spanner instance with six nodes and varying amounts of data in each (shown in gray). Cloud Spanner may have placed data into this distribution to balance the read/write workload across nodes, not just the amount of data across nodes.

FIGURE 7.4 Cloud Spanner distributes splits across servers to avoid hotspots.

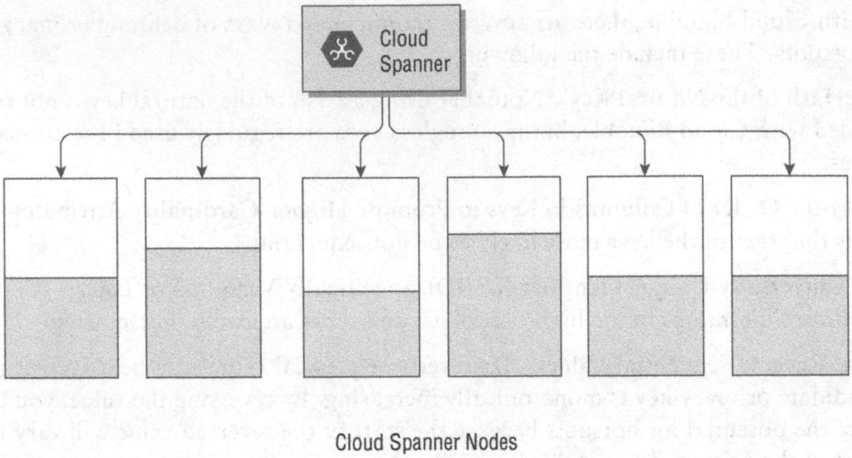

Cloud Spanner Nodes

Secondary Indexes

Cloud Spanner provides for secondary indexes on columns or groups of columns other than the primary key. An index is automatically created for the primary key, but you have to define any secondary indexes specifically.

Secondary indexes are useful when filtering in a query using a WHERE clause. If the column referenced in the WHERE clause is indexed, the index can be used for filtering rather than scanning the full table and then filtering. Secondary indexes are also useful when you need to return rows in a sort order other than the primary key order.

When a secondary index is created, the index will store the following:

- All primary key columns from the base table
- All columns included in the index
- Any additional columns specified in a STORING clause

The STORING clause allows you to specify additional columns to store in an index but not include those columns as part of the index. For example, if you wanted a secondary index on the customer table by postal code, you could create it as follows:

```
CREATE INDEX CustomerByPostalCode ON Customers(PostalCode);
```

If you frequently need to refer to the customer's last name when you look up by postal code, you can have the secondary index store the last name along with the postal code by specifying the LastName column in the STORING clause of the CREATE INDEX command, such as in the following line of code:

```
CREATE INDEX CustomerByPostalCode ON Customers(PostalCode)STORING (LastName);
```

Since the index has the primary key columns, the secondary index columns, and the additional `LastName` column, any query that references only those columns can be performed by retrieving data from the index only and not from the base table as well.

When Cloud Spanner develops an execution plan to retrieve data, it will usually choose the optimal set of indexes to use. If testing indicates that the best option is not being selected by the query, you can specify a `FORCE_INDEX` clause in the `SELECT` query to have Cloud Spanner use the specified index. Consider the following query:

```
SELECT CustomerID, LastName, PostalCode
FROM Customers
WHERE PostalCode  = '99221'
```

This query would benefit from using a secondary index on the `PostalCode` column. If the Cloud Spanner execution plan builder does not choose to use that index, you can force its use by specifying a `FORCE_INDEX` clause using the index directive syntax:

```
SELECT CustomerID, LastName, PostalCode
FROM Customers@{FORCE_INDEX=CustomerByPostalCode}
WHERE PostalCode  = '99221'
```

Query Best Practices

Here are some other best practices to keep in mind when using Cloud Spanner.

Use Query Parameters

When a query is executed, Cloud Spanner builds an execution plan. This involves analyzing statistics about the distribution of data, existing secondary indexes, and other characteristics of the tables in the query. If a query is repeated with changes to only some filter criteria, such as a postal code, then you can avoid rebuilding the query execution plan each time the query is executed by using *parameterized queries*.

Consider an application function that returns a list of customer IDs for a given postal code. The query can be written by using literal values for the postal code as in the following snippet:

```
SELECT CustomerID
FROM Customers
WHERE PostalCode  = '99221'
```

If this query is repeated with changes only to the literal value, you can use a query parameter instead of the literal values. A parameter is specified using the @ sign followed by the parameter name, such as the following:

```
SELECT CustomerID
FROM Customers
WHERE PostalCode  = @postCode
```

The value of the parameter is specified in the params field of the ExecuteSQL or ExecuteStreamingSQL API request.

Use *EXPLAIN PLAN* to Understand Execution Plans

A *query execution plan* is a series of steps designed to retrieve data and respond to a query. Since Cloud Spanner stores data in splits that are distributed across a cluster, execution plans have to incorporate local execution of subplans—that is, subplans are executed on each node, and then the results are aggregated across all nodes.

Figure 7.5 shows a logical example of an execution plan for a query that selects the name of songs from a table of songs.

FIGURE 7.5   An example query execution plan

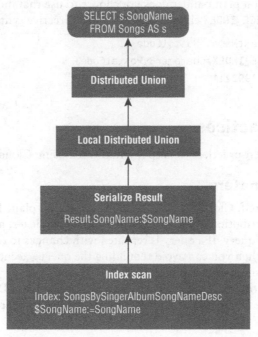

Source: https://cloud.google.com/spanner/docs/query-execution-plans

To see an execution plan from the GCP console, select a Cloud Spanner instance and database, run a query from the console, and use the Explanation option to list the plan.

Avoid Long Locks

When executing a transaction, the database may use locks to protect the integrity of data. There are some situations in which you should use locking read/write transactions, including

- If a write depends on the result of one or more reads, the reads and the write should be in a read/write transaction.

- If several (more than one) write operations have to be committed together, the writes should be in a read/write transaction.

- If there may be one or more writes depending on the results of a read, the operations should be in a read/write transaction.

When using read/write transactions, you want to keep the number of rows read to a minimum. This is because during a read/write transaction, no other processes can modify those rows until the transaction commits or rolls back. Avoid full table scans or large joins within a read/write transaction. If you do need to perform a large read, do it within a read-only transaction that does not lock rows.

Designing BigQuery Databases for Data Warehousing

BigQuery is an analytical database designed for data warehousing, machine learning (ML), and related analytic operations. Although BigQuery uses standard SQL as a query language, it is not a relational database. Some relational data modeling practices are applicable to BigQuery databases, and others are not. In this section, you'll see how to design BigQuery databases that scale while remaining performant and cost-effective. Specifically, this section covers the following:

- Schema design for data warehousing

- Clustered and partitioned tables

- Querying data

- External data access

- BigQuery ML

The focus here is on leveraging BigQuery features to support large-scale data warehousing. Additional features of BigQuery are discussed in Chapter 2.

Schema Design for Data Warehousing

Data warehousing is the practice of creating and using databases for primarily analytic operations. This is distinct from databases designed for transaction processing, such as an e-commerce application for selling products or an inventory management system for tracking those products.

Types of Analytical Datastores

The term *data warehousing* is sometimes used broadly to include a range of data stores for supporting analysis. These include the following:

Data Warehouses   These are centralized, organized repositories of analytical data for an organization.

Data Marts   These are subsets of data warehouses that focus on particular business lines or departments.

Data Lakes   These are less structured data stores for raw and lightly processed data.

BigQuery is designed to support data warehouses and data marts. Data lakes may be implemented using object storage, such as Cloud Storage, or NoSQL databases, such as Cloud Bigtable.

Projects, Datasets, and Tables

At the highest levels, BigQuery data is organized around projects, datasets, and tables.

Projects are the high-level structure used to organize the use of GCP services and resources. The use of APIs, billing, and permissions are managed at the project level. From a BigQuery perspective, projects contain datasets and sets of roles and permissions for working with BigQuery.

Datasets exist within a project and are containers for tables and views. When you create a dataset, you specify a geographic location for that dataset. The location of a dataset is immutable. Access to tables and views are defined at the dataset level. For example, a user with read access to a dataset will have access to all tables in the dataset.

Tables are collections of rows and columns stored in a columnar format, known as *Capacitor format*, which is designed to support compression and execution optimizations. After data is encoded in Capacitor format, it is written to the Colossus distributed filesystem.

BigQuery tables are subject to the following limitations:

- Table names within a dataset must be unique.

- When you are copying a table, the source and destination table must be in the same location.

- When you are copying multiple tables to a single destination table, all source tables must have the same schema.

Tables support the following data types for columns:

Array: An ordered list of zero or more elements of a non-array type

Bool: Boolean TRUE or FALSE

Bytes: Variable-length binary data

Date: A calendar date

Datetime: Represents a year, month, day, hour, minute, second, and subsecond; this data type does not include time zone

Numeric: An exact numeric value with 38 digits of precision and 9 decimal digits

Float64: Double-precision approximate numeric values with fractional components

INT64: Numeric values without fractional components

Geography: A collection of points, lines, and polygons representing a point set or subset of the earth's surface

String: Variable-length characters; must be UTF-8 encoded

Struct: Container of ordered typed fields

Time: A time independent of a date

Timestamp: A point in time with microsecond precision and that includes time zone

Most of these are atomic units or scalar values, but the array and struct types can store more complex structures.

Although BigQuery supports joins and data warehouses often use joins between fact tables and dimension tables, there are advantages to denormalizing a data model and storing related data together. In BigQuery, you can do this with nested and repeated columns.

A column that contains nested and repeated data is defined as a `RECORD` data type and is accessed as a `STRUCT` in SQL. Data that is in object-based schema formats, such as JavaScript Object Notation (JSON) and Apache Avro files, can be loaded directly into BigQuery while preserving their nested and repeated structures.

BigQuery supports up to 15 levels of nested structs.

Clustered and Partitioned Tables

BigQuery is most cost-efficient when you can minimize the amount of data scanned to retrieve queries. BigQuery does not have indexes like relational databases or document databases, but it does support partitioning and clustering, both of which can help limit the amount of data scanned during queries.

Partitioning

Partitioning is the process of dividing tables into segments called *partitions*. By segmenting data, BigQuery can take advantage of metadata about partitions to determine which of them should be scanned to respond to a query. BigQuery has three partition types:

- Ingestion time partitioned tables
- Timestamp partitioned tables
- Integer range partitioned tables

When a table is created with *ingestion time partitioning*, BigQuery loads data into a daily partition and creates new partitions each day. A data-based timestamp is stored in a pseudo-column called `_PARTITIONTIME`, which can be referenced in `WHERE` clauses to limit scanning to partitions created within a specified time period.

Timestamp partitioned tables partition based on a `DATE` or `TIMESTAMP` column in a table. Partitions have data from a single day. Rather than using `_PARTITIONTIME`, queries over timestamp partition tables reference the `DATE` or `TIMESTAMP` column used to partition data. Rows with null values in the `DATE` or `TIMESTAMP` column are stored in a `__NULL__` partition, and rows that have dates outside the allowed range are stored in a partition called `__UNPARTITIONED__`.

Timestamp partitioned tables have better performance than sharded tables, which use separate tables for each subset of data rather than separate partitions.

Integer range partition tables are partitioned based on a column with an INTEGER data type. Integer range partitions are defined with the following:

- An INTEGER column
- Start value of the range of partitions
- End value of the range of partitions
- Interval of each range within a partition

The total number of partitions created is the difference between the end value and start value divided by the interval size. For example, if the start value is 0, the end value is 500, and the interval is 25, then there will be 20 partitions. As with timestamped partitioned tables, the __NULL__ and __UNPARTITIONED__ partitions are used for rows that do not fit in the other partitions.

When you create any of type of partitioned table, you can specify that any query against that table must include a filter based on the partition structure.

Clustering

In BigQuery, *clustering* is the ordering of data in its stored format. When a table is clustered, one to four columns are specified along with an ordering of those columns. By choosing an optimal combination of columns, you can have data that is frequently accessed together collocated in storage. Clustering is supported only on partitioned tables, and it is used when filters or aggregations are frequently used.

Once a clustered table is created, the clustering columns cannot be changed. Clustering columns must be one of the following data types:

- Date
- Bool
- Geography
- INT64
- Numeric
- String
- Timestamp

Both partitioning and clustering can significantly improve the efficiency of filtering and aggregation queries.

Querying Data in BigQuery

BigQuery supports two types of queries: interactive and batch queries. *Interactive queries* are executed immediately, whereas *batch queries* are queued up and run when resources are available. BigQuery runs queries interactively by default.

The advantage of using batch queries is that resources are drawn from a shared resource pool and batch queries do not count toward the concurrent rate limit, which is 100 concurrent queries. *Dry-run queries*, which just estimate the amount of data scanned, also do not count against that limit. Queries can run up to six hours but not longer.

Queries are run as jobs, similar to jobs run to load and export data. To run queries, users will need the `bigquery.jobs.create` permission, which can be granted by assigning one of the `bigquery.user`, `bigquery.jobUser`, or `bigquery.admin` roles.

Like Cloud Spanner, BigQuery supports the use of parameterized queries. BigQuery uses a similar syntax, too. A parameter is specified by an @ character followed by the name of the parameter.

It is possible to query multiple tables at once in BigQuery by using a wildcard in a table name within the `FROM` clause of a SQL query. The wildcard character is the * character. For example, consider a dataset that includes the following tables:

- `myproject.mydataset.dwtable1`
- `myproject.mydataset.dwtable2`
- `myproject.mydataset.dwtable3`
- `myproject.mydataset.dwtable4`
- `myproject.mydataset.dwtable5`

A single query can take into account all of these tables by using the `FROM` clause:

```
FROM `myproject.mydataset.dwtable*`
```

Wildcard queries work only on tables and not views. External tables are not supported either.

External Data Access

BigQuery can access data in external sources, known as *federated sources*. Instead of first loading data into BigQuery, you can create a reference to an external source. External sources can be Cloud Bigtable, Cloud Storage, and Google Drive.

When accessing external data, you can create either permanent or temporary external tables. Permanent tables are those that are created in a dataset and linked to an external source. Dataset-level access controls can be applied to these tables. When you are using a temporary table, a table is created in a special dataset and will be available for approximately 24 hours. Temporary tables are useful for one-time operations, such as loading data into a data warehouse.

The following permissions are required to query an external table in BigQuery:

- `bigquery.tables.create`
- `bigquery.tables.getdata`
- `bigquery.jobs.create`

Querying Cloud Bigtable Data from BigQuery

To query data stored in Cloud Bigtable, you will first need to specify a URI for the table you want to query. The URI includes the project ID of the project containing the Cloud

Bigtable instance, the instance ID, and the table names. When working with external Cloud Bigtable data, users must have the following roles:

- `bigquery.dataViewer` at the dataset level or higher
- `bigquery.user` role at the project level or higher to run query jobs
- `bigtable.reader` role, which provides read-only access to table metadata

Performance of reading from Cloud Bigtable tables will depend on the number of rows read, the amount of data read, and the level of parallelization.

When an external Cloud Bigtable has column families, the column families are represented within BigQuery as an array of columns.

Querying Cloud Storage Data from BigQuery

BigQuery supports several formats of Cloud Storage data:

- Comma-separated values
- Newline-delimited JSON
- Avro
- Optimized Row Columnar (ORC)
- Parquet
- Datastore exports
- Firestore exports

Data files may be in Regional, Multi-Regional, Nearline, or Coldline storage.

When you create a reference to a Cloud Storage data source, you specify a URI that identifies a bucket name and a filename.

To query data from Cloud Storage, users must have the `storage.objects.get` permission. If they are querying using wildcards in the table name, they will also need the `storage.objects.list` permission.

Querying Google Drive Data from BigQuery

Data from Google Drive can be queried from the following formats:

- Comma-separated values
- Newline-delimited JSON
- Avro
- Google Sheets

Data sources are referenced using a URI that includes the Google Drive file ID of the data file. An OAuth scope is required to register and query an external data source in Google Drive. Users must be granted View access to the Google Drive file that is the source of external data.

BigQuery ML

BigQuery extends standard SQL with the addition of machine learning (ML) functionality. This allows BigQuery users to build ML models in BigQuery rather than programming models in Python, R, Java, or other programming languages outside of BigQuery.

Currently, BigQuery supports several ML algorithms, including the following:

- Linear regression
- Binary logistic regression
- Multiclass logistic regression
- K-means clustering
- TensorFlow models

The basic steps for using BigQuery ML are as follows:

1. Create a dataset to store the model.
2. Examine and preprocess data to map it to a form suitable for use with an ML algorithm.
3. Divide your dataset into training, validation, and testing datasets.
4. Create a model using training data and the CREATE MODEL command.
5. Evaluate the model's precision, recall, accuracy, and other properties with the ML.EVALUATE function.
6. When the model is sufficiently trained, use the ML.PREDICT function to apply the model to make decisions.

There is much more to machine learning than this brief summary of BigQuery ML. For additional details on preparing data, building models, and evaluating them, see Chapter 9, "Deploying Machine Learning Pipelines," and Chapter 11, "Measuring, Monitoring, and Troubleshooting Machine Learning Models."

Exam Essentials

Understand Cloud Bigtable is a nonrelational database based on a sparse three-dimensional map. The three dimensions are rows, columns, and cells. When you create a Cloud Bigtable instance, you specify a number of type of nodes. These nodes manage metadata about the data stored in the Cloud Bigtable database, whereas the actual data is stored outside of the nodes on the Colossus filesystem. Within the Colossus filesystem, data is organized into sorted string tables, or SSTables, which are called *tablets*.

Understand how to design row-keys in Cloud Bigtable. In general, it is best to avoid monotonically increasing values or lexicographically close strings at the beginning of keys. When a using a multitenant Cloud Bigtable database, it is a good practice to use a tenant prefix in the row-key. String identifiers, such as a customer ID or a sensor ID, are good candidates for a row-key. Timestamps may be used as part of a row-key, but they should not be the entire row-key or the start of the row-key. Moving timestamps from the front of a row-key so that another attribute is the first part of the row-key is an example of *field promotion*. In general, it is a good practice to promote, or move toward the front of the key, values that are highly varied. Another way to avoid hotspots is to use salting.

Know how to use tall and narrow tables for time-series databases.   Keep names short; this reduces the size of metadata since names are stored along with data values. Store few events within each row, ideally only one event per row; this makes querying easier. Also, storing multiple events increases the chance of exceeding maximum recommended row sizes. Design row-keys for looking up a single value or a range of values. Range scans are common in time-series analysis. Keep in mind that there is only one index on Cloud Bigtable tables.

Know when to use interleaved tables in Cloud Spanner.   Use interleaved tables with a parent-child relationship in which parent data is stored with child data. This makes retrieving data from both tables simultaneously more efficient than if the data were stored separately and is especially helpful when performing joins. Since the data from both tables is co-located, the database has to perform fewer seeks to get all the needed data.

Know how to avoid hotspots by designing primary keys properly.   Monotonically increasing keys can cause read and write operations to happen in few servers simultaneously instead of being evenly distributed across all servers. Options for keys include using the hash of a natural key; swapping the order of columns in keys to promote higher-cardinality attributes; using a universally unique identifier (UUID), specifically version 4 or later; and using bit-reverse sequential values.

Know the differences between primary and secondary indexes.   Primary indexes are created automatically on the primary key. Secondary indexes are explicitly created using the CREATE INDEX command. Secondary indexes are useful when filtering in a query using a WHERE clause. If the column referenced in the WHERE clause is indexed, the index can be used for filtering rather than scanning the full table and then filtering. Secondary indexes are also useful when you need to return rows in a sort order other than the primary key order. When a secondary index is created, the index will store all primary key columns from the base table, all columns included in the index, and any additional columns specified in a STORING clause.

Understand the organizational structure of BigQuery databases.   Projects are the high-level structure used to organize the use of GCP services and resources. Datasets exist within a project and are containers for tables and views. Access to tables and views are defined at the dataset level. Tables are collections of rows and columns stored in a columnar format, known as *Capacitor format*, which is designed to support compression and execution optimizations.

Understand how to denormalize data in BigQuery using nested and repeated fields. Denormalizing in BigQuery can be done with nested and repeated columns. A column that contains nested and repeated data is defined as a RECORD datatype and is accessed as a STRUCT in SQL. BigQuery supports up to 15 levels of nested STRUCTs.

Know when and why to use partitioning and clustering in BigQuery.   Partitioning is the process of dividing tables into segments called *partitions*. BigQuery has three partition types: ingestion time partitioned tables, timestamp partitioned tables, and integer range partitioned tables. In BigQuery, clustering is the ordering of data in its stored format. Clustering is supported only on partitioned tables and is used when filters or aggregations are frequently used.

Understand the different kinds of queries in BigQuery.   BigQuery supports two types of queries: interactive and batch queries. Interactive queries are executed immediately, whereas batch queries are queued and run when resources are available. The advantage of using these batch queries is that resources are drawn from a shared resource pool and batch queries do not count toward the concurrent rate limit, which is 100 concurrent queries. Queries are run as jobs, similar to jobs run to load and export data.

Know that BigQuery can access external data without you having to import it into BigQuery first.   BigQuery can access data in external sources, known as federated sources. Instead of first loading data into BigQuery, you can create a reference to an external source. External sources can be Cloud Bigtable, Cloud Storage, and Google Drive. When accessing external data, you can create either permanent or temporary external tables. Permanent tables are those created in a dataset and linked to an external source. Temporary tables are useful for one-time operations, such as loading data into a data warehouse.

Know that BigQuery ML supports machine learning in BigQuery using SQL.   BigQuery extends standard SQL with the addition of machine learning functionality. This allows BigQuery users to build machine learning models in BigQuery rather than programming models in Python, R, Java, or other programming languages outside of BigQuery.

Review Questions

You can find the answers in the appendix.

1. You are investigating long latencies in Cloud Bigtable query response times. Most queries finish in less than 20 ms, but the 99th percentile queries can take up to 400 ms. You examine a Key Visualizer heatmap and see two areas with bright colors indicating hotspots. What could be causing those hotspots?

   A. Improperly used secondary index

   B. Less than optimal partition key

   C. Improperly designed row-key

   D. Failure to use a read replica

2. An IoT startup has hired you to review their Cloud Bigtable design. The database stores data generated by over 100,000 sensors that send data every 60 seconds. Each row contains all the data for one sensor sent during an hour. Hours always start at the top of the hour. The row-key is the sensor ID concatenated to the hour of the day followed by the date. What change, if any, would you recommend to this design?

   A. Use one row per sensor and 60-second datasets instead of storing multiple datasets in a single row.

   B. Start the row keyrow-key with the day and hour instead of the sensor ID.

   C. Allow hours to start an any arbitrary time to accommodate differences in sensor clocks.

   D. No change is recommended.

3. Your company has a Cloud Bigtable database that requires strong consistency, but it also requires high availability. You have implemented Cloud Bigtable replication and specified single-cluster routing in the app profile for the database. Some users have noted that they occasionally receive query results inconsistent with what they should have received. The problem seems to correct itself within a minute. What could be the cause of this problem?

   A. Secondary indexes are being updated during the query and return incorrect results when a secondary index is not fully updated.

   B. You have not specified an app configuration file that includes single-cluster routing and use of replicas only for failover.

   C. Tablets are being moved between nodes, which can cause inconsistent query results.

   D. The row-key is not properly designed.

4. You have been tasked with migrating a MongoDB database to Cloud Spanner. MongoDB is a document database, similar to Cloud Firestore. You would like to maintain some of the document organization of the MongoDB design. What data type, available in Cloud Spanner, would you use to define a column that can hold a document-like structure?

   A. Array

   B. String

   C. STRUCT

   D. JSON

5. An application using a Cloud Spanner database has several queries that are taking longer to execute than the users would like. You review the queries and notice that they all involve joining three or more tables that are all related hierarchically. What feature of Cloud Spanner would you try in order to improve the query performance?

    A. Replicated clusters

    B. Interleaved tables

    C. STORING clause

    D. Execution plans

6. A Cloud Spanner database is using a natural key as the primary key for a large table. The natural key is the preferred key by users because the values are easy to relate to other data. Database administrators notice that these keys are causing hotspots on Cloud Spanner nodes and are adversely affecting performance. What would you recommend in order to improve performance?

    A. Keep the data of the natural key in the table but use a hash of the natural key as the primary key

    B. Keep the natural key and let Cloud Spanner create more splits to improve performance

    C. Use interleaved tables

    D. Use more secondary indexes

7. You are using a UUID as the primary key in a Cloud Spanner database. You have noticed hotspotting that you did not anticipate. What could be the cause?

    A. You have too many secondary indexes.

    B. You have too few secondary indexes.

    C. You are using a type of UUID that has sequentially ordered strings at the beginning of the UUID.

    D. You need to make the maximum length of the primary key longer.

8. You are working for a financial services firm on a Cloud Bigtable database. The database stores equity and bond trading information from approximately 950 customers. Over 10,000 equities and bonds are tracked in the database. New data is received at a rate of 5,000 data points per minute. What general design pattern would you recommend?

    A. Tall and narrow table

    B. One table for each customer

    C. One table for equities and one for bonds

    D. Option A and Option B

    E. Option A and Option C

9. You have been brought into a large enterprise to help with a data warehousing initiative. The first project of the initiative is to build a repository for all customer-related data, including sales, finance, inventory, and logistics. It has not yet been determined how the data will be used. What Google Cloud storage system would you recommend that the enterprise use to store that data?

    A. Cloud Bigtable

    B. BigQuery

    C. Cloud Spanner

    D. Cloud Storage

10. Data is streaming into a BigQuery table. As the data arrives, it is added to a partition that was automatically created that day. Data that arrives the next day will be written to a different partition. The data modeler did not specify a column to use as a partition key. What kind of partition is being used?

   A. Ingestion time partitioned tables

   B. Timestamp partitioned tables

   C. Integer range partitioned tables

   D. Clustered tables

11. You are designing a BigQuery database with multiple tables in a single dataset. The data stored in the dataset is measurement data from sensors on vehicles in the company's fleet. Data is collected on each vehicle and downloaded at the end of each shift. After that, it is loaded into a partitioned table. You want to have efficient access to the most interesting data, which you define as a particular measurement having a value greater than 100.00. You want to cluster on that measurement column, which is a FLOAT64. When you define the table with a timestamped partitioned table and clustering on the measurement column, you receive an error. What could that error be?

   A. You cannot use clustering on an external table.

   B. You cannot use clustering with a FLOAT64 column as the clustering key.

   C. The table is not the FLOAT64 partition type.

   D. The clustering key must be an integer or timestamp.

12. What data formats are supported for external tables in Cloud Storage and Google Drive?

   A. Comma-separated values only

   B. Comma-separated values and Avro

   C. Comma-separated values, Avro, and newline-delimited JSON

   D. Comma-separated values, Avro, newline-delimited JSON, and Parquet

Chapter

8

Understanding Data Operations for Flexibility and Portability

---

GOOGLE CLOUD PROFESSIONAL DATA ENGINEER EXAM OBJECTIVES COVERED IN THIS CHAPTER INCLUDE THE FOLLOWING:

✓ **4.4 Ensuring flexibility and portability. Considerations include:**

- Mapping to current and future business requirements

- Designing for data and application portability (e.g., multi-cloud, data residency requirements)

- Data staging, cataloging, and discovery

Data engineers are responsible for many aspects of the data lifecycle in addition to determining and designing storage systems. Data may be operated on in several ways:

- Cataloged
- Preprocessed
- Visualized
- Explored
- Processed with workflows

In this chapter, we will discuss how to use the Data Catalog, a metadata management service supporting the discovery and management of datasets in Google Cloud. Then we will turn our attention to Cloud Dataprep, a preprocessing tool for transforming and enriching data. Next, we will look at Data Studio for visualizing data and Cloud Datalab for interactive exploration and scripting. In each case, we will also discuss business requirements of typical use cases.

Cataloging and Discovery with Data Catalog

Enterprises accumulate vast amounts of data, and one of the challenges that comes with that is keeping track of information about datasets. For example, there may be hundreds of Cloud Storage buckets and folders that contain thousands of files. The people responsible for managing data need to keep track of information such as the contents of the data files, the version of the schema if the data is structured, how the data in one file relates to data in other files, who has access to the data, and so on. This kind of metadata about the datasets is crucial for understanding what data is available, what it means, and how it can be used.

Data Catalog is a GCP metadata service for data management. It is fully managed, so there are no servers to provision or configure. Its primary function is to provide a single, consolidated view of enterprise data. Metadata is collected automatically during ingest operations to BigQuery and Cloud Pub/Sub as well through APIs and third-party tools. BigQuery metadata is collected on datasets, tables, and views. Cloud Pub/Sub topic metadata is also automatically collected.

Data Catalog is currently in beta. Until it is available for general release, it is unlikely that there will be questions about it on the Professional Data Engineer exam. Nonetheless, data engineers should understand Data Catalog in general because metadata management is essential for compliance, lifecycle data management, and other data engineering tasks.

Before you can use Data Catalog to capture metadata, you need to enable the Data Catalog API in a project that contains the resources created or accessed via the API.

Searching in Data Catalog

The search capabilities in Data Catalog are based on the same search technology that Google uses with Gmail and Google Drive, so it should be familiar to most users of Google services. With the Data Catalog search capabilities, users can filter and find native metadata, which is captured from the underlying storage system that houses the subject data and user-generated metadata that is collected from tags. Tagging is discussed in the next section.

To be able to search metadata with Data Catalog, a user will need permissions to read metadata for the subject assets, such as a BigQuery dataset of a Pub/Sub topic. It is important to remember that Data Catalog is collecting and searching metadata, not the data in the dataset, table, topic, and so forth. Figure 8.1 shows an example overview page of Data Catalog.

FIGURE 8.1   Users can search and browse data assets from the Data Catalog overview page.

When metadata is collected from underlying storage systems, Data Catalog is a read-only service. Any changes to the metadata must be made through the underlying storage system. Data Catalog will collect metadata automatically from several resources within a project, including the following:

- Cloud Storage
- Cloud Bigtable
- Google Sheets
- BigQuery
- Cloud Pub/Sub

Metadata can also be collected manually.

Tagging in Data Catalog

Tags are commonly used in GCP and other public clouds to store metadata about a resource. Tags are used for a wide range of metadata, such as assigning a department or team to all resources that they create in a project or specifying a data classification level to a Cloud Storage bucket or object.

Data Catalog uses templates to help manage user-defined metadata. Figure 8.2 shows an example tag template, which includes template details as well as tag attributes.

FIGURE 8.2   Example Data Catalog tag template

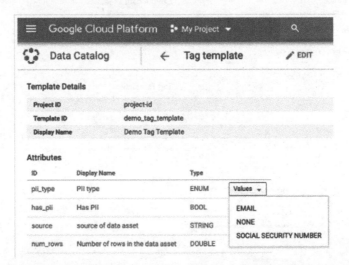

Source: https://cloud.google.com/data-catalog/docs/quickstarts/quickstart-search-tag

Data Preprocessing with Dataprep

Analysts and data engineers often spend significant amounts of time preparing data for analysis. *Cloud Dataprep* is a managed service designed to help reduce the time required to prepare data for analysis by providing tools to explore, cleanse, and transform data. There are no servers to provision or configure.

Typical business requirements that drive the use of Cloud Dataprep include the need to analyze datasets that may not be in a format suitable for analysis. This could be due to something as simple as the need for data in different formats as well as more complicated scenarios, such as the need to detect inconsistent or poor-quality data.

 Cloud Dataprep is a partner service developed by Trifacta. Before you can use it, a project administrator will have to agree to its license and data access terms.

Cloud Dataprep is an interactive tool that relies on dragging and dropping components within a workflow rather than programming scripts. Users can read data directly from Cloud Storage and BigQuery as well as upload data from their local machines. When data is uploaded, Cloud Dataprep attempts to automatically detect the schema, the data types of values, the distribution of numeric data, and missing or anomalous values. Figure 8.3 shows the kind of summary data that users will see when working with Cloud Dataprep.

FIGURE 8.3 Cloud Dataprep shows statistics about the distribution of data in attributes.

Source: https://cloud.google.com/dataprep/docs/html/Job-Details-Page_57344846?hl=ES-MX

Cleansing Data

Cleansing data can be tedious job. It often requires careful attention to detail about data virtually anywhere in a dataset. In some cases, only a small number of values in a column are missing or incorrectly formatted, and sometimes every value in a column needs to be corrected. Also, there are many ways that data can be incorrect, and each way requires a different procedure to correct.

The main cleansing operations in Cloud Dataprep center around altering column names, reformatting strings, and working with numeric values. Here are some example cleansing tasks that can be performed with Cloud Dataprep:

- Renaming columns
- Changing the datatype of a column
- Copying from one column to another
- Removing and deduplicating data
- Modifying strings
- Extracting values from strings
- Formatting dates
- Applying conditional transformations

The cleansing phase of working with a dataset is often iterative. You may find some data formats that you want to change and then begin to explore the data only to realize that additional anomalies are in the dataset that you need to correct. The interactive nature of Cloud Dataprep supports this kind of ad hoc, iterative sequence of steps.

Discovering Data

Another step in processing data for analysis and machine learning is identifying patterns and inconsistencies in your datasets. Cloud Dataprep supports this process by providing for the following:

- Filtering data
- Locating outliers
- Deriving aggregates, such as counts
- Calculating values across columns
- Comparing strings

In addition to performing data cleansing and discovery operations interactively, users can capture sequences of operations in a structure known as a *recipe*.

Enriching Data

Sometimes, datasets need to be augmented with additional columns. For example, datasets may need to be joined or appended together before using them for analysis or machine learning model building. Cloud Dataprep supports several types of enrichment operations, including the following:

- Adding two columns
- Generating primary keys
- Adding lookup data
- Appending datasets
- Joining datasets
- Adding metadata

In the case of adding metadata, Cloud Dataprep can work with data outside the data in datasets. For example, you can reference source file path and filename, creation data, date of importing, and other metadata attributes.

Importing and Exporting Data

Cloud Dataprep can import a number of flat file formats, including

- Microsoft Excel format (XLS/XLSX)
- CSV
- JSON, including nested
- Plain text
- Tab-separated values (TSV)
- Parquet

The service can also read CSV and JSON files compressed with GZIP, BZIP, and Snappy. Avro files compressed with Snappy can also be imported.

Cloud Dataprep does not change source data, but it is possible to export data after preparing it. Data can be exported to the following:

- CSV
- JSON
- Avro
- BigQuery tables

Users can write compressed CSV and JSON files using GZIP or BZIP.

When data is imported, Cloud Dataprep creates a reference to the dataset, except when data is uploaded from a local device, in which case a copy of the dataset is created.

Structuring and Validating Data

Cloud Dataprep has functionality for more advanced transformations, including the following:

- Reshaping data
- Splitting columns
- Creating aggregations
- Pivoting data
- Manipulating arrays
- Manipulating JSON

There are also tools for validating data, including profiling source data. Profiles include information about

- Mismatched values in columns
- Missing values in columns
- Statistical breakout by quartile

Once data has been prepared using Cloud Dataprep, you can then move on to visualize the data with Data Studio.

Visualizing with Data Studio

Data Studio is a reporting and visualization tool. The tool is organized around reports, and it reads data from data sources and formats the data into tables and charts. Figure 8.4 shows an example report generated by Data Studio.

Many business use cases will require the use of Data Studio, including data warehouse reporting and monitoring with dashboards. The three basic tasks in Data Studio are connecting to data sources, visualizing data, and sharing reports.

Connecting to Data Sources

Data Studio uses the concept of a connector for working with datasets. Datasets can come in a variety of forms, including a relational database table, a Google Sheet, or a BigQuery table. Connectors provide access to all or a subset of columns in a data source. Connectors typically require you to authorize access to data.

FIGURE 8.4   An example report showing Google Analytics data

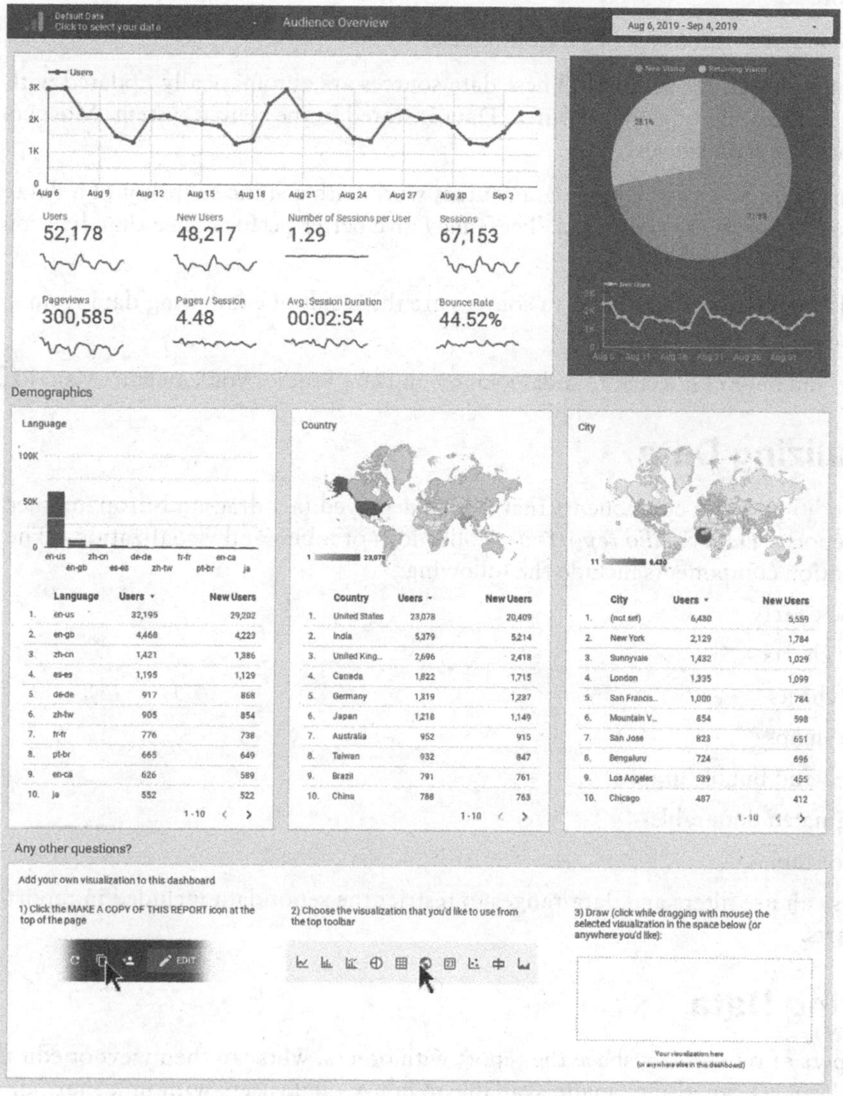

Source: https://datastudio.google.com/gallery?category=marketing

There are three kinds of connectors:

Google Connectors   These are provided by Google for accessing data from other Google services, including Analytics, Ads, Sheets, and BigQuery.

Partner Connectors   These connectors are developed by third parties, and they provide access to non-Google data such as Facebook, GitHub, and Reddit data sources.

Community Connectors   These connectors are developed by anyone with a need to access a data source.

There are also three types of data sources:

Live Connection Data Sources   These data sources are automatically updated with changes to the underlying data source. Data is stored in the source system. Most connectors work with live data sources.

Extracted Data Sources   These data sources work with a static snapshot of a dataset, which can be updated on demand. These may give better performance than live connection data sources.

Blended Data Sources   These data sources are the result of combining data from up to five data sources.

Once you have connected to a data source in Data Studio, you can start visualizing data.

Visualizing Data

Data Studio provides components that can be deployed in a drag-and-drop manner to create reports. *Data Studio reports* are collections of tables and visualizations. The visualization components include the following:

- Line charts
- Bar charts
- Pie charts
- Geo maps
- Area and bubble graphs
- Paginated data tables
- Pivot tables

Users can use filters and data ranges to restrict the set of data included in report tables and charts.

Sharing Data

Developers of reports can share the report with others, who can then view or edit the report. Reports can also be made available to non-Google users with link sharing.

Data Studio provides the option to schedule the running of a report and the generation of a PDF file, which can be emailed to recipients.

Exploring Data with Cloud Datalab

Cloud Datalab is an interactive tool for exploring and transforming data. Cloud Datalab runs as an instance of a container. Users of Cloud Datalab create a Compute Engine instance, run the container, and then connect from a browser to a Cloud Datalab notebook, as shown in Figure 8.5.

FIGURE 8.5   An example Cloud Datalab notebook

← → C   ⓘ localhost:8081/tree/datalab

⠿ Apps   M Datalab-as-a-Servic...   ⓢ DevSite Element Sty...   ▣ styles.md - Code Se...   🐝 Be

🔬 Google Cloud Datalab

➕ Notebook   ➕ Folder   ⬆ Upload

☐   🏠 / datalab

☐   📁 ..

☐   📁 docs

☐   📁 notebooks

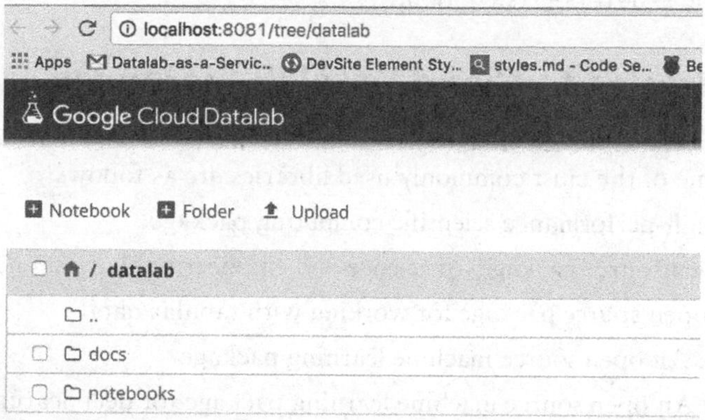

Source: https://cloud.google.com/datalab/docs/quickstart

Cloud Datalab containers run an instance of a Jupyter Notebook.

 NOTE   Cloud Datalab has recently been rebranded AI Platform Notebooks. You may see either name used in the Google Cloud Professional Data Engineer exam.

Jupyter Notebooks

Jupyter Notebooks are documents that can contain code as well as text. Code and text are located in cells. All text and code within a cell are treated as a single unit. For example, when a cell is executed, all code in the cell is executed.

Jupyter Notebooks are widely used in data science, machine learning, and other tasks that lend themselves to interactive, iterative development. Jupyter Notebooks support a variety of programming languages, including Python and SQL.

Managing Cloud Datalab Instances

It is a relatively simple task to create and use Cloud Datalab instances. With the Cloud software development kit (SDK) already installed, including the optional Datalab component, a user can create a Cloud Datalab instance with the datalab create command. For example:

```
datalab create --machine-type n1-highmem-2 my-datalab-instance-1
```

Once the instance is created, the user can connect using the datalab connect command. The default port for connecting is 8081, but that can be changed by specifying the --port option in the datalab create command. The datalab list command provides a list of all running instances.

A Datalab instance can be deleted using the datalab delete command. By default, this command does not delete the persistent disk attached to the instance, assuming that the disk's configuration is also set to the default. To delete the persistent instance as well, users need to specify the `--delete-disk` option.

Adding Libraries to Cloud Datalab Instances

Data scientists and machine learning engineers often need to import libraries when working with Python. Some of the most commonly used libraries are as follows:

Numpy: A high-performance scientific computing package

Scipy: An open source package for science and engineering that uses numpy

Pandas: An open source package for working with tabular data

Scikit Learn: An open source machine learning package

TensorFlow: An open source machine learning package for deep learning

Many of the commonly used packages are available in Cloud Datalab, but when a user needs to add others, this is done by using either the `conda install` command or the `pip install` command. For example, to install the data analysis package `scikit-data`, a user would specify the following command in a Jupyter Notebook cell:

```
!conda install scikit-data
```

This command runs the conda installer to download the `scikit-data` package. Some libraries are not available through the conda installer; in that case, the `pip` installer can be used. For example, the topological data analysis tool is currently not available through the conda installer, so `pip` should be used to install that library:

```
!pip install scikit-tda
```

The `!` character at the beginning of the command indicates to Jupyter Notebook that the command should be run as a shell command, not a Python statement.

In some cases, exploratory data analysis is an end in itself, but in many cases, it is the first step to defining a workload that will be repeated. In those cases, you can use Cloud Composer to orchestrate those workloads.

Orchestrating Workflows with Cloud Composer

Cloud Composer is a fully managed workflow orchestration service based on Apache Airflow. *Workflows* are defined as directed acyclic graphs (DAGs), which are specified in Python. Workflows can make use of many GCP services, including the following:

- BigQuery
- Cloud Dataflow
- Cloud Dataproc

- Cloud Datastore
- Cloud Storage
- Cloud Pub/Sub
- AI Platform

  Elements of workflows can run on premises and in other clouds as well as in GCP.

Airflow Environments

Apache Airflow is a distributed platform, and it requires several GCP services. When it is deployed, the GCP resources deployed are known as a *Cloud Composer environment*. Environments are stand-alone deployments based on Kubernetes Engine. There can be multiple Cloud Composer environments in a single project.

Environments can be created in the GCP console or by using the command line. The SDK command to create an environment is gcloud beta composer.

 As of this writing, this service is in beta release. By the time you read this, the word "beta" may have been dropped from the command. Also, some parameters may have changed.

When you create an instance, you can specify node configuration and network configuration, as well as environment variables.

Creating DAGs

Airflow DAGs are defined in Python as a set of operators and operator relationships. An operator specifies a single task in a workflow. The most commonly used operators are as follows:

BashOperator: Executes a command in the Bash shell

PythonOperator: Executes a Python function

EmailOperator: Sends an email message

SimpleHTTPOperator: Sends HTTP requests

Database operators: Includes PostgresOperator, MySQLOperator, SQLiteOperator, and JdbcOperator

Sensor: Waits for a certain event, such as a specific time or the creation of a file or other resource

The order of operators is specified using the >> symbol. For example, assuming that you have created a write_files_python PythonOperator and a delete_temp_files_bash BashOperator, you can have write_files_python executed first followed by delete_temp_files_bash as follows:

```
write_files_python >> delete_temp_files_bash
```

Airflow Logs

The Airflow environment creates two types of logs: Airflow logs and streaming logs. *Airflow logs* are associated with a single DAG task. These files are stored in the Cloud Storage logs folder of the Cloud Composer environment. Logs are retained after an environment is shut down. You will need to delete logs manually. *Streaming logs* are a superset of Airflow logs. These logs are stored in Stackdriver and can be viewed using the Logs viewer. You can also use log-based metrics for monitoring and alerting. Airflow generates several logs, including the following:

Airflow-datbase-init-job: For database initialization

Airflow-scheduler: For logs generated by the scheduler

Airflow-webserver: For logs generated by the web interface

Airflow-worker: For logs generated as DAGs are executed

Airflow-monitoring: For logs generated by Airflow monitoring

Airflow: For otherwise uncategorized logs

To summarize, the key points about Cloud Composer are that it is a workflow orchestration service that runs within Kubernetes Engine and executes tasks specified in a Python script composed of operators that execute tasks. Tasks can be executed on a schedule, manually, or in response to an external event.

Exam Essentials

Know that Data Catalog is a metadata service for data management. Data Catalog is fully managed, so there are no servers to provision or configure. Its primary function is to provide a single, consolidated view of enterprise data. Metadata is collected automatically during ingest operations to BigQuery and Cloud Pub/Sub, as well through APIs and third-party tools.

Understand that Data Catalog will collect metadata automatically from several GCP sources. These sources include Cloud Storage, Cloud Bigtable, Google Sheets, BigQuery, and Cloud Pub/Sub. In addition to native metadata, Data Catalog can collect custom metadata through the use of tags.

Know that Cloud Dataprep is an interactive tool for preparing data for analysis and machine learning. Cloud Dataprep is used to cleanse, enrich, import, export, discover, structure, and validate data. The main cleansing operations in Cloud Dataprep center around altering column names, reformatting strings, and working with numeric values. Cloud Dataprep supports this process by providing for filtering data, locating outliers, deriving aggregates, calculating values across columns, and comparing strings.

Be familiar with Data Studio as a reporting and visualization tool. The Data Studio tool is organized around reports, and it reads data from data sources and formats the data into tables and charts. Data Studio uses the concept of a connector for working with datasets. Datasets can come in a variety of forms, including a relational database table, a Google Sheet, or a BigQuery table. Connectors provide access to all or to a subset of columns in a data source. Data Studio provides components that can be deployed in a drag-and-drop manner to create reports. Reports are collections of tables and visualization.

Understand that Cloud Datalab is an interactive tool for exploring and transforming data. Cloud Datalab runs as an instance of a container. Users of Cloud Datalab create a Compute Engine instance, run the container, and then connect from a browser to a Cloud Datalab notebook, which is a Jupyter Notebook. Many of the commonly used packages are available in Cloud Datalab, but when users need to add others, they can do so by using either the conda `install` command or the pip `install` command.

Know that Cloud Composer is a fully managed workflow orchestration service based on Apache Airflow.   Workflows are defined as directed acyclic graphs, which are specified in Python. Elements of workflows can run on premises and in other clouds as well as in GCP. Airflow DAGs are defined in Python as a set of operators and operator relationships. An operator specifies a single task in a workflow. Common operators include BashOperator and PythonOperator.

Review Questions

You can find the answers in the appendix.

1. Analysts and data scientists at your company ask for your help with data preparation. They currently spend significant amounts of time searching for data and trying to understand the exact definition of the data. What GCP service would you recommend that they use?

    A. Cloud Composer

    B. Data Catalog

    C. Cloud Dataprep

    D. Data Studio

2. Machine learning engineers have been working for several weeks on building a recommendation system for your company's e-commerce platform. The model has passed testing and validation, and it is ready to be deployed. The model will need to be updated every day with the latest data. The engineers want to automate the model building process that includes running several Bash scripts, querying databases, and running some custom Python code. What GCP service would you recommend that they use?

    A. Cloud Composer

    B. Data Catalog

    C. Cloud Dataprep

    D. Data Studio

3. A business intelligence analyst has just acquired several new datasets. They are unfamiliar with the data and are especially interested in understanding the distribution of data in each column as well as the extent of missing or misconfigured data. What GCP service would you recommend they use?

    A. Cloud Composer

    B. Cloud Catalog

    C. Cloud Dataprep

    D. Data Studio

4. Line-of-business managers have asked your team for additional reports from data in a data warehouse. They want to have a single report that can act as a dashboard that shows key metrics using tabular data as well as charts. What GCP service would you recommend?

    A. Cloud Composer

    B. Data Catalog

    C. Cloud Dataprep

    D. Data Studio

5. You are using Cloud Dataprep to prepare datasets for machine learning. Another team will be using the data that you prepare, and they have asked you to export your data from Cloud Dataprep. The other team is concerned about file size and asks you to compress the files using GZIP. What formats can you use in the export file?

    A. CSV only

    B. CSV and JSON only

    C. CSV and AVRO only

    D. JSON and AVRO only

6. The finance department in your company is using Data Studio for data warehouse reporting. Their existing reports have all the information they need, but the time required to update charts and tables is longer than expected. What kind of data source would you try to improve the query performance?

    A. Live data source

    B. Extracted data source

    C. Compound data source

    D. Blended data source

7. A DevOps team in your company uses Data Studio to display application performance data. Their top priority is timely data. What kind of connection would you recommend they use to have data updated in reports automatically?

    A. Live data source

    B. Extracted data source

    C. Compound or blended data source

    D. Extracted or live data source

8. A machine learning engineer is using Data Studio to build models in Python. The engineer has decided to use a statistics library that is not installed by default. How would you suggest that they install the missing library?

    A. Using `conda install` or `pip install` from a Cloud shell

    B. Using `conda install` or `pip install` from within a Jupyter Notebook

    C. Use the Linux package manager from within a Cloud shell

    D. Download the source from GitHub and compile locally

9. A DevOps engineer is working with you to build a workflow to load data from an on-premises database to Cloud Storage and then run several data preprocessing and analysis programs. After those are run, the output is loaded into a BigQuery table, an email is sent to managers indicating that new data is available in BigQuery, and temporary files are deleted. What GCP service would you use to implement this workflow?

    A. Cloud Dataprep

    B. Cloud Dataproc

    C. Cloud Composer

    D. Data Studio

10. You have just received a large dataset. You have comprehensive documentation on the dataset and are ready to start analyzing. You will do some visualization and data filtering, but you also want to be able to run custom Python functions. You want to work interactively with the data. What GCP service would you use?

    A. Cloud Dataproc

    B. Cloud Datalab

    C. Cloud Composer

    D. Data Studio

Chapter 9

Deploying Machine Learning Pipelines

GOOGLE CLOUD PROFESSIONAL DATA ENGINEER EXAM OBJECTIVES COVERED IN THIS CHAPTER INCLUDE THE FOLLOWING:

3. **Operationalizing machine learning models**

✓ 3.2 **Deploying an ML pipeline. Considerations include:**

- Ingesting appropriate data
- Retraining of machine learning models (Cloud AI, BigQuery ML, Kubeflow, Spark ML)
- Continuous evaluation

Data engineers are increasingly working with machine
learning (ML) pipelines. In this chapter, we will review
the structure of ML pipelines and describe several ways to
implement those pipelines in GCP.

ML pipelines include several stages, beginning with data ingestion and preparation,
then data segregation, followed by model training and evaluation. As in other software
development processes, models, like other software, should be deployed and monitored in a
structured manner.

GCP provides multiple ways to implement ML pipelines. General-purpose computing
resources, such as Compute Engine and Kubernetes Engine, can be used to implement
ML pipelines. Managed services, such as Cloud Dataflow and Cloud Dataproc, are also
available as well as specialized ML services, such as Cloud ML.

Structure of ML Pipelines

Machine learning projects begin with a problem definition. This could involve how to
improve sales revenue by making product recommendations to customers, how to evaluate
medical images to detect tumors, or how to identify fraudulent financial transactions.
These are three distinct types of problems, but they can all be solved using machine
learning techniques deployed via ML pipelines.

The stages of a machine learning pipeline are as follows:

- Data ingestion
- Data preparation
- Data segregation
- Model training
- Model evaluation
- Model deployment
- Model monitoring

Although the stages are listed in a linear manner, ML pipelines are more cyclic than
linear, as shown in Figure 9.1. This is a difference with dataflow pipelines, like those used
to ingest, transform, and store data, which are predominantly linear.

FIGURE 9.1 ML pipelines are usually executed in cycles.

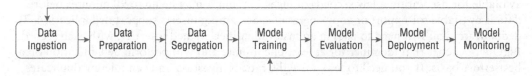

Data Ingestion

Data ingestion for machine learning can be either batch or streaming.

Batch Data Ingestion

Batch data ingestion should use a dedicated process for ingesting each distinct data source. For example, one process may ingest sales transactions from an e-commerce site, whereas another process ingests data about customers from another source. Batch ingestion is often done on a relatively fixed schedule, much like many data warehouse extraction, load, and transformation (ELT) processes. It is important to be able to track which batch data comes from, so you must include a batch identifier with each record that is ingested. This is considered a best practice, and it allows you to compare results across datasets more easily.

Batch data can be stored in several ways. Cloud Storage is a good option since it can store unstructured data as well as file-based, semi-structured, and structured data, such as database extracts. The lifecycle management features of Cloud Storage are also helpful. You can define policies to migrate batches of data to Nearline or Coldline storage after it has been processed by later stages of the data ingestion pipeline. Object storage is also a good option for *data lakes*, which are repositories of a wide variety of data from different sources and in different formats, which are then stored with minimal processing. If your organization is already using a well-designed data lake, you can take advantage of its services, like metadata cataloging, for storing machine learning data well.

Streaming Data Ingestion

Cloud Pub/Sub is designed for scalable messaging, including *streaming data ingestion*. There are several advantages to using Cloud Pub/Sub for streaming data ingestion. Cloud Pub/Sub is a fully managed, serverless service that is available globally. Clients can publish up to 1000 MB/second, and subscribers can consume up to 2000 MB/second for pull subscriptions and 100 MB/second for push subscriptions. Message attributes are made up of key-value pairs. Keys are restricted to 256 bytes, but values can be as large as 1024 bytes.

Cloud Pub/Sub is a good option for ingesting streaming data that will be stored in a database, such as Bigtable or Cloud Firebase, or immediately consumed by machine learning processes running in Cloud Dataflow, Cloud Dataproc, Kubernetes Engine, or Compute Engine.

When using BigQuery, you have the option of using streaming inserts. Data is usually available for use within a few seconds of ingesting, but it may be up to 90 minutes before data is available for export or copy operations. Streaming inserts support deduplication. To deduplicate, you will need to pass in an insert identifier, named insertID, with each record. BigQuery caches that identifier for at least one minute and will perform deduplication on a best-effort basis. If you need to maximize the rate of ingestion and can tolerate duplicates, then not passing in a value for insertID will allow for higher ingestion rates. Data can be ingested into ingestion time partitioned tables as well as tables partitioned on a date or timestamp column.

Once data has been ingested into GCP, the next step is preparing that data for use with machine learning algorithms.

Data Preparation

Data preparation is the process of transforming data from its raw form into a structure and format that is amenable to analysis by machine learning algorithms. There are three steps to data preparation:

- Data exploration
- Data transformation
- Feature engineering

Data Exploration

Data exploration is the first step to working with a new data source or a data source that has had significant changes. The goal of this stage is to understand the distribution of data and the overall quality of data.

To understand the distribution of data, we can look at basic descriptive statistics of numeric attributes, such as minimum, maximum, mean, and mode. Histograms are also useful. When working with non-numeric data, it can help to understand the number of distinct values in an attribute, which is known as the *cardinality* of the attribute, and the frequency of each of those values.

Overall quality of data is assessed by determining the number of missing or invalid values in a dataset. If some attributes of a record are missing, you may want to discard the data or use a default value, depending on the use case. Similarly, if there is an invalid value of an attribute, such as an invalid country code, you may be able to determine the correct value by looking at other attributes, such as the name of a city and province or state.

As noted in Chapter 8, "Understanding Data Operations for Flexibility and Portability," Cloud Dataprep is designed to support this kind of exploration, as well as data transformation. Cloud Data Fusion, a fully managed, code-free data integration service in GCP, is also recommended for this kind of data exploration.

Data Transformation

Data transformation is the process of mapping data from its raw form into data structures and formats that allow for machine learning. Transformations can include the following:

- Replacing missing values with a default value
- Replacing missing values with an inferred value based on other attributes in a record
- Replacing missing values with an inferred value based on attributes in other records
- Changing the format of numeric values, such as truncating or rounding real numbers to integers
- Removing or correcting attribute values that violate business logic, such as an invalid product identifier
- Deduplicating records
- Joining records from different data sets
- Aggregating data, such as summing values of metrics into hour or minute totals

Cloud Dataprep can be used for interactive data transformation, and it is especially useful when you're working with new datasets. For large volumes of data or cases in which the set of needed transformations is well defined, Cloud Dataflow is a good option for implementing transformations. Cloud Dataflow supports both batch and stream processing.

Feature Engineering

Feature engineering is the process of adding or modifying the representation of features to make implicit patterns more explicit. For example, if a ratio of two numeric features is important to classifying an instance, then calculating that ratio and including it as a feature may improve the model quality. Feature engineering is especially important when you are using models that employ some kind of linear separation to make predictions. For example, consider datasets with two features that are labeled as positive or negative. The dataset could be plotted on an x-y axis. If a binary classifier can find a line that separates positive from negative examples, this is called a *linear problem*. Figure 9.2 shows an example of a linear-separable set of instances.

FIGURE 9.2   An example of a dataset that can be classified with a linear model

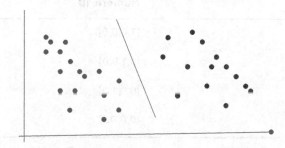

Now consider Figure 9.3. There is no straight line that you can draw to separate the two classes of instances.

FIGURE 9.3   An example of a dataset that cannot be classified with a linear model

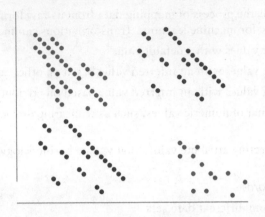

In cases such as the one shown in Figure 9.3, you can create new features that allow you to represent each instance in a higher dimensional space where a linear model can separate the instances. One way to do this is to use a *cross product*, which is created by multiplying two or more numeric features. For example, if we have two numeric features, *x* and *y*, we can multiply them to create a new feature *z*; that is, z = x * y. Now, instead of representing each instance in a two-dimensional space, it is represented in a three-dimensional space. Cross products encode information about nonlinearity, so linear models can be used to build a classifier.

This characteristic is also common to *cross-categorical features*. For example, an online retailer building a model to predict how much a customer will spend might use a combination of a postal code and a credit rating to create a new feature. Assuming that there are 1,000 postal codes and four categories of credit ratings, a cross of these features would create a new feature with 4,000 possible values.

Another common feature engineering technique is *one-hot encoding*. This process maps a list of categorical values to a series of binary numbers that have a single value set to 1 and all other values set to 0. For example, refer to Table 9.1.

TABLE 9.1   One-hot encoding of a categorical feature

Category	Numeric ID
Good Credit	[1,0,0,0]
Fair Credit	[0,1,0,0]
Poor Credit	[0,0,1,0]
No Credit History	[0,0,0,1]

One-hot encoding is often used with neural networks and other algorithms that do not work directly with categorical values. Decision trees and random forests work directly with categorical values, so one-hot encoding is not necessary.

Data Segregation

Data segregation is the process splitting a data set into three segments: training, validation, and test data.

Training Data

Machine learning algorithms create models, which are functions that map from some input to a predicted output. The mappings are generated based on data rather than by manually programming them. The data used to generate these mappings is known as the *training data*.

Validation Data

Although machine learning algorithms can learn some values, known as *parameters*, from training data, there are some values that are specified by a machine learning engineer. These values are known as hyperparameters. *Hyperparameters* are values that configure a model, and they can include the number of layers in a neural network or the maximum depth of trees in a random forest model. Hyperparameters vary by machine learning algorithm. See Figure 9.4 and Figure 9.5 for examples of hyperparameters.

FIGURE 9.4   Neural networks have hyperparameters to specify the number of layers and the number of nodes in each layer.

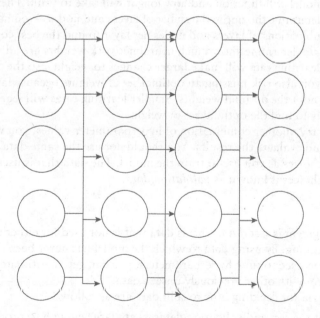

Hyperparameters:
Layers: 4
Nodes per Layer: 5

FIGURE 9.5   Random forest models have hyperparameters specifying the maximum number of trees to build and the maximum depth of trees.

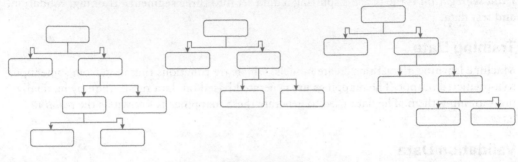

Hyperparameters:
Maximum Number of Trees: 3
Maximum Depth of Trees: 4

The *validation data* set is used to tune hyperparameters. This is often done by experimenting with different values for hyperparameters. For example, in neural networks, you can specify the number of layers and number of nodes in each layer of neural networks, as well as a learning rate.

The number of layers and number of nodes in each layer of a neural network determine both how well a model will function and how long it will take to train. There is no calculation available to determine the optimal number of layers and nodes—you have to experiment with different combinations of layers and nodes per layer to find the best configuration.

The *learning rate* determines how much neural network weights are adjusted when training. A large learning rate will make larger changes to weights, so the model may learn faster. However, you also risk missing an optimal set of weights because large changes in weights can overshoot the optimal weights. Smaller learning rates will learn more slowly but are more likely to find the optimal set of weights.

Each time you try another combination of hyperparameter values, you will need to train the model and evaluate the results. You should not use the same data to assess your hyperparameter choices as you use to train the model. The data that is used for evaluating hyperparameter choices is known as *validation data*.

Test Data

The third data segment is *test data*. This is data that is not used for either training or hyperparameter tuning. By using data to which the model has never been exposed and that has never been used to tune hyperparameters, you can get an estimate of how well the model will perform with other previously unseen data.

The main criteria for deciding how to split data are as follows:

- Ensuring that the test and validation datasets are large enough to produce statistically meaningful results

- Ensuring that the test and validation datasets are representative of the data as a whole

- Ensuring that the training dataset is large enough for the model to learn from in order to make accurate predictions with reasonable precision and recall

After data is segmented, the next step in ML pipelines is model training.

Model Training

Model training is the process of using training data to create a model that can be used to make predictions. This is sometimes called *fitting a model to the data*. Part of the model training phase is performing hyperparameter tuning, which we discussed earlier.

Feature Selection

Feature selection is another part of model training. This is the process of evaluating how a particular attribute or feature contributes to the predictiveness of a model. The goal is to have features of a dataset that allow a model to learn to make accurate predictions. Features are selected to do the following:

- Reduce the time and amount of data needed to train a model

- Make models easier to understand

- Reduce the number of features that have to be considered; this is known as the *curse of dimensionality*

- Reduce the risk of overfitting the model to the training data, which in turn would reduce the model accuracy on data not encountered during training

There are a number of different algorithms for selecting features. The simplest approach is to train a model with each subset of features and see which subset has the best performance. Although it is simple and easy to implement, this naive approach is not scalable.

Another approach is to start with a subset of features, measure its performance, and then make an incremental modification in the subset of features. If the performance of the modified subset is better, the modification is retained, and the process is repeated. Otherwise, the modification is discarded, and another one is tried. This is technique is known as *greedy hill climbing*.

There are many other approaches to feature selection based on information theory, correlations among features, as well as heuristics.

Underfitting, Overfitting, and Regularization

Two problems that can occur during model training are underfitting and overfitting.

Underfitting creates a model that is not able to predict values of training data correctly or new data that was not used during training. If the model performs poorly across multiple algorithms, and when evaluating the model using the same data that was used to train it, then that is underfitting, and it is likely caused by insufficient training data. The problem of underfitting may be corrected by increasing the amount of training data, using a different machine learning algorithm, or modifying hyperparameters. In the case of changing hyperparameters, this could include using more nodes or layers in a neural network, which is a collection of interconnected artificial neurons used to make a calculation, or increasing the number and depth of trees in a random forest—in other words, a collection decision trees, which are an ordered conjunction of features that determine a label.

Overfitting occurs when a model fits the training data too well. This happens when there is noise in the data and the model fits the noise as well as the correct data points. *Noise* is a term borrowed from signal processing to describe data points that are in the dataset but that are not generated by the underlying processes being modeled. A problem in the network, for instance, could corrupt a measurement sent from a sensor, in which case that data point would be noise. For an example, see Figure 9.6. Overfitting can occur when training data and validation data are not distinct or when training datasets are too small.

FIGURE 9.6   The dashed line is a linear model that does not overfit, and the solid line fits the model to an outlier data point that causes the model to overfit.

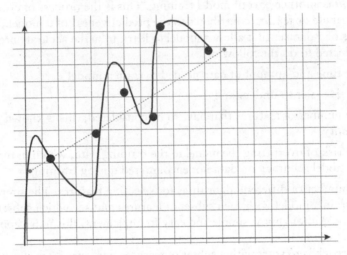

One way to compensate for the impact of noise in the data and reduce the risk of overfitting is by introducing a penalty for data points that make the model more complicated. This process is called *regularization*. Two kinds of regularization are L1 regularization, which is also known as *Lasso Regularization*, for Least Absolute Shrinkage and Selection Operator, and L2, or *Ridge Regression*.

Both L1 and L2 regularization add a penalty to the function that computes errors in a prediction, which is called the *cost function*. Machine learning algorithms use these cost functions to improve the quality of prediction. In L1 regularization, the penalty is based on magnitude or absolute value of coefficients in a model. In L2 regularization, the penalty is based on the square of the magnitude of the coefficient.

L1 regularization can shrink a feature's coefficient to zero, effectively eliminating the feature from consideration.

Model Evaluation

There are a variety of ways to understand and evaluate the quality of a machine learning model, including

- Individual evaluation metrics
- K-fold cross validation

- Confusion matrices
- Bias and variance

Individual Evaluation Metrics

Machine learning models can be evaluated based on a number of metrics, including the following:

Accuracy   This is the measure of how often a machine learning algorithm makes a correct prediction, specifically

Accuracy = (True Positive + True Positive) / Total Predicted

Precision   This is the proportion of positive cases that were correctly identified. This measure is also known as the *positive predictive value*. The formula is as follows:

Precision = True Positive / (True Positive + False Positive)

Recall   This is the number of actual positive cases that were correctly identified as opposed to negative cases identified as positive. The formula for recall is as follows:

Recall = True Positive / (True Positive + False Negative)

F1 Score   This is a measure that combines precision and recall. The formula for calculating the F measure is as follows:

2 * ((precision * recall) / (precision + recall))

There are trade-offs to optimizing precision or recall. The F1 score combines both precision and recall, so it is often used to evaluate models.

K-Fold Cross Validation

K-fold cross validation is a technique for evaluating model performance by splitting a data set into k segments, where k is an integer. For example, if a dataset were split into five equal-sized subsets, that would be a fivefold cross-validation dataset.

K-fold cross-validation datasets are used as follows. The dataset is shuffled or randomly sorted and split into k groups. One group is held out for evaluation purposes, and the remaining groups are used to train the model. When the model is trained, it is evaluated using the dataset that was held out. The evaluation results are stored, and the process is repeated, holding out another group and training with the remaining groups until all groups have been used for evaluation.

The value of k should be chosen so that each segment is representative of the dataset at large. In practice, setting k to 10 seems to work well in many cases.

When k is set equal to the number of records in a dataset, that is called *leave-one-out-cross-validation*.

Confusion Matrices

Confusion matrices are used with classification models to show the relative performance of a model. In the case of a binary classifier, a confusion matrix would be 2×2, with one column and one row for each value. Figure 9.7 shows an example confusion matrix for a binary classifier. The columns indicate the predicted value, and the rows indicate the actual value.

FIGURE 9.7   A confusion matrix for a classifier making 100 predictions (n = 100)

In this example, there are a total of 100 predictions. There were a total of 70 Yes instances, with 65 of those correctly predicted as Yes and 5 predicted as No. There were a total of 30 No instances. Twenty-six No instances were correctly predicted, and the prediction of the 4 others was incorrect.

One advantage of using a confusion matrix is that it helps to see quickly the accuracy of a model.

Bias and Variance

The errors made by predictive models can be understood in terms of bias and variance. Data scientists typically run many cycles of training models with different sets and sizes of training datasets. This allows them to understand bias and variance better.

Bias is the difference between the average prediction of a model and the correct prediction of a model. Models with high bias tend to have oversimplified representations of the process that generates the training data; this is underfitting the model. When data scientists run training models with different datasets, bias is measured by the difference of the average predicted value from a target value.

Variance is the variability in model predictions. It helps to understand how model prediction differs across multiple training datasets. It does not measure how accurate a prediction is from a target value, but rather the variability of a model to predict. Models with high variance tend to overfit training data so that the model works well when making predictions on the training data, but it does not generalize to data that the model has not seen before.

Ideally, models should have both low bias and low variance, and this is achieved by lowering the mean squared error (MSE) of the model by working through multiple training datasets.

Model Deployment

Machine learning models are programs not unlike other programs. When they are deployed, they should be managed using the same best practices used for manually coded applications, including version control, testing, and continuous integration and deployment.

Model Monitoring

Machine learning models should be monitored like other applications. *Performance monitoring* should be used to understand how well the model is using resources. Stackdriver Monitoring can be used to collect metrics on resource utilization, and Stackdriver Logging can be used to capture information on events that occur while the model is running.

In addition to performance monitoring, models should be monitored for accuracy. This can be done using the model to predict the value of new instances on which the model was not trained. For example, if a model was deployed one week ago and new data has become available since then, and the actual values of the predicted feature are known, then that new data can be used to assess the accuracy of the model.

Keep in mind, however, that even if the model does not change, the accuracy of the model can change if there are changes in the process or the entity being modeled. For example, consider that a model is developed to predict how much a customer will spend on a particular type of product. The model is trained with data collected at some point in time. Now imagine that the company changes its pricing strategy. The data used to train the model does not reflect how customers respond to the new pricing strategy and therefore will make predictions based on the prior strategy. In this case, the model should be updated by training it on the data collected since the new strategy was adopted.

ML pipelines are abstractions that can be implemented in several ways in GCP.

GCP Options for Deploying Machine Learning Pipeline

Data engineers have multiple options for deploying machine learning workflows in GCP, from running custom programs in Compute Engine to using a fully managed machine learning service. In this section, we'll look at four options that take advantage of the machine learning capabilities of several different GCP services. They are as follows:

- Cloud AutoML
- BigQuery ML
- Kubeflow
- Spark Machine Learning

Each option is particularly well suited to a specific workload, as you'll see.

Cloud AutoML

Cloud AutoML is a machine learning service designed for developers who want to incorporate machine learning into their applications without having to learn many of the details of ML. The service uses a GUI to train and evaluate models, which reduces the level of effort required to get started building models. There are several AutoML products, including the following:

- AutoML Vision
- AutoML Video Intelligence (in beta as of this writing)
- AutoML Natural Language
- AutoML Translation
- AutoML Tables (in beta as of this writing)

AutoML Vision has several capabilities:

AutoML Vision Classification   This service enables users to train their own machine learning models to classify images.

AutoML Vision Edge - Image Classification   This capability enables users to build custom image classification models that can be deployed to edge devices. This is useful if an application requires local classification and real-time responses to the results of the classification.

AutoML Vision Object Detection   This feature is used to train models to detect objects in images and provide information about those objects, such as their location in the image.

AutoML Vision Edge - Object Detection   This feature enables object detection capabilities at the edge of a distributed system that includes cloud and remote or edge processing.

AutoML Video Intelligence Classification can be used to train machine learning models to classify segments of video using a custom set of labels. AutoML Video Intelligence Object Tracking supports the training of machine learning models that can detect and track multiple objects through video segments.

AutoML Natural Language enables developers to deploy machine learning applications that can analyze documents and classify them, identify entities in the text, and determine sentiment or attitudes from text.

AutoML Translation provides developers with the ability to create custom translation models. This is particularly useful if you are developing a translation application for a domain with its own nomenclature, such a field of science or engineering.

AutoML Tables builds machine learning models based on structured data. AutoML provides tools to clean and analyze datasets, including the ability to detect missing data and determine the distribution of data for each feature. It also performs common feature engineering tasks such as normalizing numeric values, creating buckets for continuous value features, and extracting date and time features from timestamps. AutoML builds models using multiple machine learning algorithms, including linear regression, deep neural network, gradient-boosted decision trees, AdaNet, and ensembles of models generated by a variety of algorithms. This approach allows AutoML Tables to determine the best algorithm for each use case.

Finally, AutoML provides comparable capabilities as BigQueryML.

BigQuery ML

BigQuery ML enables users of the analytical database to build machine learning models using SQL and data in BigQuery datasets. Making machine learning methods available through SQL functions, combined with not having to move data, is a key advantage to using BigQuery ML over other options.

BigQuery ML can be accessed through the following:

- BigQuery web user interface
- bq command-line tool
- BigQuery REST API
- External tools, including Jupyter Notebooks

BigQuery ML supports several types of machine learning algorithms, including

- Linear regression for forecasting
- Binary logistic regression for classification with two labels
- Multiple logistic regression for classification with more than two labels
- K-means clustering for segmenting datasets
- TensorFlow model importing to allow BigQuery users access to custom TensorFlow models

Sometimes, a use case could make use of either AutoML Tables or BigQueryML. AutoML Tables may be a better option when you want to optimize your model, without a lot of experimentation, with different algorithms and feature engineering. If you have many features, AutoML maybe a better option since it automates common feature engineering tasks. AutoML typically takes longer to return a model since it tests a variety of models, so if you need to minimize model generation time, then consider BigQueryML.

Kubeflow

Kubeflow is an open source project for developing, orchestrating, and deploying scalable and portable machine learning workloads. Kubeflow is designed for the Kubernetes platform. Kubeflow originally began life as a tool to help run TensorFlow jobs on Kubernetes, but it expanded to a multicloud framework for running ML pipelines. Kubeflow can be used to run machine learning workloads in multiple clouds or in a hybrid cloud environment.

Kubeflow includes the following components:

- Support for training TensorFlow models
- TensorFlow Serving, which is used to deploy trained models and make them available to other services
- A JupyterHub installation, which is a platform for spawning and managing multiple instances of a single-user Jupyter Notebook server
- Kubeflow Pipelines, which are used to define machine learning workflows

Kubeflow Pipelines are descriptions of machine learning workflows, including all the components needed to execute a workflow. Pipelines are packaged as Docker images.

Kubeflow is a good choice for running machine learning workloads if you are already working with Kubernetes Engine and have some experience with building machine learning models. Kubeflow supports the scalable use of machine learning models but does not provide some of the features of AutoML or the simplicity of BigQuery ML.

Spark Machine Learning

Cloud Dataproc is a managed Spark and Hadoop service. Included with Spark is a machine learning library called *MLib*. If you are already using Cloud Dataproc or a self-managed Spark cluster, then using Spark MLib may be a good choice for running machine learning workloads.

Spark MLib contains several tools, including

- Machine learning algorithms for classification, regression, clustering, and collaborative filtering, which are used with recommendation engines

- Support for feature engineering, data transformation, and dimensionality reduction

- ML pipelines for executing multistep workloads

- Other utilities, such as math libraries and other data management tools

Spark MLib's API supports the chaining together of multiple steps in a machine learning pipeline. Pipelines are constructed from several types of components, including

Data Frames   Tabular structures for storing data in memory

Transformers   Applies functions to data frames, including applying a machine learning model to generate predictions

Estimators   Algorithms that are used to apply machine learning algorithms to create models

Parameters   Used by transformers and estimators

Spark MLib has a wide variety of machine learning algorithms. If you need an algorithm not available in other GCP machine learning services, consider using Spark MLib. The available algorithms include the following:

- Support vector machines for classification

- Linear regression for forecasting

- Decision trees, random forests, and gradient-boosted trees for classification

- Naive Bayes for classification

- K-means clustering and streaming k-means for segmenting

- Latent Dirichlet allocation for segmenting

- Singular value decomposition and principal component analysis for dimensionality reduction

- Frequent Pattern (FP)–growth and association rules for frequent pattern mining

Data engineers have a variety of options for running their machine learning workloads in GCP. Cloud AutoML is designed for developers who want to build on existing machine learning models and tools that automate some machine learning tasks, like feature engineering. BigQuery ML allows SQL users to build models within BigQuery and avoid having to export data and develop models using Python or Java. Kubeflow supports deploying scalable ML pipelines in Kubernetes. Spark MLib is a comprehensive set of machine learning tools that can be used when deploying Cloud Dataproc clusters.

Cloud AutoML and Cloud BigQuery are readily used by developers and analysts with limited or no experience building machine learning models. Both Kubeflow and Spark MLib require some knowledge of machine learning techniques and practices.

Exam Essentials

Know the stages of ML pipelines.   Data ingestion, data preparation, data segregation, model training, model evaluation, model deployment, and model monitoring are the stages of ML pipelines. Although the stages are listed in a linear manner, ML pipelines are more cyclic than linear, especially relating to training and evaluation.

Understand batch and streaming ingestion.   Batch data ingestion should use a dedicated process for ingesting each distinct data source. Batch ingestion often occurs on a relatively fixed schedule, much like many data warehouse ETL processes. It is important to be able to track which batch data comes from, so include a batch identifier with each record that is ingested. Cloud Pub/Sub is designed for scalable messaging, including ingesting streaming data. Cloud Pub/Sub is a good option for ingesting streaming data that will be stored in a database, such as Bigtable or Cloud Firebase, or immediately consumed by machine learning processes running in Cloud Dataflow, Cloud Dataproc, Kubernetes Engine, or Compute Engine. When using BigQuery, you have the option of using streaming inserts.

Know the three kinds of data preparation.   The three kinds of data preparation are data exploration, data transformation, and feature engineering. Data exploration is the first step in working with a new data source or a data source that has had significant changes. The goal of this stage is to understand the distribution of data and the overall quality of data. Data transformation is the process of mapping data from its raw form into data structures and formats that allow for machine learning. Transformations can include replacing missing values with a default value, changing the format of numeric values, and deduplicating records. Feature engineering is the process of adding or modifying the representation of features to make implicit patterns more explicit. For example, if a ratio of two numeric features is important to classifying an instance, then calculating that ratio and including it as a feature may improve the model quality. Feature engineering includes the understanding of key attributes (features) that are meaningful for machine learning objectives at hand. This includes dimensional reduction.

Know that data segregation is the process splitting a dataset into three segments: training, validation, and test data.   Training data is used to build machine learning models.

Validation data is used during hyperparameter tuning. Test data is used to evaluate model performance. The main criteria for deciding how to split data are to ensure that the test and validation datasets are large enough to produce statistically meaningful results, that test and validation datasets are representative of the data as a whole, and that the training dataset is large enough for the model to learn to make accurate predictions with reasonable precision and recall.

Understand the process of training a model.   Know that feature selection is the process of evaluating how a particular attribute or feature contributes to the predictiveness of a model. The goal is to have features of a dataset that allow a model to learn to make accurate predictions. Know that underfitting creates a model that is not able to predict values of training data correctly or new data that was not used during training.

Understand underfitting, overfitting, and regularization.   The problem of underfitting may be corrected by increasing the amount of training data, using a different machine learning algorithm, or modifying hyperparameters. Understand that overfitting occurs when a model fits the training data too well. One way to compensate for the impact of noise in the data and reduce the risk of overfitting is by introducing a penalty for data points, which makes the model more complicated. This process is called regularization. Two kinds of regularization are L1 regularization, which is also known as Lasso Regularization, for Least Absolute Shrinkage and Selection Operator, and L2 or Ridge Regression.

Know ways to evaluate a model.   Methods for evaluation a model include individual evaluation metrics, such as accuracy, precision, recall, and the F measure; k-fold cross-validation; confusion matrices; and bias and variance. K-fold cross-validation is a technique for evaluating model performance by splitting a data set into k segments, where k is an integer. Confusion matrices are used with classification models to show the relative performance of a model. In the case of a binary classifier, a confusion matrix would be 2×2, with one column and one row for each value.

Understand bias and variance.   Bias is the difference between the average prediction of a model and the correct prediction of a model. Models with high bias tend to have over-simplified models; this is underfitting the model. Variance is the variability in model predictions. Models with high variance tend to overfit training data so that the model works well when making predictions on the training data but does not generalize to data that the model has not seen before.

Know options for deploying machine learning workloads on GCP.   These options include Cloud AutoML, BigQuery ML, Kubeflow, and Spark MLib. Cloud AutoML is a machine learning service designed for developers who want to incorporate machine learning in their applications without having to learn many of the details of ML. BigQuery ML enables users of the analytical database to build machine learning models using SQL and data in BigQuery datasets. Kubeflow is an open source project for developing, orchestrating, and deploying scalable and portable machine learning workloads. Kubeflow is designed for the Kubernetes platform. Cloud Dataproc is a managed Spark and Hadoop service. Included with Spark is a machine learning library called MLib, and it is a good option for machine learning workloads if you are already using Spark or need one of the more specialized algorithms included in Spark MLib.

Review Questions

You can find the answers in the appendix.

1. You have been tasked with helping to establish ML pipelines for your department. The models will be trained using data from several sources, including several enterprise transaction processing systems and third-party data provider datasets. Data will arrive in batches. Although you know the structure of the data now, you expect that it will change, and you will not know about the changes until the data arrives. You want to ensure that your ingestion process can store the data in whatever structure it arrives in. After the data is ingested, you will transform it as needed. What storage system would you use for batch ingestion?

    A. Cloud Storage

    B. Cloud Spanner

    C. Cloud Dataprep

    D. Cloud Pub/Sub

2. A startup company is building an anomaly detection service for manufacturing equipment. IoT sensors on manufacturing equipment transmit data on machine performance every 30 seconds. The service will initially support up to 5,000 sensors, but it will eventually grow to millions of sensors. The data will be stored in Cloud Bigtable after it is preprocessed and transformed by a Cloud Dataflow workflow. What service should be used to ingest the IoT data?

    A. Cloud Storage

    B. Cloud Bigtable

    C. BigQuery Streaming Insert

    D. Cloud Pub/Sub

3. A machine learning engineer has just started a new project. The engineer will be building a recommendation engine for an e-commerce site. Data from several services will be used, including data about products, customers, and inventory. The data is currently available in a data lake and stored in its raw, unprocessed form. What is the first thing you would recommend the machine learning engineer do to start work on the project?

    A. Ingest the data into Cloud Storage

    B. Explore the data with Cloud Dataprep

    C. Transform the data with Cloud Dataflow

    D. Transform the data with BigQuery

4. A machine learning engineer is in the process of building a model for classifying fraudulent transactions. They are using a neural network and need to decide how many nodes and layers to use in the model. They are experimenting with several different combinations of number of nodes and number of layers. What data should they use to evaluate the quality of models being developed with each combination of settings?

    A. Training data

    B. Validation data

    C. Test data

    D. Hyperparameter data

5. A developer with limited knowledge of machine learning is attempting to build a machine learning model. The developer is using data collected from a data lake with minimal data preparation. After models are built, they are evaluated. Model performance is poor. The developer has asked for your help to reduce the time needed to train the model and increase the quality of model predictions. What would you do first with the developer?

    A. Explore the data with the goal of feature engineering

    B. Create visualizations of accuracy, precision, recall, and F measures

    C. Use tenfold cross-validation

    D. Tune hyperparameters

6. A developer has built a machine learning model to predict the category of new stories. The possible values are politics, economics, business, health, science, and local news. The developer has tried several algorithms, but the model accuracy is poor even when evaluating the model on using the training data. This is an example of what kind of potential problem with a machine learning model?

    A. Overfitting

    B. Underfitting

    C. Too much training data

    D. Using tenfold cross-validation for evaluation

7. A developer has built a machine learning model to predict the category of new stories. The possible values are politics, economics, business, health, science, and local news. The developer has tried several algorithms, but the model accuracy is quite high when evaluating the model using the training data but quite low when evaluating using test data. What would you recommend to correct this problem?

    A. Use confusion matrices for evaluation

    B. Use L1 or L2 regularization when evaluating

    C. Use L1 or L2 regularization when training

    D. Tune the hyperparameters more

8. Your e-commerce company deployed a product recommendation system six months ago. The system uses a machine learning model trained using historical sales data from the previous year. The model performed well initially. When customers were shown product recommendations, the average sale value increased by 14 percent. In the past month, the model has generated an average increase of only 2 percent. The model has not changed since it was deployed six months ago. What could be the cause of the decrease in effectiveness, and what would you recommend to correct it?

   A. The model is overfitting—use regularization.

   B. The data used to train the model is no longer representative of current sales data, and the model should be retrained with more recent data.

   C. The model should be monitored to collect performance metrics to identity the root cause of the decreasing effectiveness of the model.

   D. The model is underfitting—train with more data.

9. A startup company is developing software to analyze images of traffic in order to understand congestion patterns better and how to avoid them. The software will analyze images that are taken every minute from hundreds of locations in a city. The software will need to identify cars, trucks, cyclists, pedestrians, and buildings. The data on object identities will be used by analysis algorithms to detect daily patterns, which will then be used by traffic engineers to devise new traffic flow patterns. What GCP service would you use for this?

   A. AutoML Vision Object Detection

   B. AutoML Vision Edge - Object Detection

   C. AutoML Video Intelligence Classification

   D. Auto ML Video Intelligence Object Tracking

10. An analyst would like to build a machine learning model to classify rows of data in a dataset. There are two categories into which the rows can be grouped: Type A and Type B. The dataset has over 1 million rows, and each row has 32 attributes or features. The analyst does not know which features are important. A labeled training set is available with a sufficient number of rows to train a model. The analyst would like the most accurate model possible with the least amount of effort on the analyst's part. What would you recommend?

   A. Kubeflow

   B. Spark MLib

   C. AutoML Tables

   D. AutoML Natural Language

11. The chief financial officer of your company would like to build a program to predict which customers will likely be late paying their bills. The company has an enterprise data warehouse in BigQuery containing all the data related to customers, billing, and payments. The company does not have anyone with machine learning experience, but it does have analysts and data scientists experienced in SQL, Python, and Java. The analysts and data scientists will generate and test a large number of models, so they prefer fast model building. What service would you recommend using to build the model?

    A. Kubeflow

    B. Spark MLib

    C. BigQuery ML

    D. AutoML Tables

12. A team of researchers is analyzing buying patterns of customers of a national grocery store chain. They are especially interested in sets of products that customers frequently by together. The researchers plan to use association rules for this frequent pattern mining. What machine learning option in GCP would you recommend?

    A. Cloud Dataflow

    B. Spark MLib

    C. BigQuery ML

    D. AutoML Tables

Chapter

10

Choosing Training and Serving Infrastructure

GOOGLE CLOUD PROFESSIONAL DATA ENGINEER EXAM OBJECTIVES COVERED IN THIS CHAPTER INCLUDE THE FOLLOWING:

3. Operationalizing machine learning models

✓ **3.3 Choosing the appropriate training and serving infrastructure. Considerations include:**

- Distributed vs. single machine
- Use of edge compute
- Hardware accelerators (e.g., GPU, TPU)

Data engineers have a wide array of options for training and serving machine learning models. GCP has a number of serverless options and specialized AI services. We discussed these topics in Chapter 9, "Deploying Machine Learning Pipelines." This chapter focuses on choosing the appropriate training and serving infrastructure for your needs when serverless or specialized AI services are not a good fit for your requirements.

The Professional Data Engineer exam guide lists three topics relating to choosing training and serving infrastructure with which you should be familiar:

- Use of hardware accelerators
- Distributed and single machine infrastructure
- Use of edge computing for serving machine learning models

We'll start with considering how to choose between distributed and single machine infrastructure.

Cloud ML Engine has been rebranded by Google as AI Platform. The two terms are used interchangeably here.

Hardware Accelerators

Advances in integrated circuit and instruction set design have led to the development of specialized computing hardware accelerators. These devices offload some of the computing workload from CPUs. Two different types of hardware accelerators are available in GCP:

- Graphics processing units (GPUs)
- Tensor processing units (TPUs)

Graphics Processing Units

Graphic processing units (GPUs) are accelerators that have multiple arithmetic logic units (ALUs), which implement adders and multipliers. Modern GPUs have thousands of ALUs. This architecture is well suited to workloads that benefit from massive parallelization, such as training deep learning models. GPUs typically increase training performance on deep learning models by a factor of 10.

GPUs and CPUs share a common design pattern: calculations use registers or shared memory for intermediate calculation results. This can lead to a von Neumann bottleneck, which is the limited data rate between a processor and memory, and slow processing. An alternative design is used by TPUs.

Tensor Processing Units

Tensor processing units (TPUs) are specialized accelerators based on ASICs and created by Google to improve the training of deep neural networks. These accelerators are designed for the TensorFlow framework. The design of TPUs is proprietary and available only through Google's cloud services or on Google's Edge TPU devices.

Compared to GPUs, TPUs perform low-precision computation with as little as 8-bit precision. Using low-precision computation allows for high throughput. In one benchmark, 1 TPU was 27 times faster at training than 8 GPUs.

TPUs are designed to scale horizontally using TPU pods, which have hundreds of TPUs functioning together. TPUs are grouped into pods, which are a two-dimensional mesh network that presents the TPUs as a single programmable resource.

TPUs reduce the impact of the von Neumann bottleneck by implementing matrix multiplication in the processor. This means that TPUs are not used for general-purpose computing tasks but are better suited than GPUs for performing large-scale multiplications and additions, which are needed for training deep learning models.

TPUs can be used with Compute Engine, Kubernetes Engine, and AI Engine.

Choosing Between CPUs, GPUs, and TPUs

CPUs, GPUs, and TPUs can be used for machine learning, but Google has provided guidelines for choosing the best option for your workload at https://cloud.google.com/tpu/docs/tpus.

CPUs are recommended for the following:

- Prototyping
- Simple models that train relatively quickly
- Models that heavily use custom TensorFlow operations written in C++
- Models that are limited by available I/O or network bandwidth of the host server

GPUs are recommended for the following:

- Models that are not built on TensorFlow
- Models with inaccessible source code or code that is difficult to change
- Models that have some custom TensorFlow operations that must run at least partially on CPUs
- Models that use TensorFlow operations not supported on TPUs; available operations are listed at https://cloud.google.com/tpu/docs/tensorflow-ops
- Medium-to-large models that can be trained with large batch sizes

TPUs are recommended for the following:

- Models dominated by matrix multiplications
- Models without custom TensorFlow operations inside the main training loop
- Models that can take weeks or months to train on CPUs or GPUS
- Large and very large models that can be trained in very large batch sizes

TPUs are not recommended for workloads that require high-precision arithmetic.

Distributed and Single Machine Infrastructure

When discussing machine learning infrastructure, it is helpful to distinguish infrastructure for training machine learning models and infrastructure for serving machine learning models. Training is a compute-intensive operation, and having sufficient computing resources can mean the difference between models that take days to train versus hours to do so. Serving machine learning models—that is, deploying them in production to make predictions—is less CPU intensive. In fact, the widely used deep learning platform TensorFlow includes TensorFlow Lite, which is a framework for running machine learning models on mobile and IoT devices.

Single Machine Model Training

Single machines are useful for training small models, developing machine learning applications, and exploring data using Jupyter Notebooks or related tools. Cloud Datalab, for example, runs instances in Compute Engine virtual machines (VMs).

NOTE   Cloud Datalab is being deprecated for the AI Platform. The Professional Data Engineer exam may reference either.

The ability to use a single instance is constrained by the available CPUs, GPUs, and memory. With GCE, you have the option of scaling the size of the virtual machine. Currently, the largest machine type, m1-ultramem-160, provides 160 vCPUs and 3.75 TB of memory.

You also have the option of offloading some of the training load from CPUs to GPUs. GPUs have high-bandwidth memory and typically outperform CPUs on floating-point operations. GCP uses NVIDIA GPUs. NVIDIA is the creator of CUDA, a parallel computing platform that facilitates the use of GPUs. As of this writing, GCP offers five GPU types:

- NVIDIA Tesla K80
- NVIDIA Tesla P4
- NVIDIA Tesla T4

- NVIDIA Tesla V100

- NVIDIA Tesla P100

The NVIDIA Tesla K80 can perform over 2.9 teraflop double-precision and over 8.7 teraFLOPS (TFLOPS) single-precision operations and has 24 GB of memory.

The NVIDIA Tesla P4 is optimized for deep learning, and it provides 5.5 TFLOPS on single-precision operations and 22 tera operations per second (TOPS) on integer operations. It has 8 GB of memory.

The NVIDIA Tesla T4 is also well suited to deep learning, and it provides over 8 TFLOPS on single-precision operations and up to 130 TOPS on int8 operations.

The NVIDIA Tesla V100 is a GPU with the equivalent performance of 32 CPUs and the ability to perform 14 TFLOPS.

Compute Engine currently supports attaching up to 8 GPUs to a single instance.

Single machines can be used to train models, as long as the resources, in terms of CPU, GPU, and memory, are sufficient for the volume of data and type of algorithm used. Of course, any time that you are using a single machine, that machine is a potential single point of failure (SPOF).

Distributed Model Training

Distributing model training over a group of servers provides for scalability and improved availability. There are a variety of ways to use distributed infrastructure, and the best choice for you depends on your specific requirements and development practices.

One way to distribute training is to use machine learning frameworks that are designed to run in a distributed environment.

TensorFlow, the deep learning framework created by Google and released as open source, allows developers to specify a distributed computing strategy when training a model. For example, TensorFlow supports both synchronous and asynchronous training. Synchronous training has all worker training on different subsets of input data and incrementally combines results. In asynchronous training, workers operate independently and update variables asynchronously.

Here are some examples of TensorFlow strategies for distributed training:

MirroredStrategy   This strategy supports synchronous distributed training on multiple GPUs on one machine. Each variable is mirrored across all GPUs.

CentralStorageStrategy   This strategy is a synchronous training technique in which variables are not mirrored and both CPU and GPUs are used.

MultiWorkerMirroredStrategy   This strategy is like the mirrored strategy, but it works across multiple nodes.

TPUStrategy   This strategy runs synchronous training on TPUs.

TensorFlow training can run on Kubernetes Engine using the TensorFlow Training Job (TFJob) custom resource. For more on TensorFlow's distributed processing model, see www.tensorflow.org/guide/distributed_training.

Alternatively, you can use distributed infrastructure to build multiple models in parallel. For example, you may have a container configured with machine learning tools that is running on GKE. You could use that container to generate models that are trained with different hyperparameters. Each of those models could be trained in parallel, with GKE managing the deployment of pods to meet the workload.

Serving Models

Serving a machine learning model is the process of making the model available to make predictions for other services. When serving models, you need to keep in mind the following:

- Latency
- Scalability
- Version management
- Online versus batch prediction

The *latency* of model predictions will be largely a function of the resources available to execute the model, the type of model, and the amount of preprocessing required. Executing a model and training a model are significantly different. For example, when building a decision tree, an algorithm will consider many instances and features. When the decision tree is used to make predictions, the model makes a series of evaluations using data passed into the model. The number of evaluations will be a function of the depth of the tree, but it will be significantly less work than building the decision tree.

Serving models from a centralized location, such as a data center, can introduce latency because input data and results are sent over the network. If an application needs real-time results, it is better to serve the model closer to where it is needed, such as an edge or IoT device. (See the next section for more on edge computing.)

Models will need to scale to meet workloads. Since this chapter is about infrastructure choices, we will focus on using Compute Engine and Kubernetes Engine. With Compute Engine, you can configure an instance group with a minimum and maximum number of VMs in the group. Compute Engine will automatically scale up or down depending on workload. Kubernetes Engine will likewise scale the number of pods running machine learning models according to workload.

Version control of machine learning models is similar to version management for other software. When you serve a model, you may want to route a small amount of traffic to a new model and the rest of the traffic to the old model. This will give you an opportunity to see how the model performs in production before rolling it out to all users. If the model performs well, you can route all traffic to the new model. Other deployment strategies, such as incremental rollout, can be used as well.

Inference may be performed in batches or online. Batch mode makes predictions for multiple instances at one time. This is useful when you have a large number of instances to evaluate and the evaluation does not have to be done in real time. For example, a retailer that categorizes customers into those likely to leave for a competitor, which is known as "churning," can use batch mode predictions. This is because the response to the classification process is not needed immediately. Instead, the retailer may send a series of customized offers over several weeks to that customer.

A model that predicts fraudulent credit card transactions, however, would need to execute in online mode. In that case, the model would need to be exposed using an API that applications could call to receive a real-time evaluation.

Edge Computing with GCP

Edge computing is the practice of moving compute and storage resources closer to the location at which it is needed, such as on a factory floor or in a field on a farm.

Edge Computing Overview

An early and conceptually simpler forerunner of edge computing is a *content distribution network (CDN)*. CDNs store data at locations close to the users of the data. For example, as shown in Figure 10.1, a global news organization might maintain CDN endpoints across the globe so that users can retrieve content from the closest endpoint rather than from a centralized system. In this use case, edge computing reduces latency for users retrieving content. This is a commonly considered factor when adopting edge computing.

FIGURE 10.1   CDNs distribute content to servers around the globe.

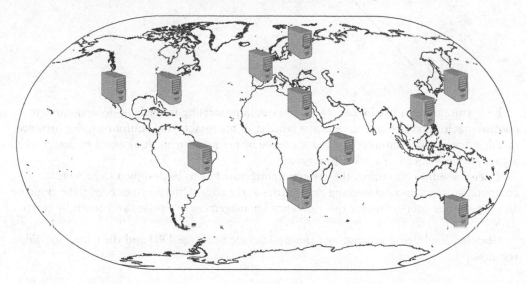

Edge computing devices can be relatively simple IoT devices, such as sensors with a small amount of memory and limited processing power. This type of device could be useful when the data processing load is light. If all raw data does not need to be stored in a central storage system, then there is no need to transmit all of it from the edge to the central storage system. Instead, the processing that is needed can be done on an edge device, and the results can be sent to the central storage system. Figure 10.2, for example, shows a set of sensors and an edge computing device that can process data locally and then send summary data to the cloud.

FIGURE 10.2 Edge computing can be used to process data locally and then send summary data to the cloud.

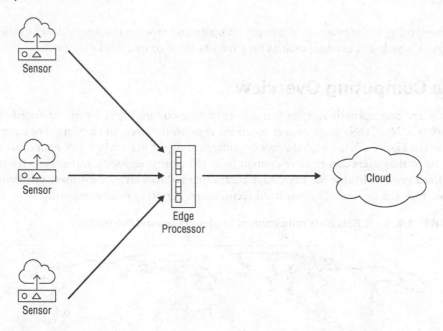

Edge computing is used when low-latency data processing is needed—for example, to control machinery such as autonomous vehicles or manufacturing equipment. For instance, an edge device could monitor the sounds made by manufacturing equipment to detect when a part does not correctly click into place.

To enable edge computing, the system architecture has to be designed to provide compute, storage, and networking capabilities at the edge while services run in the cloud or an on-premises data center for the centralized management of devices and centrally stored data.

Google Cloud's edge computing offerings include the Edge TPU and the Cloud IoT Edge services.

Edge Computing Components and Processes

Google Cloud IoT Edge computing consists of three basic components:

- Edge device, which interacts with and senses its environment
- Gateway device, which processes data on behalf of IoT devices
- Cloud platform, such as GCP

Edge devices provide three kinds of data:

- Metadata, such as the device ID, model number, and serial number
- State information about the status of the device
- Telemetry, which is data collected by the device

Before a device is incorporated into an IoT processing system, it must be provisioned and configured. Provisioning includes bootstrapping the device and collecting basic identifying information. For security, the device should be authenticated using a token, key, or other mechanism. The device should also receive authorizations, which define the operations the device is allowed to perform. The device should also be tracked in a central device registry.

After a device is provisioned and it starts collecting data, the data is then processed on the device. The kinds of operations performed can include converting data formats, validating data with business logic rules, summarizing data, and enhancing datasets with additional attributes.

After local processing, the data is transmitted to a gateway. Gateways can manage network traffic across protocols. For example, some IoT devices may not have full network stacks and may communicate with the gateway over other protocols, such as Bluetooth. The gateway in that case receives data over Bluetooth and transmits it to a cloud service over a TCP/IP network.

Data sent to the cloud is ingested by one of a few different kinds of services. In GCP, IoT data can be ingested using the following services:

- Cloud Pub/Sub for scalable ingestion
- IoT Core MQTT, a Message Queue Telemetry Transport broker that uses an industry-standard binary protocol
- Stackdriver Monitoring and Stackdriver Logging, which can also be used to ingest and process metrics and log messages

AI Platform is a managed service that can be used to support deploying machine learning models to the edge. It addresses several factors that you need to consider when making inferences at the edge, including the following:

- Serving prediction
- Restricting access to functionality based on authorizations

- Enforcing quotas on users
- Managing API keys
- Deploying new models

AI Platform also exposes REST APIs so that models can be used for online predictions.

Edge TPU

Edge TPU is a hardware device available from Google for implementing edge computing. Edge TPU performs inference, so it is used to serve models. Training models occurs in the cloud or other centralized computing service. This device is an application-specific integrated circuit (ASIC) designed for running AI services at the edge. Edge TPU is designed to work with Cloud TPU and Google Cloud services. In addition to the hardware, Edge TPU includes software and AI algorithms. Here are some use cases for Edge TPU:

- Image processing in a manufacturing environment
- Robotic control
- Anomaly detection in time series data
- Voice recognition and response

The TensorFlow Lite and Android Neural Network API machine learning frameworks can be used to run models on edge devices.

Cloud IoT

Cloud IoT is Google's managed service for IoT services. The platform provides services for integrating edge computing with centralized processing services. Device data is captured by the Cloud IoT Core service, which can then publish the data to Cloud Pub/Sub for streaming analytics. Data can also be stored in BigQuery for analysis or used for training new machine learning models in Cloud ML. Data provided through Cloud IoT can also be used to trigger Cloud Functions and associated workflows.

Figure 10.3 shows the reference architecture for Cloud IoT.

The reference architecture for Cloud IoT includes the following:

- Cloud IoT Core for device management
- Cloud ML Engine for training and deploying machine learning models
- Cloud Dataflow for streaming and batch analytics
- Cloud Pub/Sub for ingestion
- BigQuery for data warehousing and ad hoc querying

Other GCP services can be used as well, including Cloud Storage for archival storage and Cloud Firestore for storing semi-structured data that will be queried.

FIGURE 10.3   Reference architecture for Cloud IoT

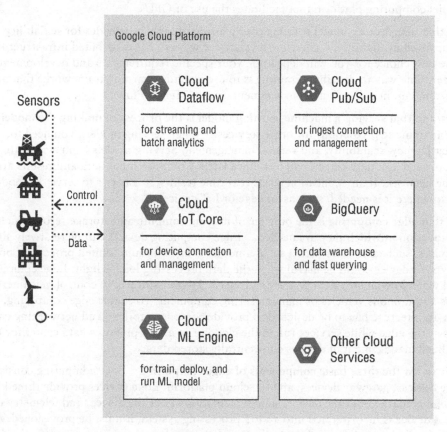

Build & train ML models in the cloud

Source: https://cloud.google.com/solutions/iot/

Exam Essentials

Understand that single machines are useful for training small models.   This includes when you are developing machine learning applications or exploring data using Jupyter Notebooks or related tools. Cloud Datalab, for example, runs instances in Compute Engine virtual machines.

Know that you also have the option of offloading some of the training load from CPUs to GPUs.   GPUs have high-bandwidth memory and typically outperform CPUs on floating-point operations. GCP uses NVIDIA GPUs, and NVIDIA is the creator of CUDA, a parallel computing platform that facilitates the use of GPUs.

Know that distributing model training over a group of servers provides for scalability and improved availability. There are a variety of ways to use distributed infrastructure, and the best choice for you will depend on your specific requirements and development practices. One way to distribute training is to use machine learning frameworks that are designed to run in a distributed environment, such as TensorFlow.

Understand that serving a machine learning model is the process of making the model available to make predictions for other services. When serving models, you need to consider latency, scalability, and version management. Serving models from a centralized location, such as a data center, can introduce latency because input data and results are sent over the network. If an application needs real-time results, it is better to serve the model closer to where it is needed, such as an edge or IoT device.

Know that edge computing is the practice of moving compute and storage resources closer to the location at which they are needed. Edge computing devices can be relatively simple IoT devices, such as sensors with a small amount of memory and limited processing power. This type of device could be useful when the data processing load is light. Edge computing is used when low-latency data processing is needed—for example, to control machinery such as autonomous vehicles or manufacturing equipment. To enable edge computing, the system architecture has to be designed to provide compute, storage, and networking capabilities at the edge while services run in the cloud or in an on-premises data center for the centralized management of devices and centrally stored data.

Be able to list the three basic components of edge computing. Edge computing consists of edge devices, gateway devices, and the cloud platform. Edge devices provide three kinds of data: metadata about the device, state information about the device, and telemetry data. Before a device is incorporated into an IoT processing system, it must be provisioned. After a device is provisioned and it starts collecting data, the data is then processed on the device. After local processing, data is transmitted to a gateway. Gateways can manage network traffic across protocols. Data sent to the cloud is ingested by one of a few different kinds of services in GCP, including Cloud Pub/Sub, IoT Core MQTT, and Stackdriver Monitoring and Logging.

Know that an Edge TPU is a hardware device available from Google for implementing edge computing. This device is an application-specific integrated circuit (ASIC) designed for running AI services at the edge. Edge TPU is designed to work with Cloud TPU and Google Cloud services. In addition to the hardware, Edge TPU includes software and AI algorithms.

Know that Cloud IoT is Google's managed service for IoT services. This platform provides services for integrating edge computing with centralized processing services. Device data is captured by the Cloud IoT Core service, which can then publish data to Cloud Pub/Sub for streaming analytics. Data can also be stored in BigQuery for analysis or used for training new machine learning models in Cloud ML. Data provided through Cloud IoT can also be used to trigger Cloud Functions and associated workflows.

Understand GPUs and TPUs.   Graphic processing units are accelerators that have multiple arithmetic logic units (ALUs) that implement adders and multipliers. This architecture is well suited to workloads that benefit from massive parallelization, such as training deep learning models. GPUs and CPUs are both subject to the von Neumann bottleneck, which is the limited data rate between a processor and memory, and slow processing. TPUs are specialized accelerators based on ASICs and created by Google to improve training of deep neural networks. These accelerators are designed for the TensorFlow framework. TPUs reduces the impact of the von Neumann bottleneck by implementing matrix multiplication in the processor. Know the criteria for choosing between CPUs, GPUs, and TPUs.

Review Questions

You can find the answers in the appendix.

1. You are in the early stages of developing a machine learning model using a framework that requires high-precision arithmetic and benefits from massive parallelization. Your data set fits within 32 GB of memory. You want to use Jupyter Notebooks to build the model iteratively and analyze results. What kind of infrastructure would you use?

    A. A TPU pod with at least 32 TPUs

    B. A single TPU

    C. A single server with a GPU

    D. A managed instance group of 4 VMs with 64 GB of memory each

2. You are developing a machine learning model that will predict failures in high-precision machining equipment. The equipment has hundreds of IoT sensors that send telemetry data every second. Thousands of the machines are in use in a variety of operating conditions. A year's worth of data is available for model training. You plan to use TensorFlow, a synchronous training strategy, and TPUs. Which of the following strategies would you use?

    A. MirroredStrategy

    B. CentralStorageStrategy

    C. MultiWorkerMirroredStrategy

    D. TPUStrategy

3. Your client has developed a machine learning model that detects anomalies in equity trading time-series data. The model runs as a service in a Google Kubernetes Engine (GKE) cluster deployed in the us-west-1 region. A number of financial institutions in New York and London are interested in licensing the technology, but they are concerned that the total time required to make a prediction is longer than they can tolerate. The distance between the serving infrastructure and New York is about 4,800 kilometers, and the distance to London is about 8,000 kilometers. This is an example of what kind of problem with serving a machine learning model?

    A. Overfitting

    B. Underfitting

    C. Latency

    D. Scalability

4. A study of global climate change is building a network of environmental sensors distributed across the globe. Sensors are deployed in groups of 12 sensors and a gateway. An analytics pipeline is implemented in GCP. Data will be ingested by Cloud Pub/Sub and analyzed using the stream processing capabilities of Cloud Dataflow. The analyzed data will be stored in BigQuery for further analysis by scientists. The bandwidth between the gateways and the GCP is limited and sometimes unreliable. The scientists have determined that they need the average temperature, pressure, and humidity measurements of each group of 12

sensors for a one-minute period. Each sensor sends data to the gateway every second. This generates 720 data points (12 sensors × 60 seconds) every minute for each of the three measurements. The scientists only need the one-minute average for temperature, pressure, and humidity. What data processing strategy would you implement?

A. Send all 720 data points for each measurement each minute to a Cloud Pub/Sub message, generate the averages using Cloud Dataflow, and write those results to BigQuery.

B. Average all 720 data points for each measurement each minute, send the average to a Cloud Pub/Sub message, and use Cloud Dataflow and write those results to BigQuery.

C. Send all 720 data points for each measurement each minute to a BigQuery streaming insert into a partitioned table.

D. Average all 720 data points for each measurement each minute, send the average to a Cloud Pub/Sub message, and use Cloud Dataflow and write those results to BigQuery.

5. Your DevOps team is deploying an IoT system to monitor and control environmental conditions in your building. You are using a standard IoT architecture. Which of the following components would you not use?

A. Edge devices

B. Gateways

C. Repeater

D. Cloud platform services

6. In the Google Cloud Platform IoT reference model, which of the following GCP services is used for ingestion?

A. Cloud Storage

B. BigQuery streaming inserts

C. Cloud Pub/Sub

D. Cloud Bigtable

7. A startup is developing a product for autonomous vehicle manufacturers that will enable its vehicles to detect objects better in adverse weather conditions. The product uses a machine learning model built on TensorFlow. Which of the following options would you choose to serve this model?

A. On GKE using TensorFlow Training (TFJob)

B. On Compute Engine using managed instance groups

C. On Edge TPU devices in the vehicles

D. On GPUs in the vehicles

8. In the Google Cloud Platform IoT reference model, which of the following GCP services is used for stream processing?

A. Cloud Storage

B. BigQuery streaming inserts

C. Cloud Pub/Sub

D. Cloud Dataflow

9. You have developed a TensorFlow model using only the most basic TensorFlow operations and no custom operations. You have a large volume of data available for training, but by your estimates it could take several weeks to train the model using a 16 vCPU Compute Engine instance. Which of the following should you try instead?

    A. A 32 vCPU Compute Engine instance

    B. A TPU pod

    C. A GKE cluster using on CPUs

    D. App Engine Second Generation

10. You have developed a machine learning model that uses a specialized Fortran library that is optimized for highly parallel, high-precision arithmetic. You only have access to the compiled code and cannot make any changes to source code. You want to use an accelerator to reduce the training time of your model. Which of the following options would you try first?

    A. A Compute Engine instance with GPUs

    B. A TPU pod

    C. A Compute Engine instance with CPUs only

    D. Cloud Functions

Chapter 11

Measuring, Monitoring, and Troubleshooting Machine Learning Models

---

GOOGLE CLOUD PROFESSIONAL DATA ENGINEER EXAM OBJECTIVES COVERED IN THIS CHAPTER INCLUDE THE FOLLOWING:

3. Operationalizing machine learning models

✓ **3.4 Measuring, monitoring, and troubleshooting machine learning models. Considerations include:**

- Machine learning terminology (e.g., features, labels, models, regression, classification, recommendation, supervised and unsupervised learning, evaluation metrics)

- Impact of dependencies of machine learning models

- Common sources of error (e.g., assumptions about data)

Machine learning has spawned a fundamentally new way to develop services. Rather than manually code logic, machine learning algorithms use data to identify patterns that can be used to predict values, classify objects, and recommend products to customers. The Google Cloud Professional Data Engineer exam expects data engineers to have some familiarity with machine learning. You do not have to be a seasoned machine learning engineer or data scientist, but you should be able to have a technical discussion with one. To that end, this chapter focuses on key concepts in machine learning. The chapter is organized into the following topics:

- Types of machine learning algorithms
- Deep learning
- Engineering machine learning models
- Common sources of error in machine learning models

Machine learning is a broad discipline with many areas of specialization. This chapter will provide a high-level overview to help you pass the Professional Data Engineer exam, but it is not a substitute for studying machine learning using resources designed for that purpose. Additional learning resources are included at the end of the chapter.

Three Types of Machine Learning Algorithms

Machine learning algorithms have traditionally been categorized into supervised, unsupervised, and reinforcement learning algorithms. We will review supervised and unsupervised algorithms and then briefly describe reinforcement learning.

Supervised Learning

Supervised learning algorithms are used to make predictions. When an ML model is used to predict a discrete value, it is known as a *classification model*. When a model is used to predict a continuous value, it is known as a *regression model*.

Classification

Supervised algorithms learn from examples. Consider the data in Table 11.1, which contains information about different kinds of animals. If you wanted to build an ML model to predict whether or not an animal is a mammal, you could use data such as that shown in the table. Supervised learning algorithms use one of the columns of data to represent the value to be predicted. For example, you would use the Mammal column for the predicted value. In ML terminology, this column is called a *label*.

TABLE 11.1   Animal classification data

Animal	Habitat	Live birth	Hair/follicles/fur	Backbone	Mammal
Whale	Aquatic	Yes	Yes	Yes	Yes
Cow	Terrestrial	Yes	Yes	Yes	Yes
Platypus	Semi-aquatic	No	Yes	Yes	Yes
Skates	Aquatic	No	No	No	No
Ray	Aquatic	Yes	No	No	No
Crow	Terrestrial	No	No	Yes	No

The simplest form of a classifier is called a *binary classifier*. A classifier that predicts if an animal is a mammal or not a mammal is an example of a binary classifier. More realistic examples of binary classifiers are those used to predict if a credit card transaction is fraudulent or legitimate, and a machine vision ML model that predicts if a medical image contains or does not contain evidence of a malignant tumor.

A *multiclass classification model* assigns more than two values. In the animal data example, a model that predicts a habitat from the other features is an example of a multiclass classifier. Another example is a classifier that categorizes news stories into one of several categories, such as politics, business, health, and technology.

Some commonly used supervised algorithms are support vector machines (SVMs), decision trees, and logistic regression.

Support vector machines (SVMs) represent instances in a multidimensional space. A simple example is a set of points in a three-dimensional grid. SVMs find a boundary between classes that maximize the distance between those classes. Figure 11.1 shows an example of a plane separating two groups of instances. If a new point were added to the space, it could be categorized based on which side of the plane it is located.

FIGURE 11.1   An example of how SVMs can be used to predict discrete values

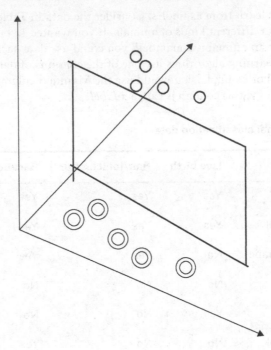

In general, when features are numerical, you can imagine that each instance is a point in an *n*-dimensional space, where *n* is the number of numerical features. Thinking of instances in terms of points located in space makes some useful concepts possible for thinking about machine learning algorithms. A *decision boundary* is a line, plane, or hyperplane that separates instances into categories.

A *decision tree* is a type of supervised learning algorithm that builds a model as a series of decisions about features, such as the amount of a transaction or the frequency of a particular word in a news story. For example, Figure 11.2 shows how a decision tree can be used to predict the type of an animal.

Logistic regression is a statistical model based on the logistic function, which produces an S-shaped curve known as a *sigmoid* and is used for binary classification. Figure 11.3 shows an example of a logistic regression model that can perform binary classification.

FIGURE 11.2   An example decision tree to predict the type of an animal

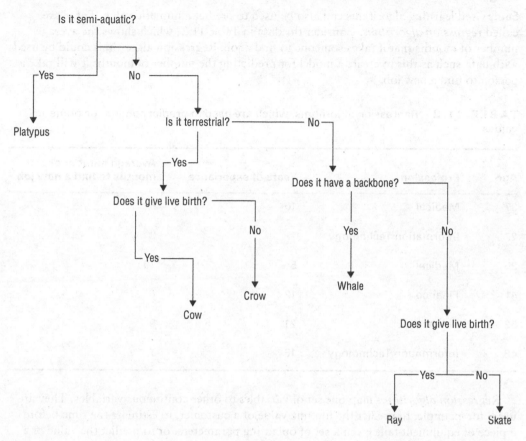

FIGURE 11.3   An example logistic regression function using a sigmoid curve

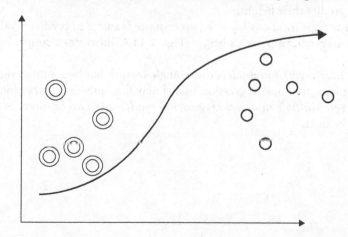

Regression

Supervised learning algorithms can also be used to predict a numeric value. These are called *regression algorithms*. Consider the data in Table 11.2, which shows the average number of months that it takes someone to find a job. Regression algorithms could be used with data such as this to create a model for predicting the number of months it will take a person to find a new job.

TABLE 11.2 Regression algorithms, which are used to predict continuous numeric values

Age	Profession	Years of experience	Average number of months to find a new job
37	Medical	10	5
22	Information Technology	1	3
25	Medical	5	10
41	Finance	12	6
52	Finance	21	9
48	Information Technology	15	7

Regression algorithms map one set of variables to other continuous variables. They are used, for example, to predict the lifetime value of a customer, to estimate the time before a piece of equipment fails given a set of operating parameters, or to predict the value of a stock at some point in the future.

Simple linear regression models use one feature to predict a value, such as using a person's age to predict their height.

Multiple linear regression models use two or more features to predict a value, such as age and gender, to predict a person's height. Figure 11.4 illustrates a simple linear regression problem.

Simple nonlinear regression models use a single feature but fit a non-straight line to data. For example, a nonlinear regression model may fit a quadratic curve (one with one bend in the curve). *Multiple nonlinear regression models* use two or more features and fit a curved line to the data.

FIGURE 11.4   A simple linear regression example

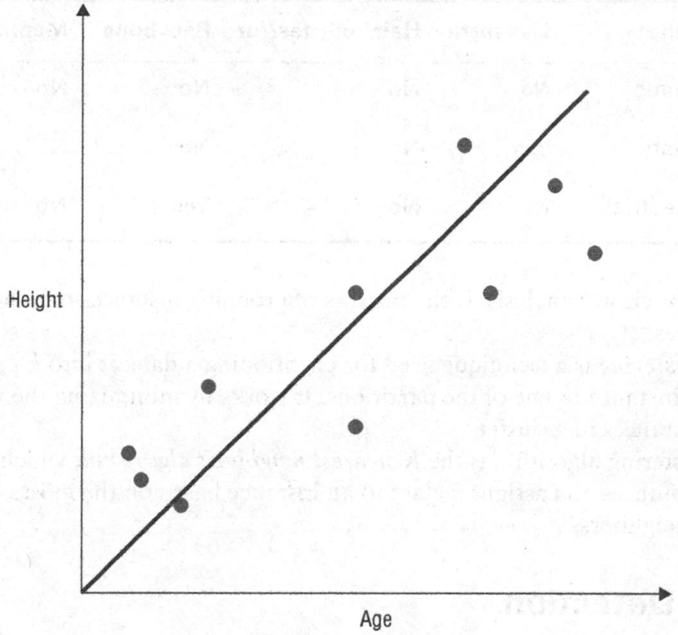

Unsupervised Learning

Unsupervised learning algorithms find patterns in data without using predefined labels. Two commonly used forms of unsupervised learning are *clustering* and *anomaly detection*.

Unsupervised algorithms learn by starting with unlabeled data and then identifying salient features, such as groups or clusters, and anomalies in a data stream. The animal data in Table 11.3 could be used to create clusters of similar animals. Unlike with supervised algorithms, there is no one feature or label that is being predicted. In this example, a clustering algorithm configured to find three groups within the Table 11.3 data may group the records based on habitat—aquatic, semi-aquatic, or terrestrial.

TABLE 11.3   Clustering algorithms, which group similar records together

Animal	Habitat	Live birth	Hair/follicles/fur	Backbone	Mammal	Cluster
Whale	Aquatic	Yes	Yes	Yes	Yes	1
Cow	Terrestrial	Yes	Yes	Yes	Yes	3
Platypus	Semi-aquatic	No	Yes	Yes	Yes	2

TABLE 11.3   Clustering algorithms, which group similar records together *(continued)*

Animal	Habitat	Live birth	Hair/follicles/fur	Backbone	Mammal	Cluster
Skates	Aquatic	No	No	No	No	1
Ray	Aquatic	Yes	No	No	No	2
Crow	Terrestrial	No	No	Yes	No	3

Clustering, or cluster analysis, is the process of grouping instances together based on common features.

K-means clustering is a technique used for partitioning a dataset into *k* partitions and assigning each instance to one of the partitions. It works by minimizing the variance between the instances in a cluster.

Another clustering algorithm is the *K-nearest neighbors algorithm*, which takes as input the *k* closest instances and assigns a class to an instance based on the most common class of the nearest neighbors.

Anomaly Detection

Anomaly detection is the process of identifying unexpected patterns in data. Anomalies come in a variety of forms. *Point anomalies* are outliers, such as a credit card transaction with an unusually large amount. *Contextual anomalies* are unusual patterns given other features of an instance. For example, purchasing a large number of umbrellas in a desert area is contextually anomalous. *Collective anomalies* are sets of instances that together create an anomaly, such as a large number of credit card transactions from different geographic areas in a short period of time.

Anomaly detection algorithms use density-based techniques, such as k-nearest neighbors, cluster analysis, and outlier detection approaches.

Reinforcement Learning

Reinforcement learning is an approach to learning that uses agents interacting with an environment and adapting behavior based on rewards from the environment. This form of learning does not depend on labels.

Reinforcement learning is modeled as an environment, a set of agents, a set of actions, and a set of probabilities of transitioning from one state to another after a particular action is taken. A reward is given after the transition from one state to another following an action.

Reinforcement learning is useful when a problem requires a balance between short-term and long-term trade-offs. It is especially useful in robotics and game playing.

Deep Learning

If you are new to machine learning, you may be surprised not to see deep learning as a type of machine learning. The categorization used here is based on the kinds of problems solved, and that leads to the supervised, unsupervised, and reinforcement learning types. *Deep learning* is not a kind of problem but a way to solve ML problems. It can be used with any of the three types of ML problems.

Deep learning uses the concept of an artificial neuron as a building block. These neurons or nodes have one or more inputs and one output. The inputs and outputs are numeric values. The output of one neuron is used as the input of one or more other neurons. A simple, single neuron model is known as a perceptron and is trained using the perceptron algorithm. By adding layers of neurons on top of each other, you can build more complex, deep networks, such as the one shown in Figure 11.5.

FIGURE 11.5   An example deep learning network

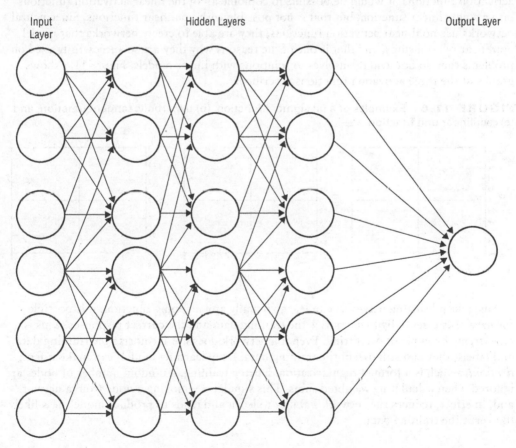

The first layer is the *input layer*. This is where feature values are input to the network. The middle layers are known as *hidden layers*. The final layer is the *output layer*. The output of that node is the output of the model.

When deep learning models are trained, parameters in each node are adjusted so that as values or signals are sent through the network, the correct value is produced by the output node. One of the most important features of neural networks is that they can learn virtually any mapping function, from inputs to outputs.

There are a few neural network and deep learning–specific terms with which you should be familiar. Each neuron in a neural network has a set of inputs and produces an output. The function that maps from inputs to outputs is known as an *activation function*. A commonly used activation function is the *rectified linear unit (ReLU)* function. When a weighted sum of inputs is equal to or less than zero, the ReLU outputs a 0. When the weighted sum of inputs is greater than zero, the ReLU outputs the weighted sum.

Other activation functions include the hyperbolic tangent (TanH) function and the sigmoid function. Both of these are nonlinear functions. If a neural network used linear activation functions, it would be possible to combine all of the linear activation functions into a single linear function, but that is not possible with nonlinear functions. Since neural networks use nonlinear activation functions, they are able to create networks that model nonlinear relationships, and that is one of the reasons why they are so successfully used on problems that do not lend themselves to solutions with linear models. Figure 11.6 shows graphs of the three activation functions described.

FIGURE 11.6   Examples of a (a) sigmoid function, (b) hyperbolic tangent function, and (c) rectilinear unit function

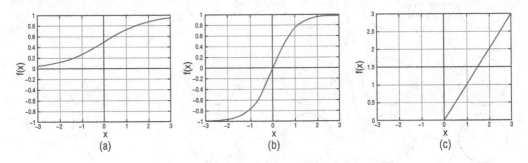

Since deep learning networks can learn virtually any mapping function, it is possible for networks essentially to memorize the training data and the correct responses. This is an extreme example of overfitting. Even if a network does not memorize the training data and labels, they can still overfit the training data. Deep learning models can make use of *dropout*, which is a form of regularization. During training, a random number of nodes are ignored when calculating weighted sums. This simulates removing a node from a network and, in effect, reduces the network's ability to learn and tends to produce models less likely to overfit the training data.

During training, the error of the prediction is propagated through the layers, and the size of the error propagated decreases with each layer. In deep networks, this can lead the *vanishing gradient problem*, which is that early layers in the network take much longer to train. Machine learning researchers have investigated many ways to tackle the vanishing gradient problem, and the most common solution is to use ReLU as an activation function.

Engineering Machine Learning Models

Using machine learning algorithms to build models is only one part of the ML process. Several steps are required to create a model that is ready to go into production. Once it is ready for production, it must be operationalized, which takes into consideration serving models at scale, monitoring model performance, and retraining models.

Model Training and Evaluation

Building an ML model is a multistep process that includes the following:

- Data collection and preparation
- Feature engineering
- Training models
- Evaluating models

You should be familiar with each of these steps for the Professional Data Engineer exam.

Data Collection and Preparation

Data collection is similar to data collection in other pipelines, but preparation is slightly different because the goal of this stage is to map data from its original representation to a representation that is suitable for the machine learning algorithm or algorithms to be used to train ML models.

Machine learning algorithms can have particular requirements. For example, a deep learning network needs to have all features represented numerically. This is not a problem when features are continuous values, such as the total value of a sale or the number of days since the customer last made a purchase. When you are working with categorical values, such as the categories of news stories or the names of sales regions, the categories will need to be mapped to a numeric representation.

One way to map categorical values to numeric values is to assign a distinct number to each categorical value. For example, if you have four sales regions—Northeast, Southeast, Northwest, and Southwest—then you could replace those names with a 1, 2, 3, and 4, respectively. This mapping should be used only when the difference in magnitude between the numbers will not affect the model training. When magnitude between values is important, you should use one-hot encoding.

One-hot encoding maps from a category to a binary representation. Each distinct value is assigned a position in a bit vector. Using the sales regions example, you could assign Northeast to [1,0,0,0], Southeast to [0,1,0,0], Northwest to [0,0,1,0], and Southwest to [0,0,0,1]. This technique is commonly used with neural networks, including deep learning networks.

Another data preparation technique is *bucketing*, which is also called *binning*. Bucketing is the process of converting a continuous feature into ranges values, and it is used to reduce the impact of minor observation errors. For example, an IoT device reporting relative humidity may generate values from 1 to 100. For your purposes, however, you may want to indicate into which of 10 buckets a measurement falls, such as 1 to 10, 11 to 20, 21 to 30, and so forth. A related concept is *quantile bucketing*, which is the process of assigning instances to buckets so that each bucket has approximately the same number of instances. This can be useful when there are many instances in a small range and many instances spread over a large range.

You may also need to address the problem of missing or anomalous data. If data is missing, you might do one of the following:

- Discard the record

- Use a default value, such as 0

- Use an inferred value, such as the average of the previous three values for that attribute in an ordered list of records

You can use similar techniques for values that are out of range, such as values greater than 10 when all values should be between 0 and 10.

Feature Engineering

Feature engineering is the process of identifying which features are useful for building models. It also includes adding new features derived from existing features. For example, a data model that predicts if a customer is going to stop buying from you and start buying from a competitor may use as features the total amount spent in the last 30 days, last 60 days, and last 90 days. Those features by themselves may not be predictive, but the ratio of the amount spent in the last 30 days to the amount spent in the last 60 and last 90 days are two additional features that could be more informative.

Recall from the earlier section "Three Types of Machine Learning Algorithms" that some algorithms find lines, planes, or hyperplanes that separate instances of a particular category. Sometimes it is not possible to find a straight line, plane, or hyperplane that separates all instances using only the original set of features. In that case, you can use cross products of features. There are two types of cross products: cross products of numeric values and cross products that use one-hot encodings.

The cross product of numeric values is the multiple of those values. For example, if a customer purchases $100 worth of goods and it has been 12 days since the previous purchase, the cross product would be 100 × 12, or 1,200. This kind of cross product can represent nonlinear features of a dataset.

A more common form of cross product uses one-hot encodings. For example, a customer may be located in the Northeast sales region, encoded as [1,0,0,0], and their preferred language is English, encoded as [0,0,0,1]. The cross product would be a 16-bit vector with a single 1 and fifteen 0s.

Another part of feature engineering is eliminating features that you know will not be predictive, such as sequentially generated identifiers. You may also want to remove some features that highly correlate with another feature.

You can also use unsupervised learning techniques to help with feature engineering. Clustering and dimension reduction are two such techniques.

Thinking of instances as points in space is also useful when thinking about clustering or grouping of related instances. A *centroid* is the mean or center of a cluster. When you use K-means clustering, you specify k, which is the number of clusters. If k is set to 5, the algorithm will find 5 centroids, one for each cluster. Those cluster centroids could be used as a feature.

Continuing with the spatial reasoning approach, when we think of instances as points in space, we typically think of the space as having one dimension per feature. This can lead to a large number of dimensions, which can then lead to inefficient training. In those cases, it is common to use a *dimension reduction technique* to produce a set of representations of the features with fewer dimensions. *Principal component analysis (PCA)* is a dimension reduction technique.

Sometimes, there are not enough instances to train a model. *Data augmentation* is the practice of introducing artificial instances by transforming existing instances. For example, you might apply transformations to images to create new images for training an object detection model.

Training Models

When a model is trained, it is presented with a training set of data. The algorithm analyzes one instance at a time and then updates the parameters of the model. In some cases, it is more efficient to analyze multiple examples before updating parameters. This is done using batches. *Batches* are instances that are grouped together and processed in a single training iteration. The number of instances in a batch is known as the *batch size*.

Some algorithms can build a model by analyzing a training set once, whereas others, such as neural networks, can benefit from multiple passes over the training data. An *epoch* is the term used to describe one full pass over a training dataset by the training algorithm. With some ML algorithms, you will specify the number of epochs to use. This is an example of a *hyperparameter*, which is a parameter that uses the number of epochs specified instead of having the model learn it.

A simple way to think of neural network training is that the networks make predictions by taking inputs, multiplying each input by a value, called a *weight*, summing those products, and using that result as the input to a function called an *activation function*. The output of the activation function becomes the input to the next layer of the network. The process continues until the output layer emits its output. That output is compared to the expected value. If the output and expected value are different, then the difference is noted. This is known as the error. For example, if a network outputs the value of 0.5 and the expected value was 0.9, then the error is 0.4.

In this example, the network produced a number that was too large, so the weights in the network should be adjusted so that they collectively produce a smaller number. There are many ways that you could adjust weights; the most common method is to adjust weights based on the size of the error. *Backpropagation* is the most widely used algorithm for training neural networks, and it uses the error and the rate of change in the error to calculate weight adjustments. The size of adjustments is partially determined by a hyperparameter called the *learning rate*. Small learning rates can lead to longer training times, but learning rates that are too large can overshoot optimal weights.

Model training often starts with a training dataset and an algorithm to produce a model, but it is also possible to start with a trained model and build on it. This is known as *transfer learning*. This technique is often used in vision and language understanding, where a model built for one purpose, such as recognizing cats in images or identifying the names of persons in text, can be used to build other models, such as a dog recognition model or identifying the names of geographic places in text.

Regularization is a set of techniques for avoiding overgeneralization by penalizing complex models, so training tends to favor less complex, and therefore less likely to overfit, models. Two kinds of regularization are L1 and L2 regularization. *L1 regularization* calculates a penalty based on the absolute value of the weights. *L2 regularization* calculates a penalty based on the sum-of-the-squares of the weights. L1 regularization should be used when you want less relevant features to have weights close to zero. L2 regularization should be used when you want outlier instances to have weights close to zero, which is especially useful when working with linear models.

Evaluating Models

Once you have built a model, you need to assess how well it performs. This process is called *evaluation*. Just as a software engineer should not deploy code that has not been tested, an ML engineer should not deploy models that have not been evaluated.

There are several metrics that are commonly used to evaluate machine learning models.

Accuracy

Accuracy is a measure of how many predictions a model correctly makes. It is usually expressed as a percentage. The formula for calculating accuracy is the total number of correct predictions divided by the total number of predictions. When accuracy is applied to a binary classifier, accuracy is expressed in terms of true positives (TP), true negatives (TN), false positives (FP), and false negatives (FN), formally written as follows:

$$\text{Accuracy} = (TP + TN) / (TP + TN + FP + FN)$$

Precision

Precision is a measure of the true positives divided by the sum of true positives and false positives. This is a measure of how well the model correctly predicts true positives and how often it classifies something as a true positive when it is not, formally written as follows:

$$\text{Precision} = TP / (TP + FP)$$

Recall

Recall is a measure of the number of true positives divided by the sum of true positives and false negatives. This is a measure of how many of actual positive examples were identified, formally written as follows:

$$\text{Recall} = TP / (TP + FN)$$

Recall is also known as sensitivity.

F1 Score

F1 score is a measure that takes into account both precision and recall. Formally, the F1 score is the harmonic mean of precision and recall:

$$\text{F1 Score} = 2 * [(\text{Precision} * \text{Recall}) / (\text{Precision} + \text{Recall})]$$

F1 scores are useful when you want to optimize a model to have balanced precision and recall. It is also a good metric to use when evaluating models built with imbalanced training sets.

The measures can be combined to produce graphical representations of a model's performance. Two common ones are the *receiver operator characteristic (ROC)* and the *area under the curve (AUC)*.

The ROC curve is plotted as the true positive rate versus that false positive rate at varying threshold settings. Figure 11.7 shows an example of an ROC. The AUC is a measure of the area under the ROC curve.

FIGURE 11.7   The ROC is the curved line, and the AUC is the area under that curve line.

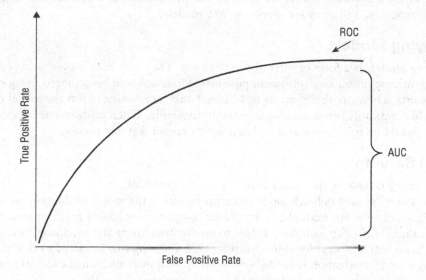

In addition to using these metrics to measure the quality of a model, it is a common practice to compare more complex models with simpler models. This gives some idea of the trade-off between improvement in the model with increased complexity. *Baseline models* are simple models used as a reference point for evaluating more complex models. For example, a linear model may be used as a baseline for a deep learning network. *Linear models* assign a weight to each feature to make predictions and include an offset from the intercept to the origin. For example, the following equation uses four features, four weights, and a bias, which is *b*:

$$y = f1 * w1 + f2 * w2 + f3 * w3 + f4 * w4 + b$$

Baseline models also demonstrate the minimal performance that you should expect from a more complex model.

Operationalizing ML Models

Once models are trained and pass evaluation, they are released into production. The process of releasing and maintaining models is known as *operationalization*. It consists of the following:

- Deploying models
- Serving models
- Monitoring models
- Retraining models

Some of the considerations are the same as you would find when operationalizing any software program, and some are specific to ML models.

Deploying Models

Deploying models is a form of software deployment. They may be deployed using continuous integration/continuous deployment pipelines. Models should be deployed using *canary deployments*. These are deployments to a limited number of users to test the model under real-world conditions before making it generally available. When problems are discovered, a model should be rolled back and replaced with a previous stable version.

Model Serving

Model serving is making the model available to other services.

Models may be used in batch mode when the results of the model evaluation are not needed immediately. For example, an insurance company may have a batch process for paying insurance claims that includes a model to predict fraudulent claims. Since the company already has a batch process for this operation, model serving can be added to that process.

When a model evaluation is needed immediately—for example, when evaluating a credit card transaction—then the model should be available through an API.

You should also consider other factors common to deploying software, including scalability, reliability, and availability. If a model is running in Compute Engine, for example, you could take advantage of managed instance groups to deploy clusters of servers and load-balance across them. If you are deploying containerized models in Kubernetes Engine, you can configure your ML services to scale as needed and within the limits of business requirements. These requirements could include limits on the size of Kubernetes clusters or on the amount of resources allocated to particular ML models.

Monitoring

ML models have the same monitoring requirements as other software but have some specific issues that need to be addressed as well.

Monitoring should include monitoring source systems that provide data to train models. If those source systems are unavailable, it could prevent the updating of models. You should also monitor for changes in the schema of input sources.

Models should be tested in the training and production environments using the same test dataset. Both tests should produce the same results.

Retraining

If the conditions that were in place when a model is trained change, the quality of predictions can degrade. For example, a model used to predict which additional clothing products a customer will buy may need to be updated as the seasons change. Models should be kept up to date to prevent the quality of predictions from degrading.

Monitoring the last update of models can help detect which among them may be at risk of becoming stale.

Common Sources of Error in Machine Learning Models

Machine learning engineers face a number of challenges when building effective models. Problems like overfitting, underfitting, and vanishing gradient can be addressed by adjusting the way that a model is trained. In other cases, the data used to train can be a source of error. Three common problems are as follows:

- Data quality
- Unbalanced training sets
- Bias in training data

These problems can occur together, making it especially important to address them before beginning model training.

Data Quality

Poor-quality data leads to poor models. The same can be said for anything derived from the data, unless steps are taken to compensate for it. Some common data quality problems are as follows:

- Missing data
- Invalid values
- Inconsistent use of codes and categories
- Data that is not representative of the population at large

It is important to analyze a dataset before using it for machine learning. Cloud Dataprep is useful for this stage of machine learning.

Unbalanced Training Sets

Some classification problems have trouble with *unbalanced datasets*, which are datasets that have significantly more instances of some categories than of others. For example, most credit card transactions are legitimate, but a small percentage are fraudulent. Let's assume that 2 percent of credit card transactions are fraudulent, and 98 percent are legitimate. If we trained a model that optimized for accuracy, then the model could predict that all transactions are legitimate, and it would have a 98 percent accuracy rate. However, it would essentially be useless.

You can deal with unbalanced datasets in several ways. You could undersample the majority class, which means that you would use fewer instances of the majority class than you would get with random sampling. Alternatively, you could oversample the minority class, in which case you would get more instances of the minority class than if you had randomly sampled. Another technique is *cost-sensitive learning*, which takes misclassification costs into account. For example, when building a decision tree, the training algorithm could take misclassification cost into account when determining a splitting factor. Hybrid algorithms use multiple strategies to compensate for unbalanced datasets.

In addition to altering how you train with unbalanced datasets, you should be careful to avoid using accuracy as an evaluation metric. A better metric for unbalanced datasets is the F1 score, which is described in the previous section, "Model Training and Evaluation."

Types of Bias

Bias is an overused word in machine learning. Sometimes, bias refers to an offset in a linear equation that adjusts the y-intercept. In other cases, it refers to a prejudice that favors something, but with merit. It is that type of bias that is addressed in this section.

Automation bias is a human bias in favor of decisions made by machines over those made by humans. These can occur as omission errors, which are when humans do not detect something missing from the machine decision. Automation bias can occur as a commission error in which humans do not detect an incorrect decision made by a machine.

Reporting bias occurs when a dataset does not accurately reflect the state of the world. Additional data should be collected until the distribution of data in a dataset reflects the distribution in the population as a whole. A related concept is *selection bias*, which is the process of choosing instances to include in ways that do not mirror the population. Selection bias by a human is a process that can result in reporting bias in a dataset.

Group attribution bias occurs when one generalizes a characteristic of an individual to a group as a whole. *In-group bias* occurs when someone favors a group to which they belong. *Out-group bias* occurs when invalid assumptions are made about a group of which the person is not a member.

When working to avoid bias, you can use tools such as the What If Tool for exploring datasets and detecting possible bias (`https://pair-code.github.io/what-if-tool/`).

Machine learning is a broad domain, spanning theoretical algorithm design to operationalizing production systems. Here are some additional resources that can help you prepare for the Professional Data Engineer exam:

See Andrew Ng's "Machine Learning" course on Cousera; as of this writing, it had been viewed by 2.8 million students: `www.coursera.org/learn/machine-learning`.

See Eric Beck, Shanqing Cai, Eric Nielsen, Michael Salib, and D. Sculley, "The ML Test Score: A Rubric for ML Production Readiness and Technical Debt Reduction," at `https://research.google/pubs/pub46555/`.

For more on supervised ML, see `https://en.wikipedia.org/wiki/Supervised_learning`.

For more on unsupervised ML, see `https://en.wikipedia.org/wiki/Unsupervised_learning`.

For more on reinforcement learning, see `https://en.wikipedia.org/wiki/Reinforcement_learning`.

For more on deep learning, see Jianqing Fan, Cong Ma, and Yiqiao Zhong, see "Selective Overview of Deep Learning," at `https://arxiv.org/pdf/1904.05526.pdf`.

Exam Essentials

Know the three types of machine learning algorithms: supervised, unsupervised, and reinforcement learning.   Supervised algorithms learn from labeled examples. Unsupervised learning starts with unlabeled data and identifies salient features, such as groups or clusters, and anomalies in a data stream. Reinforcement learning is a third type of machine learning algorithm that is distinct from supervised and unsupervised learning. It trains a model by interacting with its environment and receiving feedback on the decisions that it makes.

Know that supervised learning is used for classification and regression.   Classification models assign discrete values to instances. The simplest form is a binary classifier that assigns one of two values, such as fraudulent/not fraudulent, or has malignant tumor/does not have malignant tumor. Multiclass classification models assign more than two values. Regression models map continuous variables to other continuous variables.

Understand how unsupervised learning differs from supervised learning.   Unsupervised learning algorithms find patterns in data without using predefined labels. Three types of unsupervised learning are clustering, anomaly detection, and collaborative filtering. Clustering, or cluster analysis, is the process of grouping instances together based on common features. Anomaly detection is the process of identifying unexpected patterns in data.

Understand how reinforcement learning differs from supervised and unsupervised techniques. Reinforcement learning is an approach to learning that uses agents interacting with an environment and adapting behavior based on rewards from the environment. This form of learning does not depend on labels. Reinforcement learning is modeled as an environment, a set of agents, a set of actions, and a set of probabilities of transitioning from one state to another after a particular action is taken. A reward is given after the transition from one state to another following an action.

Understand the structure of neural networks, particularly deep learning networks. Neural networks are systems roughly modeled after neurons in animal brains and consist of sets of connected artificial neurons or nodes. The network is composed of artificial neurons that are linked together into a network. The links between artificial neurons are called connections. A single neuron is limited in what it can learn. A multilayer network, however, is able to learn more functions. A multilayer neural network consists of a set of input nodes, hidden nodes, and an output layer.

Know machine learning terminology.   This includes general machine learning terminology, such as baseline and batches; feature terminology, such as feature engineering and bucketing; training terminology, such as gradient descent and backpropagation; and neural network and deep learning terms, such as activation function and dropout. Finally, know model evaluation terminology such as precision and recall.

Know common sources of errors, including data-quality errors, unbalanced training sets, and bias.   Poor-quality data leads to poor models. Some common data-quality problems are missing data, invalid values, inconsistent use of codes and categories, and data that is not representative of the population at large. Unbalanced datasets are ones that have significantly more instances of some categories than of others. There are several forms of bias, including automation bias, reporting bias, and group attribution.

Review Questions

You can find the answers in the appendix.

1. You are building a machine learning model to predict the sales price of houses. You have 7 years of historical data, including 18 features of houses and their sales price. What type of machine learning algorithm would you use?

   A. Classifier

   B. Regression

   C. Decision trees

   D. Reinforcement learning

2. You have been asked to build a machine learning model that will predict if a news article is a story about technology or another topic. Which of the following would you use?

   A. Logistic regression

   B. K-means clustering

   C. Simple linear regression

   D. Multiple linear regression

3. A startup is collecting IoT data from sensors placed on manufacturing equipment. The sensors send data every five seconds. The data includes a machine identifier, a timestamp, and several numeric values. The startup is developing a model to identify unusual readings. What type of unsupervised learning technique would they use?

   A. Clustering

   B. K-means

   C. Anomaly detection

   D. Reinforcement learning

4. You want to study deep learning and decide to start with the basics. You build a binary classifier using an artificial neuron. What algorithm would you use to train it?

   A. Perceptron

   B. SVM

   C. Decision tree

   D. Linear regression

5. A group of machine learning engineers has been assigned the task of building a machine learning model to predict the price of gold on the open market. Many features could be used, and the engineers believe that the optimal model will be complex. They want to understand the minimum predictive value of a model that they can build from the data that they have. What would they build?

   A. Multiclass classifier

   B. K clusters

   C. Baseline model

   D. Binary classifier

6. You are preparing a dataset to build a classifier. The data includes several continuous values, each in the range 0.00 to 100.00. You'd like to have a discrete feature derive each continuous value. What type of feature engineering would you use?

    A. Bucketing

    B. Dimension reduction

    C. Principal component analysis

    D. Gradient descent

7. You have been tasked with developing a classification model. You have reviewed the data that you will use for training and testing and realize that there are a number of outliers that you think might lead to overfitting. What technique would you use to reduce the impact of those outliers on the model?

    A. Gradient descent

    B. Large number of epochs

    C. L2 regularization

    D. Backpropagation

8. You have built a deep learning neural network that has 8 layers, and each layer has 100 fully connected nodes. The model fits the training data quite well with an F1 score of 98 out of 100. The model performs poorly when the test data is used, resulting in an F1 score of 62 out of 100. What technique would you use to try to improve performance of this model?

    A. User more epochs

    B. Dropout

    C. Add more layers

    D. ReLU

9. Your team is building a classifier to identify counterfeit products on an e-commerce site. Most of the products on the site are legitimate, and only about 3 percent of the products are counterfeit. You are concerned that, as is, the dataset will lead to a model that always predicts that products are legitimate. Which of the following techniques could you use to prevent this?

    A. Undersampling

    B. Dropout

    C. L1 regularization

    D. AUC

10. You are reviewing a dataset and find that the data is relatively high quality. There are no missing values and only a few outliers. You build a model based on the dataset that has high accuracy, precision, and recall when applied to the test data. When you use the model in production, however, it renders poor results. What might have caused this condition?

    A. Applying L1 regularization

    B. Applying dropout

    C. Reporting bias

    D. Automation bias

Chapter

12

Leveraging Prebuilt Models as a Service

GOOGLE CLOUD PROFESSIONAL DATA
ENGINEER EXAM OBJECTIVES COVERED
IN THIS CHAPTER INCLUDE THE
FOLLOWING:

3. Operationalizing machine learning models

✓ 3.1   Leveraging pre-built ML models as a service.
Considerations include:

- ML APIs (e.g., Vision AI, Speech AI)
- Customizing ML APIs (e.g., AutoML Vision, Auto ML text)
- Conversational experiences (e.g., Dialogflow)

Google Cloud Platform provides several services that use pretrained machine learning models to help developers build and deploy intelligent services more quickly. The services are broadly grouped into the following categories:

- Sight
- Conversation
- Language
- Structured data

These services are available through APIs or Cloud AutoML services. Cloud AutoML uses the APIs to provide easier-to-use services such as AutoML Vision. Those services are described in Chapter 9, "Deploying Machine Learning Pipelines." This chapter focuses on the structure and use of the intelligence APIs.

Sight

GCP has two APIs for working with sight-related intelligence: Vision AI and Video AI. There is some similarity between the services. For example, both services provide functions to identify objects and filter content. In addition, the Video Intelligence AI has video-specific features, such as tracking objects across frames and transcribing audio.

Vision AI

The Vision AI API is designed to analyze images and identify text using OCR, to enable the search of images, and to filter explicit images. Images are sent to Vision AI by specifying a URI path to an image or by sending the image data as Base64-encoded text.

There are three options for calling the Vision AI API: Google-supported client libraries, REST, and gRPC. Google recommends using the client libraries, which are available for C#, Go, Java, Node.js, Python, PHP, and Ruby.

For each image sent to the API, the following operations can be performed:

- Detecting text in images
- Detecting handwriting in images
- Detecting text in PDF, TIFF, and other types of files
- Detecting faces

- Detecting hints for suggested vertices for a cropped region of an image
- Detecting image properties
- Detecting landmarks
- Detecting logos
- Detecting multiple objects
- Detecting explicit content (Safe Search)
- Detecting web entities and pages

The following code from the Google documentation shows an example of detecting labels in a JPEG file using Python and the Vision AI API. The script starts with importing io, os, and vision libraries, and then it instantiates a client. A variable is created to hold the filename (file_name), the file is opened, and the content of the file is read into a variable (content). The content is mapped to a Vision AI API image data structure and then passed to the label detection service, which returns a list of labels. The script ends with printing the list of labels.

```
import io
    import os
    # Imports the Google Cloud client library
    from google.cloud import vision
    from google.cloud.vision import types

    # Instantiates a client
    client = vision.ImageAnnotatorClient()

    # The name of the image file to annotate
    file_name = os.path.abspath('resources/wakeupcat.jpg')

    # Loads the image into memory
    with io.open(file_name, 'rb') as image_file:
        content = image_file.read()
    image = types.Image(content=content)

    # Performs label detection on the image file
    response = client.label_detection(image=image)
    labels = response.label_annotations
    print('Labels:')
    for label in labels:
        print(label.description)
```

Source: https://github.com/GoogleCloudPlatform/python-docs-samples/blob/
master/vision/cloud-client/quickstart/quickstart.py

Other functions in the Vision AI API function in similar ways. For example, to detect landmarks in an image, you could replace the two lines of label detection from the previous snippet with the following:

```
response = client.landmark_detection(image=image)
Landmarks = response.landmark_annotations
```

Vision AI also provides for batch processing. This is done by using the Vision AI API to submit an offline, or asynchronous, request. That process starts a long-running job that does not immediately return a response. When the job completes, annotations are stored in a file in a Cloud Storage bucket. Up to 2,000 images can be submitted with a single API call. Multiple features, such as labels, landmarks, and logos, can be detected with a single API call.

Video AI

Video AI provides models that can extract metadata; identify key persons, places, and things; and annotate video content. This service has pretrained models that automatically recognize objects in videos. Specifically, this API can be used to perform the following:

- Identifying objects, locations, activities, animal species, products, and so on
- Detecting shot changes
- Detecting explicit content
- Tracking objects
- Detecting text
- Transcribing videos

Videos are sent to the Video AI API by specifying a URI path to a video or by encoding the image data as a Base64 text and passing it into the content field of the request when using the REST API. The gRPC client can accept binary data directly. Google recommends embedding Base64-encoded files into a variable in code and passing that variable into API function calls.

The following sample code from the Google documentation shows an example of invoking the Video AI API for label detection. The script imports libraries and creates a video client instance, and it specifies the label detection operation and a URI to the video file to process. The video-processing operation is invoked with a timeout. When the operation finishes, a set of segment labels is returned. For each segment label, the script prints entity descriptions and categories. The script also displays the time range in the video of each segment, along with confidence scores for the predictions.

```
from google.cloud import videointelligence
    video_client = videointelligence.VideoIntelligenceServiceClient()
    features = [videointelligence.enums.Feature.LABEL_DETECTION]
    operation = video_client.annotate_video(
        'gs://cloud-samples-data/video/cat.mp4', features=features)
    print('\nProcessing video for label annotations:')
```

```
    result = operation.result(timeout=120)
    print('\nFinished processing.')

    # first result is retrieved because a single video was processed
    segment_labels = result.annotation_results[0].segment_label_annotations
    for i, segment_label in enumerate(segment_labels):
        print('Video label description: {}'.format(
            segment_label.entity.description))
        for category_entity in segment_label.category_entities:
            print('\tLabel category description: {}'.format(
                category_entity.description))

        for i, segment in enumerate(segment_label.segments):
            start_time = (segment.segment.start_time_offset.seconds +
                          segment.segment.start_time_offset.nanos / 1e9)
            end_time = (segment.segment.end_time_offset.seconds +
                        segment.segment.end_time_offset.nanos / 1e9)
            positions = '{}s to {}s'.format(start_time, end_time)
            confidence = segment.confidence
            print('\tSegment {}: {}'.format(i, positions))
            print('\tConfidence: {}'.format(confidence))
        print('\n')
```

Source: https://github.com/GoogleCloudPlatform/python-docs-samples/blob/
master/video/cloud-client/quickstart/quickstart.py

The Video AI API also includes a service for transcribing audio tracks in a video. That service supports the following:

- Ability to include up to 30 alternative translations for a word, listed in descending order of confidence
- Profanity filtering
- Transcription hints, which are unusual phrases used in the audio that may be otherwise difficult to transcribe
- Audio track detection
- Support for identifying multiple speakers in a video
- Automatically adding punctuation

This API supports several video formats, including MOV, MPEG4, MP4, AVI, and formats that can be decoded from FFmpeg, an open source suite of libraries supporting cross-platform use of video, audio, and multimedia files.

Conversation

Three APIs support conversation services:

- Dialogflow
- Cloud Text-to-Speech API
- Cloud Speech-to-Text API

Dialogflow is used for creating conversational interfaces, whereas the other services can be used for interactive or batch processing that transforms speech to text and text to speech.

Dialogflow

Dialogflow is used for chatbots, interactive voice response (IVR), and other dialogue-based interactions with human speech. This service is based on natural language–understanding technology that is used to identify entities in a conversation and extract numbers, dates, and time, as well as custom entities that can be trained using examples. Dialogflow also provides prebuilt agents that can be used as templates.

A *Dialogflow Agent* is a virtual agent that participates in a conversation. Conversations can be audio or text based. Agents can be configured with the following:

- Agent settings for language options and behavior control
- Intents for categorizing a speaker's, or end user's, intentions
- Entities to identify and extract data from interactions
- Knowledge to parse documents, such as FAQs
- Integrations for applications that process end-user interactions
- Fulfillment to connect the service to integrations

A key component of Dialogflow is intents. *Intents* categorize a speaker's intention for a single statement in a conversation. The speaker's statement is assigned an intent classification. For example, a question about the weather may be mapped to a forecast intent, which would then be configured to process that statement to extract information, such as the time and location of the desired weather forecast. Intents are structures that include the following:

- Training phrases
- Actions
- Parameters to support extraction
- Responses to provide the speaker with answers

Dialogflow also supports contexts to model natural language contexts. *Contexts* help match intent. Contexts are used to analyze anaphora, which are words that refer to other entities. For example, in the phrase "they went to the store," *they* refers to some group of people presumably mentioned earlier in the conversation. Context is used to resolve that reference to the entities mentioned earlier.

Dialogflow is accessible through REST, gRPC, and client libraries. Client libraries are available for C#, Go, Java, Node.js, PHP, Python, and Ruby.

Cloud Text-to-Speech API

GCP's Cloud Text-to-Speech API maps natural language texts to human-like speech. The API works with more than 30 languages and has more than 180 humanlike voices. The service is based on speech synthesis technology called WaveNet, which is a deep generative model developed by DeepMind.

The API works with plain text or Speech Synthesis Markup Language (SSML) and audio files, including MP3 and WAV files. To generate speech, you call a synthesize function of the API. That function returns a Base64-encoded string that has to be decoded into an audio file. Linux users can use the Base64 command-line utility to perform that conversion.

One of the parameters needed for synthesis is a voice specification. The voices vary by language, gender, and, in some languages, dialects, such as French as spoken in France versus French as spoken in Canada. Supported languages include Arabic, Czech, Danish, Dutch, English, French, Greek, Hindi, Hungarian, Indonesian Italian, Korean, Mandarin Chinese, Norwegian, Polish, Portuguese, Swedish, Turkish, and Vietnamese. These are available in standard voice or WaveNet voice, which is higher quality. WaveNet synthesis costs more than standard.

Another synthesis parameter is the device specification. Cloud Text-to-Speech can optimize the generated speech for particular devices, such as wearable devices, headphones, small Bluetooth speakers, and large home entertainment devices.

Cloud Speech-to-Text API

The Cloud Speech-to-Text API is used to convert audio to text. The service is based on deep learning technology and supports 120 languages and variants. The service can be used for transcribing audio files as well as for supporting voice-activated interfaces. Cloud Speech-to-Text automatically detects the language being spoken. This feature is in beta, but it is already available for a large number of languages. Generated text can be returned as a stream of text or in batches as a text file.

The service has several pretrained models that are optimized for particular kinds of speech, including the following:

- Voice commands
- Phone calls
- Video
- Default voice for other domains

Other features of the service include noise handling; automatic punctuation; speaker diarization, which identifies the speaker of each utterance; and the ability to handle streaming audio.

Google has several recommendations for best results. Audio should be captured at a sampling rate of 16,000 Hz or higher. Use a lossless codec, such as FLAC or LINEAR16, for recording and transmitting audio. When recording multiple individuals, use a separate channel for each individual. If the speakers are using a specialized vocabulary, use word and phrase hints to improve accuracy. Finally, for short queries or commands, use the StreamingRecognize function with single_utterance set to true.

The Cloud Speech-to-Text API can be called using client libraries. You can also use the gcloud ml speech command from the command line.

Language

GCP has two APIs to support language processing: a translation and an analysis service.

Translation

Google's translation technology is available for use through the Cloud Translation API. The basic version of this service, Translation API Basic, enables the translation of texts between more than 100 languages. An advanced API, Translation API Advanced, is also available that supports customization for domain-specific and context-specific terms and phrases.

Translation API Basic can translate text and HTML content between languages. It can automatically detect languages, so users do not need to specify the source language. The basic API supports REST but not gRPC. Translation API Basic has several client APIs, including ones for C#, Go, Java, Python, Node.js, PHP, and Ruby.

Translation API Advanced has most of the features of Translation API Basic, plus support for glossaries, batch translations, custom models, and a gRPC API.

The following code example shows a Python function for translating a text. This function begins by importing libraries and creating an instance of a translation client. Next, the text is decoded to UTF-8 if needed. The call to the function translate_client.translate does the actual translation to the target languages, which are passed as parameters. The function finishes with printing results of the translation and related data.

```
def translate_text(target, text):
    """Translates text into the target language.

    Target must be an ISO 639-1 language code.
    See https://g.co/cloud/translate/v2/translate-reference#supported_languages
    """
    from google.cloud import translate_v2 as translate
    translate_client = translate.Client()

    if isinstance(text, six.binary_type):
        text = text.decode('utf-8')
```

```
# Text can also be a sequence of strings, in which case this method
# will return a sequence of results for each text.
result = translate_client.translate(
    text, target_language=target)

print(u'Text: {}'.format(result['input']))
print(u'Translation: {}'.format(result['translatedText']))
print(u'Detected source language: {}'.format(
    result['detectedSourceLanguage']))
```

Source: https://github.com/GoogleCloudPlatform/python-docs-samples/blob/master/translate/cloud-client/snippets.py

Batch translations are also supported by Translation API Advanced for HTML and plain-text files. Source files are located in a Cloud Storage bucket, and output files are written to a different Cloud Storage bucket.

In addition to translating text, Google Cloud Language provides an API for text analysis, referred to as Natural Language.

Natural Language

The Natural Language API uses machine learning–derived models to analyze texts. With this API, developers can extract information about people, places, events, addresses, and numbers, as well as other types of entities. The service can be used to find and label fields within semi-structured documents, such as emails. It also supports sentiment analysis.

The Natural Language API has a set of more than 700 general categories, such as sports and entertainment, for document classification. It can also be combined with other machine learning services, like Speech-to-Text API, to extract information from audio content.

For more advanced users, the service performs syntactic analysis that provides parts of speech labels and creates parse trees for each sentence. Users of the API can specify domain-specific keywords and phrases for entity extraction and custom labels for content classification. It is also possible to use spatial structure understanding to improve the quality of entity extraction. For example, you may be able to take advantage of the layout of text to improve custom entity extraction.

The API can support working with up to 5,000 classification labels and 1 million documents. Documents may be up to 10 MB in size.

The Natural Language API includes functions to perform a variety of text analysis operations, including the following:

- Identifying entities
- Analyzing sentiment associated with each entity
- Analyzing sentiment of the overall text
- Generating syntactic analysis, including parts-of-speech tags and syntax trees
- Classifying documents into categories

Here are some example high-level content categories:

- Arts and Entertainment
- Autos and Vehicles
- Business and Industrial
- Computer and Electronics
- Food and Drink
- Games
- Health
- People and Society
- Law and Government
- News

Each of these high-level categories have finer-grained categories as well; here is a small set of examples:

- /Business & Industrial/Chemicals Industry/Plastics & Polymer
- /Computers & Electronics/Computer Hardware/Computer Drives & Storage
- /Food & Drink/Food/Grains & Pasta
- /Games/Table Games/Billiards
- /Health/Medical Facilities & Services/Medical Procedures
- /People & Society/Kids & Teens/Children's Interests
- /Law & Government/Public Safety
- /News/Business News/Financial Markets News

For applications that could benefit from text classification and information extraction, the Natural Language API can provide general functionality and pretrained models that can be customized for domain-specific texts.

Structured Data

GCP has three machine learning services for structured data: AutoML Tables, which was described earlier in Chapter 9, and the Recommendations AI API and Cloud Inference API.

Recommendations AI API

The *Recommendations AI API* is a service for suggesting products to customers based on their behavior on the user's website and the product catalog of that website. The service builds a recommendation model specific to the site. Recommendations AI is currently in beta.

The product catalog contains information on products that are sold to customers, such as names of products, prices, and availability. End-user behavior is captured in logged events, such as information about what customers search for, which products they view, and which products they have purchased.

The two primary functions of the Recommendations AI API are ingesting data and making predictions. Data is ingested using either the `catalogItems.create` function for individual items or the `catalogItems.import` method for bulk loading. Google recommends providing as much detail as possible and updating the product catalog information as needed to keep the model up to date with the actual product catalog.

Customer activity records also need to be ingested. Users events that are useful for the recommendation service include clicking a product, adding an item to a shopping cart, and purchasing a product. Customer events can be recorded using a JavaScript pixel placed on the website to record actions, using the Google Tag Manager to tag and record events, or sending events directly to the Recommendations AI API using the `userEvents.write` method.

In addition to loading data, users of the Recommendations AI API will need to specify some configuration parameters to build a model, including recommendation types. Recommendation types are one of the following:

Others you may like: These are additional items that the customer is most likely to purchase.

Frequently bought together: These are items often purchased during the same session.

Recommended for you: This predicts the next product with which the customer is likely to engage.

Recently viewed: This is simply a set of catalog IDs of products with which the customer has recently interacted.

You will also need to specify an optimization objective. There are three such objectives:

Click-through rate (CTR): This is the default optimization, and it maximizes the likelihood that the user engages the recommendation.

Revenue per order: This is the default objective for the frequently bought together recommendation type, and it cannot be used with other types.

Conversion rate: This rate maximizes the likelihood that the user purchases the recommended product.

The Recommendations AI API tracks metrics to help you evaluate the performance of recommendations made. The metrics include the following:

Total revenue from all recorded purchase events: This is the sum of all revenue from all purchases.

Recommender-engaged revenue: This is the revenue from purchase events that include at least one recommended item.

Recommendation revenue: This is the revenue from recommended items.

Average order value (AOV): This is the average of orders from all purchase events.

Recommender-engaged AOV: This is the average value of orders that include at least one recommended item.

Click-through rate: This is the number of product views from a recommendation.

Conversion rate: This is the number of times that an item was added to a cart divided by the total number of recommendations.

Revenue from recommendations: This is the total revenue from all recommendations.

The Recommendations AI API is tailored for interacting with customers on an e-commerce site. The Cloud Inference API is a machine learning service designed to help analyze time-series data.

 The Recommendations AI API is in beta release as of this writing.

Cloud Inference API

Many activities and operations of interest to business can be captured in time-series data. This can include tracking the number of customers visiting a website or physical store in some time period, collecting sensor measurements from manufacturing machinery, and collecting telemetry data from fleet vehicles. The Cloud Inference API provides real-time analysis of time-series data. The Cloud Inference API is currently in alpha.

The Cloud Inference API provides for processing time-series datasets, including ingesting from JSON formats, removing data, and listing active datasets. It also supports inference queries over datasets, including correlation queries, variation in frequency over time, and probability of events given evidence of those events in the dataset.

 The Cloud Inference API is in alpha release as of this writing.

Exam Essentials

Understand the functionality of the Vision AI API.   The Vision AI API is designed to analyze images and identify text, enable the search of images, and filter explicit images. Images are sent to the Vision AI API by specifying a URI path to an image or by sending the image data as Base64-encoded text. There are three options for calling the Vision AI API: Google-supported client libraries, REST, and gRPC.

Understand the functionality of the Video Intelligence API.   The Video Intelligence API provides models that can extract metadata; identify key persons, places, and things; and annotate video content. This service has pretrained models that automatically recognize objects in videos. Specifically, this API can be used to identify objects, locations, activities, animal species, products, and so on, and detect shot changes, detect explicit content, track objects, detect text, and transcribe videos.

Understand the functionality of Dialogflow.   Dialogflow is used for chatbots, interactive voice response (IVR), and other dialogue-based interactions with human speech. The service is based on natural language–understanding technology that is used to identify entities in a conversation and extract numbers, dates, and time, as well as custom entities that can be trained using examples. Dialogflow also provides prebuilt agents that can be used as templates.

Understand the functionality of the Cloud Text-to-Speech API. GCP's Cloud Text-to-Speech API maps natural language texts to human-like speech. The API works with more than 30 languages and has more than 180 humanlike voices. The API works with plain-text or Speech Synthesis Markup Language (SSML) and audio files, including MP3 and WAV files. To generate speech, you call a synthesize function of the API.

Understand the functionality of the Cloud Speech-to-Text API. The Cloud Speech-to-Text API is used to convert audio to text. This service is based on deep learning technology and supports 120 languages and variants. The service can be used for transcribing audios as well as for supporting voice-activated interfaces. Cloud Speech-to-Text automatically detects the language being spoken. Generated text can be returned as a stream of text or in batches as a text file.

Understand the functionality of the Cloud Translation API. Google's translation technology is available for use through the Cloud Translation API. The basic version of this service, Translation API Basic, enables the translation of texts between more than 100 languages. There is also an advanced API, Translation API Advanced, which supports customization for domain-specific and context-specific terms and phrases.

Understand the functionality of the Natural Language API. The Natural Language API uses machine learning–derived models to analyze texts. With this API, developers can extract information about people, places, events, addresses, and numbers, as well as other types of entities. The service can be used to find and label fields within semi-structured documents, such as emails. It also supports sentiment analysis. The Natural Language API has a set of more than 700 general categories, such as sports and entertainment, for document classification. For more advanced users, the service performs syntactic analysis that provides parts of speech labels and creates parse trees for each sentence. Users of the API can specify domain-specific keywords and phrases for entity extraction and custom labels for content classification.

Understand the functionality of the Recommendations AI API. The Recommendations AI API is a service for suggesting products to customers based on their behavior on the user's website and the product catalog of that website. The service builds a recommendation model specific to the site. The product catalog contains information on products that are sold to customers, such as names of products, prices, and availability. End-user behavior is captured in logged events, such as information about what customers search for, which products they view, and which products they have purchased. There are two primary functions the Recommendations AI API: ingesting data and making predictions.

Understand the functionality of the Cloud Inference API. The Cloud Inference API provides real-time analysis of time-series data. The Cloud Inference API provides for processing time-series datasets, including ingesting from JSON formats, removing data, and listing active datasets. It also supports inference queries over datasets, including correlation queries, variation in frequency over time, and probability of events given evidence of those events in the dataset.

Review Questions

You can find the answers in the appendix.

1. You are building a machine learning model to analyze unusual events in traffic through urban areas. Your model needs to distinguish cars, bikes, pedestrians, and buildings. It is especially important that the model be able to identify and track moving vehicles. Video will be streamed to your service from cameras mounted on traffic lights. What GCP service would you use for the object analysis and tracking?

    A. Cloud Video Intelligence API

    B. Cloud Vision API

    C. Cloud Inference API

    D. Cloud Dataflow

2. A startup is building an educational support platform for students from ages 5–18. The platform will allow teachers to post assignments and conduct assessments. Students will be able to upload content, including text and images. The founder of the startup wants to make sure that explicit images are not uploaded. What GCP service would you use?

    A. Cloud Video Intelligence API

    B. Cloud Vision API

    C. Cloud Inference API

    D. Cloud Dataprep

3. You are using the Cloud Vision API to detect landmarks in images. You are using the batch processing with asynchronous requests. The source images for each batch is in a separate Cloud Storage bucket. There are between 1 and 5,000 images in each bucket. Each batch request processes one bucket. All buckets have the same access controls. Sometimes, the operations succeed and sometimes they fail. What could be the cause of the errors?

    A. Cloud Video Intelligence API

    B. Some buckets have more than 2,000 images.

    C. There is an issue with IAM settings.

    D. Images have to be uploaded directly from a device, not a Cloud Storage bucket.

4. Your team is building a chatbot to support customer support. Domain experts from the customer support team have identified several kinds of questions that the system should support, including questions about returning products, getting technical help, and asking for product recommendations. You will use Dialogflow to implement the chatbot. What component of Dialogflow will you configure to support the three question types?

    A. Entities

    B. Fulfillments

    C. Integrations

    D. Intents

5. A developer asks for your help tuning a text-to-speech service that is used with a health and wellness app. The app is designed to run on watches and other personal devices. The sound quality is not as good as the developer would like. What would you suggest trying to improve the quality of sound?

    A. Change the device specification to optimize for a wearable device

    B. Change from standard to WaveNet-quality voice

    C. Encode the text in Base64

    D. Options A and B

    E. Options A, B, and C

6. A developer asks for your help tuning a speech-to-text service that is used to transcribe text recorded on a mobile device. The quality of the transcription is not as good as expected. The app uses LINEAR16 encoding and a sampling rate of 12,000 Hz. What would you suggest to try to improve the quality?

    A. Use WaveNet option

    B. Increase the sampling rate to at least 16,000 Hz

    C. Use Speech Synthesis Markup Language to configure conversion parameters

    D. Options A and B

7. You have developed a mobile app that helps travelers quickly find sites of interest. The app uses the GCP Translation service. The initial release of the app used the REST API, but adoption has grown so much that you need higher performance from the API and plan to use gRCP instead. What changes do you need to make to the way that you use the Translation service?

    A. Use the WaveNet option

    B. Use Translation API Basic

    C. Use Translation API Advanced

    D. Option A or B

8. You are experimenting with the GCP Translation API. You have created a Jupyter Notebook and plan to use Python 3 to build a proof-of-concept system. What are the first two operations that you would execute in your notebook to start using the Translation API?

    A. Import Translation libraries and create a translation client

    B. Create a translation client and encode text in UTF-8

    C. Create a translation client, and set a variable to TRANSLATE to pass in as a parameter to the API function call

    D. Import Translation libraries, and set a variable to TRANSLATE to pass in as a parameter to the API function call

9. You have been hired by a law firm to help analyze a large volume of documents related to a legal case. There are approximately 10,000 documents ranging from 1 to 15 pages in length. They are all written in English. The lawyers hiring you want to understand who is mentioned in each document so that they can understand how those individuals worked together. What functionality of the Natural Language API would you use?

   A. Identifying entities

   B. Analyzing sentiment associated with each entity

   C. Analyzing sentiment of the overall text

   D. Generating syntactic analysis

10. As a founder of an e-commerce startup, you are particularly interested in engaging with your customers. You decide to use the GCP Recommendations AI API using the "others you may like" recommendation type. You want to maximize the likelihood that users will engage with your recommendations. What optimization objective would you choose?

    A. Click-through rate (CTR)

    B. Revenue per order

    C. Conversation rate

    D. Total revenue

11. Your e-commerce startup has been growing rapidly since its launch six months ago. You are starting to notice that the rate of revenue growth is slowing down. Your board of directors is asking you to develop a strategy to increase revenue. You decide to personalize each customer's experience. One of the ways in which you plan to implement your strategy is by showing customers products that they are likely to interact with next. What recommendation type would you use?

    A. Others you may like

    B. Frequently bought together

    C. Recommended for you

    D. Recently viewed

12. You work for an enterprise with a large fleet of vehicles. The vehicles are equipped with several sensors that transmit data about fuel utilization, speed, and other equipment operating characteristics. The chief of operations has asked you to investigate the feasibility of building a predictive maintenance application that can help identify breakdowns before they occur. You decide to prototype an anomaly detection model as a first step. You want to build this as quickly as possible, so you decide to use a machine learning service. Which GCP service would you use?

    A. Cloud Inference API

    B. AutoML Tables

    C. AutoML Vision

    D. Cloud Anomaly Detection API

Appendix

Answers to Review Questions

Chapter 1: Selecting Appropriate Storage Technologies

1. **D.** The correct answer is D. Stackdriver Logging is the best option because it is a managed service designed for storing logging data. Neither Option A nor B is as good a fit because the developer would have to design and maintain a relational data model and user interface to view and manage log data. Option C, Cloud Datastore, would not require a fixed data model, but it would still require the developer to create and maintain a user interface to manage log events.

2. **B.** The correct answer is B. Cloud Dataflow is a stream and batch processing service that is used for transforming data and processing streaming data. Option A, Cloud Dataproc, is a managed Hadoop and Spark service and not as well suited as Cloud Dataflow for the kind of stream processing specified. Option C, Cloud Dataprep, is an interactive tool for exploring and preparing data sets for analysis. Option D, Cloud SQL, is a relational database service, so it may be used to store data, but it is not a service specifically for ingesting and transforming data before writing to a database.

3. **A.** The correct answer is A, Cloud Storage, because the data in the files is treated as an atomic unit of data that is loaded into RStudio. Options B and C are incorrect because those are document databases and there is no requirement for storing the data in semi-structured format with support for fully indexed querying. Also, MongoDB is not a GCP service. Option D is incorrect because, although you could load CSV data into a Bigtable table, the volume of data is not sufficient to warrant using Bigtable.

4. **C.** The correct answer is C, BigQuery, which is a managed analytical database service that supports SQL and scales to petabyte volumes of data. Options A and B are incorrect because both are used for transaction processing applications, not analytics. Option D is incorrect because Bigtable does not support SQL.

5. **C.** The correct answer is C. Bigtable is the best storage service for IoT data, especially when a large number of devices will be sending data at short intervals. Option A is incorrect, because Cloud SQL is designed for transaction processing at a regional level. Option B is incorrect because Cloud Spanner is designed for transaction processing, and although it scales to global levels, it is not the best option for IoT data. Option D is incorrect because there is no need for indexed, semi-structured data.

6. **C.** The correct answer is C because the requirements call for a semi-structured schema. You will need to search players' possessions and not just look them up using a single key because of the requirement for facilitating trading. Option A is not correct. Transactional databases have fixed schemas, and this use case calls for a semi-structured schema. Option B is incorrect because it does not support indexed lookup, which is needed for searching. Option D is incorrect. Analytical databases are structured data stores.

7. **A.** The correct answer is A. Cloud Bigtable using the HBase API would minimize migration efforts, and since Bigtable is a managed service, it would help reduce operational costs. Option B is incorrect. Cloud Dataflow is a stream and batch processing service, not a database. Options C and D are incorrect. Relational databases are not

likely to be appropriate choices for an HBase database, which is a wide-column NoSQL database, and trying to migrate from a wide-column to a relational database would incur unnecessary costs.

8. C. The correct answer is C because the FASTQ files are unstructured since their internal format is not used to organize storage structures. Also, 400 GB is large enough that it is not efficient to store them as objects in a database. Options A and B are incorrect because a NoSQL database is not needed for the given requirements. Similarly, there is no need to store the data in a structured database like Cloud Spanner, so Option D is incorrect.

9. D. The correct answer is D because the output is structured, will be queried with SQL, and will retrieve a large number of rows but few columns, making this a good use case for columnar storage, which BigQuery uses. Options A and B are not good options because neither database supports SQL. Option C is incorrect because Cloud Storage is used for unstructured data and does not support querying the contents of objects.

10. B. The correct answer is B. Bigtable is a wide-column NoSQL database that supports semi-structured data and works well with datasets over 1 TB. Options A, D, and C are incorrect because they all are used for structured data. Option D is also incorrect because Cloud SQL does not currently scale to 40 TB in a single database.

11. B. The correct answer is B, write data to a Cloud Pub/Subtopic, which can scale automatically to existing workloads. The ingestion process can read data from the topic and data and then process it. Some data will likely accumulate early in every minute, but the ingestion process can catch up later in the minute after new data stops arriving. Option A is incorrect; Cloud Dataflow is a batch and stream processing service—it is not a message queue for buffering data. Option C is incorrect; Cloud SQL is not designed to scale for ingestion as needed in this example. Option D is incorrect; Cloud Dataprep is a tool for cleaning and preparing datasets for analysis.

12. A. The correct answer is A. This is a good use case for key-value databases because the value is looked up by key only and the value is a JSON structure. Option B is incorrect. Analytical databases are not a type of NoSQL database. Option C is not a good option because wide-column databases work well with larger databases, typically in the terabyte range. Option D is incorrect because the data is not modeled as nodes and links, such as a network model.

13. D. The correct answer is D. A document database could store the volume of data, and it provides for indexing on columns other than a single key. Options A and C do not support indexing on non-key attributes. Option B is incorrect because analytical is not a type of NoSQL database.

14. B. The correct answer is B; OLAP data models are designed to support drilling down and slicing and dicing. Option A is incorrect; OLTP models are designed to facilitate storing, searching, and retrieving individual records in a database. Option C is incorrect; OLAP databases often employ denormalization. Option D is incorrect; graph data models are used to model nodes and their relationships, such as those in social networks.

15. C. The correct answer is C. Cloud Spanner is the only globally scalable relational database for OLTP applications. Options A and B are incorrect because Cloud SQL will not meet the scaling requirements. Options B and D are incorrect because Cloud Datastore does not support OLTP models.

Chapter 2: Building and Operationalizing Storage Systems

1. B. The correct answer is B, Cloud SQL Proxy. Cloud SQL Proxy provides secure access to Second Generation instances without you having to create allow lists or configure SSL. The proxy manages authentication and automatically encrypts data. Option A is incorrect because TLS is the successor to SSL. It can be used to encrypt traffic, but it would require the DBA to manage certificates, so it is not as good an answer as Option B. Option C is incorrect; using an IP address does not ensure encryption of data. Option D is incorrect; there is no such thing as an auto-encryption feature in Cloud SQL.

2. B. The correct answer is B. Maintenance could be occurring. Maintenance on read replicas is not restricted to the maintenance window of the primary instance or to other windows, so it can occur anytime. That would make the read replica unavailable. Option A is incorrect because a database administrator would have to promote a read replica, and the problem stated that there is no pattern detected and DBAs were not performing database operations. Option C is incorrect; backups are not performed on read replicas. Option D is incorrect; Cloud SQL instances do not fail over to a read replica.

3. B. The correct answer is B, 65%. Options A and C are not recommended levels for any Cloud Spanner configuration. Option D, 45%, is the recommend CPU utilization for a multi-regional Cloud Spanner instance.

4. A. The correct answer is A. Since each node can store 2 TB, it will require at least 10 nodes. Options B and D are incorrect because they are more nodes than needed. Answer C is incorrect; five is not sufficient for storing 20 TB of data.

5. B. The correct answer is B. The database is multitenant, so each tenant, or customer, will query only its own data, so all that data should be in close proximity. Using customer ID first accomplishes this. Next, the sensor ID is globally unique, so data would be distributed evenly across database storage segments when sorting based on sensor ID. Since this is time-series data, virtually all data arriving at the same time will have timestamps around the same time. Using a timestamp early in the key could create hotspots. Using sensor ID first would avoid hotspots but would require more scans to retrieve customer data because multiple customers' data would be stored in each data block.

6. D. The correct answer is D. Description can be represented in a string. Health consists of three properties that are accessed together, so they can be grouped into an entity. Possessions need a recursive representation since a possession can include sets of other possessions. Options A and B are incorrect; character state requires multiple properties, and so it should not be represented in a single string. Option B is also incorrect, because possessions are complex objects and should not be represented in strings. Option C is incorrect; description is an atomic property and does not need to be modeled as an entity.

7. D. The correct answer is D—no entities are returned. The query requires a composite index, but the question stated that no additional indexes were created. All other answers are wrong because querying by property other than a key will only return entities found in an index.

8. A. The correct answer is A. Setting shorter TTLs will make keys eligible for eviction sooner, and a different eviction policy may lead to more evictions. For example, switching from an eviction policy that evicts only keys with a TTL to a policy that can evict any key may reduce memory use.

9. A. The correct answer is A. Regional storage is sufficient for serving users in the same geographic location and costs less than multi-regional storage. Option B is incorrect because it does not minimize cost, and there is no need for multi-regional storage. Options C and D are incorrect because Nearline and Coldline are less expensive only for infrequently accessed data.

10. C. The correct answer is C. A data retention policy will ensure that files are not deleted from a storage bucket until they reach a specified age. Options A and B are incorrect because files can be deleted from Coldline or multi-regional data unless a data retention policy is in place. Option D is incorrect because a lifecycle policy will change the storage type on an object but not prevent it from being deleted.

11. B. The correct answer is B, installing the Stackdriver Monitoring agent. This will collect application-level metrics and send them to Stackdriver for alerting and charting. Option A is incorrect because Stackdriver Logging does not collect metrics, but you would install the Stackdriver Logging agent if you also wanted to collect database logs. Option C is incorrect; Stackdriver Debug is for analyzing a running program. Option D is incorrect; by default, you will get only instance metrics and audit logs.

12. C. The correct answer is C. The queries are likely scanning more data than needed. Partitioning the table will enable BigQuery to scan only data within a partition, and clustering will improve the way column data is stored. Option A is incorrect because BigQuery organizes data according to table configuration parameters, and there is no indication that queries need to order results. Option B is incorrect; Standard SQL dialect has more SQL features but none of those are used. Also, it is unlikely that the query execution plan would be more efficient with Standard SQL. Option D is incorrect; it would actually require more data to be scanned and fetched because BigQuery uses a columnar data storage model.

13. A. The correct answer is A. You probably did not include the pseudo-column _PARTITIONTIME in the WHERE clause to limit the amount of data scanned. Options B and D are incorrect; the format of the file from which data is loaded does not affect the amount of data scanned. Option C is incorrect; the distinction between active and long-term data impacts only the cost of storage, not the execution of a query.

14. D. The correct answer is D. Stackdriver Monitoring collects metrics, and the slot metrics are the ones that show resource utilization related to queries. Options A and B are incorrect; logging does not collect the metrics that are needed. Option C is incorrect because CPU utilization is not a metric associated with a serverless service like BigQuery.

15. A. The correct answer is A. Since the files have sequential names, they may be loading in lexicographic order, and this can create hotspots. Option B is incorrect; the volume of data, not the format, will determine upload speed. Option C is incorrect; there should be no noticeable difference between the command-line SDK and the REST API. Option D is incorrect; writing to multi-regional storage would not make the uploads faster.

Chapter 3: Designing Data Pipelines

1. C. The correct answer is C, Cloud Pub/Sub, which is a scalable, managed messaging queue that is typically used for ingesting high-volume streaming data. Option A is incorrect; Cloud Storage does not support streaming inserts, but Cloud Pub/Sub is designed to scale for high-volume writes and has other features useful for stream processing, such as acknowledging and processing a message. Option B is incorrect; Cloud SQL is not designed to support high volumes of low-latency writes like the kind needed in IoT applications. Option D is incorrect; although BigQuery has streaming inserts, the database is designed for analytic operations.

2. B. The correct answer is B. The transformation stage is where business logic and filters are applied. Option A is incorrect; ingestion is when data is brought into the GCP environment. Option C is incorrect—that data should be processed, and problematic data removed before storing the data. Answer D is incorrect; by the analysis stage, data should be fully transformed and available for analysis.

3. B. The correct answer is B. Cloud Dataflow supports Python and is a serverless platform. Option A is incorrect because, although it supports Python, you have to create and configure clusters. Option C is incorrect; Cloud Spanner is a horizontally scalable global relational database. Option D is incorrect; Cloud Dataprep is an interactive tool for preparing data for analysis.

4. C. The correct answer is C; the new code disabled message acknowledgments. That caused Cloud Pub/Sub to consider the message outstanding for up to the duration of the acknowledgment wait time and then resend the message. Options A and B are incorrect; changing the subscription or topic IDs would cause problems but not the kind described. Option D is incorrect because the type of subscription does not influence whether messages are delivered multiple times.

5. A. The correct answer is A; messages may be delivered multiple times and therefore processed multiple times. If the logic were not idempotent, it could leave the application in an incorrect state, such as that which could occur if you counted the same message multiple times. Options B and C are incorrect; the order of delivery does not require idempotent operations. Option D is incorrect; the time between messages is not a factor in requiring logic to be idempotent.

6. A. The correct answer is A; a sliding window would have the data for the past four minutes. Option B is incorrect because tumbling windows do not overlap, and the requirement calls for using the last four messages so the window must slide. Options C and D are not actually names of window types.

7. A. The correct answer is A; you should use CloudPubSubConnector and Kafka Connect. The connector is developed and maintained by the Cloud Pub/Sub team for this purpose. Option B is incorrect since this is a less direct and efficient method. Option C requires maintaining a service. Option D is incorrect because there is no such service.

8. C. The correct answer is C. Use Cloud Dataflow templates to specify the pattern and provide parameters for users to customize the template. Option A is incorrect since this would require users to customize the code in the script. Options B and D are incorrect because Cloud Dataproc should not be used for this requirement. Also, Option D is incorrect because there are no Cloud Dataproc templates.

9. D. The correct answer is D. You should create an ephemeral cluster for each job and delete the cluster after the job completes. Option A is incorrect because that is a more complicated configuration. Option B is incorrect because it keeps the cluster running instead of shutting down after jobs complete. Option C is incorrect because it keeps the clusters running after the jobs complete.

10. A. The correct answer is A, Cloud Composer, which is designed to support workflow orchestration. Options B and C are incorrect because they are both implementations of the Apache Beam model that is used for executing stream and batch processing program. Option D is incorrect; Cloud Dataproc is a managed Hadoop and Spark service.

11. B. The correct answer is B. The data could be stored in Cloud Bigtable, which provides consistent, scalable performance. Option A is incorrect because Cloud Storage is an object storage system, not a database. Option C is incorrect, since Cloud Datastore is a document-style NoSQL database and is not suitable for a data warehouse. Option D is incorrect; Cloud Dataflow is not a database.

12. D. The correct answer is D. With change data capture, each change is a source system captured and recorded in a data store. Options A, B, and C all capture the state of source systems at a point in time and do not capture changes between those times.

Chapter 4: Designing a Data Processing Solution

1. B. The correct answer is B. IoT sensors can write data to a Cloud Pub/Sub topic. When a message is written, it can trigger a Cloud Function that runs the associated code. Cloud Functions can execute the Python validation check, and if the validation check fails, the message is removed from the queue. Option A is incorrect; Cloud Storage is not a for streaming ingestion. Option C is incorrect because BigQuery is an analytical database that could be used in later stages but not during ingest. Answer D is incorrect because Cloud Storage is not a suitable choice for high-volume streaming ingestion, and BigQuery is not suitable for storing data during ingestion.

2. A. The answer is A. This scenario calls for full control over the choice of the operating system, and the application is moving from a physical server so that it is not containerized. Compute Engine can run the application in a VM configured with Ubuntu 14.04 and the additional packages. Option B is incorrect because the application is not containerized (although it may be modified to be containerized). Option C is incorrect because the application cannot run in one of the language-specific runtimes of App Engine Standard. Option D is incorrect because the Cloud Functions product runs code in response to events and does not support long-running applications.

3. B. The correct answer is B, Kubernetes Engine, because the application will be designed using containerized microservices that should be run in a way that minimizes DevOps overhead. Option A is incorrect because Compute Engine would require more DevOps work to manage your own Kubernetes Cluster or configure managed instance groups to run different containers needed for each microservice. Options C and D are incorrect because App Engine Standard and Cloud Functions do not run containers.

4. C. The correct answer is C. Mean time between failure is used for measuring reliability. Options A and B are incorrect because they are related to utilization and efficiency but unrelated to reliability. Option D is incorrect, since mean time to recovery is used as a metric for restoring service after an outage. Mean time to recovery is important and would likely be included in negotiations, but it is not used as a measure of reliability.

5. C. The correct answer is C. A global load balancer is needed to distribute workload across multiple regions. Options A and B are incorrect because there is no indication in the requirements that object storage or a message queue is required. Option D is incorrect because there is no indication that a hybrid cloud is needed that would necessitate the use of a VPN or direct connect option.

6. A. The correct answer is A. The purpose of this queue is to list rooms on the platform so that as long each message is processed at least once, the room will appear in the listing. Options B and D are incorrect because processing does not have to be exactly once because listing a room is an idempotent operation. For example, adding a listing of the same room twice does not change the listing since duplicate listing messages are dropped by the application. Option C is incorrect because no ordering is implied in the requirements.

7. C. The correct answer is C. Machines of different types have different failure characteristics and therefore will have their own models. Option A is incorrect; randomly distributing messages will mix metrics from different types of machines. Option B is incorrect because identifiers in close proximity are not necessarily from machines of the same type. Option D is incorrect; routing based on timestamp will mix metrics from different machine types.

8. B. The correct answer is B. The description of independent services, using SOAP, and deployed on virtual machines fits the definition of an SOA architecture. Answer A is incorrect; since there are multiple components, it is not a monolithic architecture. Option C could be a possibility, but it is not the best fit since the application uses SOAP and is deployed on VMs. Option D is incorrect because the application does not use a serverless deployment.

9. C. The correct answer is C. Microservices would allow each function to be deployed independently in its own container. Option A is incorrect; a monolithic architecture would make the update problems worse. Option B is incorrect, because hub-and-spoke is a message broker pattern. Option D is incorrect; pipelines are abstractions for thinking about workflows—they are not a type of architecture.

10. A. The correct answer is A. An assessment should be done first. Options B, C, and D are all parts of a data warehouse migration plan but come after the assessment phase.

11. A. The correct answer is A. Data sources, the data model, and ETL scripts would all be included. Options B and D are incorrect; technical requirements do not include information about business sponsors and their roles. Option C is incorrect because more than data sources should be included.

12. C. The correct answer is C. The company is incurring an opportunity cost because if they had migrated to a modern cloud-based data warehouse, the team would have had opportunities to develop new reports. Options A and B are incorrect; although they are kinds of expenses, they require expenditure of funds to be either a capital or an operating cost. Option D is not a type of cost.

13. C. The correct answer is C. Denormalization reduces the number of joins required and nested, and repeated fields can be used to store related data in a single row. Option A is incorrect; BigQuery does use Colossus, but that does not change the number of joins. Option B is incorrect; BigQuery does use columnar storage, but that does not affect the number of joins. Option D is incorrect; federated storage allows BigQuery to access data stored outside of BigQuery, but it does not change the need for joins.

14. D. The correct answer is D. Prioritizing low-risk use cases will allow the team to make progress on migrating while minimizing the impact if something goes wrong. Options A, B, and C are incorrect because they do not give priority to minimizing risk; other factors are prioritized in each case.

15. B. The correct answer is B. The set of tasks to verify a correct data warehouse migration include verifying schemas, data loads, transformations, and queries, among other things. Option A is incorrect because more is required than just verifying schemas and data loads. Options C and D are incorrect; the backlog of feature requests is important but not relevant to verifying the migration.

Chapter 5: Building and Operationalizing Processing Infrastructure

1. C. The correct answer is C. A managed instance group will provision instances as required to meet the load and stay within the bounds set for the number of instances. Option A is incorrect; Cloud Functions are for event-driven processing, not continually monitoring metrics. Option B is incorrect because it is not the most efficient way to scale instances. Option D is incorrect, since the requirements call for Compute Engine instances, not a Hadoop/Spark cluster.

2. B. The correct answer is B. Autohealing uses a health check function to determine whether an application is functioning correctly, and if not, the instance is replaced. Option A is incorrect; autoscaling adds or removes instances based on instance metrics. Option C is incorrect; redundancy is a feature of instance groups, but it is not the mechanism that replaces poorly performing nodes. Option D is incorrect; eventual consistency describes a model for storing writes in a way that they will eventually be visible to all queries.

3. C. The correct answer is C, defining an instance template using the gcloud compute instance-templates create command. Options A and B are incorrect, since there is no need to create each instance individually. Option D is incorrect. cbt is the command-line utility for working with Cloud Bigtable.

4. A. The correct answer is A; Kubernetes uses pods as the smallest deployable unit. Options B and C are incorrect because deployments and replicas are Kubernetes abstractions, but they are not used as the mechanism for logically encapsulating containers. Option D is incorrect, since pods and containers are not synonymous.

5. A. The correct answer is A; the kubectl scale deployment command specifying the desired number of replicas is the correct command. Option B is incorrect, since this would set the number of replicas to 2. Options C and D are incorrect; there is no gcloud containers scale deployment command.

6. C. The correct answer is C, using two clusters with one dedicated for receiving write operations and the other responsible for batch processing. Options A and B are incorrect because you do not specify the operating system used in Bigtable. Option D is incorrect; a cluster cannot have multiple node pools in the same zone.

7. D. The correct answer is D; the number of master nodes cannot be changed. Options A and B are incorrect; there is no --num-masters or --add-masters parameter in the gcloud dataproc clusters update command. Option C is incorrect; cbt is the command-line utility for working with Cloud Bigtable.

8. A. The correct answer is A; the total CPU utilization by the deployment is used as the basis for making scaling decisions. Option B is incorrect; some CPUs in the cluster may be used by other deployments. Options C and D are incorrect because the decision is based on overall utilization, not any individual pod.

9. A. The correct answer is A; app.yaml is the configuration file used to specify the runtime. Option B is incorrect; queue.yaml is used to configure task queues. Option C is incorrect; dispatch.yaml is used to override routing rules. Option D is incorrect; cron.yaml is used to schedule tasks.

10. B. The correct answer is B. The --max-instances parameter limits the number of concurrently executing function instances. Option A is incorrect; --limit is not a parameter used with function deployments. Option C is incorrect; labels are not used to control configuration of functions. Option D is incorrect; language-specific parameters are not used to configure Cloud Functions.

11. D. The correct answer is D; data access logs have a 30-day data retention period. Options A, B, and C are incorrect; they all have 400-day retention periods.

12. C. The correct answer is C; Stackdriver Monitoring collects performance metrics. Option A is incorrect; Stackdriver Debugger is used to inspect the state of running code. Option B is incorrect; Stackdriver Logging is used to collect semi-structured data about events. Option D is incorrect; Stackdriver Trace is used to collect information about the time required to execute functions in a call stack.

13. B. The correct answer is B; Stackdriver Logging is used to collect semi-structured data about events. Option A is incorrect; Stackdriver Debugger is used to inspect the state of running code. Option C is incorrect; Stackdriver Monitoring is used to collect performance metrics. Option D is incorrect; Stackdriver Trace is used to collect information about the time required to execute functions in a call stack.

14. D. The correct answer is D; Stackdriver Trace is used to collect information about the time required to execute functions in a call stack. Option A is incorrect; Stackdriver Debugger is used to inspect the state of running code. Option B is incorrect; Stackdriver Logging is used to collect semi-structured data about events. Option C is incorrect; Stackdriver Monitoring is used to collect performance metrics.

15. B. The correct answer is B; maxNumWorkers specifies the maximum number of instances that can be run for a Cloud Dataflow pipeline. Option A is incorrect; numWorkers is the initial number of workers. Option C is incorrect; streaming specifies whether streaming mode is enabled. Option D is incorrect; it is not an actual parameter.

Chapter 6: Designing for Security and Compliance

1. C. The correct answer is C. This is an appropriate use case for primitive roles because there are few users working in a development environment, not production, and working with data that does not contain sensitive information. In this case, there is no need for fine-grained access controls. Options A and B are incorrect because they would require more administration, and fine-grained access controls are not needed. Option D is incorrect; access control lists are used with Cloud Storage resources and should be used only when roles are insufficient.

2. A. The correct answer is A; the iam.roles.create permission is needed to create custom roles. Option B is incorrect; it is not an actual permission. Options C and D are incorrect; they are examples of fictitious roles, not permissions.

3. C. The correct answer is C. A service account associated with the application should have the roles/storage.objectCreator assigned to it. Options A and B are incorrect; those are identities associated with actual users. Option D is incorrect; access control lists can be assigned to a bucket, but roles are assigned to identities.

4. B. The correct answer is B. Policy A applies to all departments, so it should be assigned at the organizational level. Policies B, C, D, and E are department specific and apply to all projects, so they can be inherited by projects when they are assigned to the departments folder. Option A is incorrect, policy A belongs at the organizational level, and each of the other policies should apply only to one department's folder. Option C is incorrect; the policies should not be assigned to individual projects. Option D is incorrect because policy A belongs at the organization level, and policies B, C, D and E belong at the folder level.

5. A. The correct answer is A. Since the application needs to read the contents of only the object, the `roles/storage.objectViewer` role is sufficient. Options B grants more permissions than needed. Option C would not allow the application to read the object. Option D has more permissions than needed.

6. B. The correct answer is B. The `roles/BigQuery.jobUser` role allows users to run jobs, including queries. Option A is incorrect because that would grant more permissions than needed. Option C is incorrect; it would allow access to table and dataset metadata. Option D is incorrect; there is no such role.

7. D. Option D is correct. You do not need to configure any settings to have data encrypted at rest in GCP. Options B, C, and D are all incorrect because no configuration is required.

8. A. The correct answer is A: AES256 or AES128 encryption. Option B is incorrect, but it is a strong encryption algorithm and could be used to encrypt data. Option C is incorrect; DES is a weak encryption algorithm that is easily broken by today's methods. Option D is incorrect; Blowfish is strong encryption algorithm designed as a replacement for DES and other weak encryption algorithms.

9. B. The correct answer is B; the data encryption key is encrypted using a key encryption key. Option A is incorrect; there are no hidden locations on disk that are inaccessible from a hardware perspective. Option C is incorrect; keys are not stored in a relational database. Option D is incorrect; an elliptic curve encryption algorithm is not used.

10. C. The correct answer is C. The risk analysis job assesses the likelihood that redacted data can be re-identified. Option A and Option B are incorrect. The results are not measures of counts or percent of times that data is redacted. Option D is incorrect. The result is not a list of InfoType patterns detected.

11. B. The correct answer is B. You should prioritize the order of scanning, starting with the most at-risk data. Option A is incorrect; identifying InfoTypes to use comes later. Option C is incorrect; a risk analysis is done after inspection. Option D is incorrect; that is not the recommended first step.

12. C. The correct answer is C; COPPA is a regulation that governs the collection of data from children under the age of 13. Option A is incorrect; HIPAA is a healthcare regulation. Option B is incorrect; GDPR is a European Union privacy regulation. Option D is incorrect; FedRAMP applies to cloud providers supplying services to U.S. federal agencies.

Chapter 7: Designing Databases for Reliability, Scalability, and Availability

1. C. The correct answer is C. Hotspots occur when a row-key design does not adequately distribute read/write load for a given query pattern. Option A is incorrect; Cloud Bigtable does not have secondary indexes. Option B is incorrect; Cloud Bigtable does not use partition keys. Options D is incorrect; the hotspots are not caused by failure to use a read replica, although using a read replica may reduce the load on the nodes with hotspots.

2. **A.** The correct answer is A. This table should be designed as a tall and narrow one with a single dataset in each row. Option B is incorrect because starting a row-key with the date and hour will lead to hotspotting. Option C is incorrect, since changing the start time will not change the parts of the design that make querying by ranges more difficult than they need to be. Option D is incorrect; the structure of rows should be changed from wide to narrow.

3. **B.** The correct answer is B. The only way to achieve strong consistency in Cloud Bigtable is by having all reads routed from a single cluster and using the other replicas only for failover. Option A is incorrect; Cloud Bigtable does not have secondary indexes. Option C is incorrect; moving tablets does not impact read consistency. Option D is incorrect; a poor row-key design can impact performance but not consistency.

4. **C.** The correct answer is C; the STRUCT data type is used to store ordered type fields, and this is the closest to a document structure. Option A is incorrect; all elements of an array are of the same data type, but items in a document may consist of different data types. Option B is incorrect because although a document could be represented in a string, it does not provide field-level access to data like a STRUCT does. Option D is incorrect; JSON is not a valid data type in Cloud Spanner.

5. **B.** The correct answer is B. Since the problematic queries involved joins of hierarchically related tables, interleaving the data of the tables could improve join performance. Option A is incorrect; Cloud Bigtable, not Cloud Spanner, uses replicated clusters. Option C is incorrect; the STORING clause is used to create indexes that can answer queries using just the index, and that would not address the join performance problem. Option D is incorrect; an execution plan might help you understand the cause of a performance problem, but it would not on its own improve query performance.

6. **A.** The correct answer is A. By using a hash of the natural key, you will avoid hotspotting and keeping the natural key data in the table will make it available to users. Option B is incorrect because Cloud Spanner automatically creates splits based on load, and if the database performance is adversely affected, then splitting is no longer sufficient to address the problem. Option C is incorrect; interleaved tables reduce the number of I/O operations performed when retrieving related data. Option D is incorrect; adding more secondary indexes will not change the hotspotting pattern of the primary index.

7. **C.** The correct answer is C. The likely cause is that you are using a UUID generator that uses time or other sequential values at the start of the key. Options A and B are incorrect because secondary indexes are not related to primary key hotspots. Option D is incorrect; UUIDs have a fixed, constant length, so the size of the string used to store them should not need to be increased.

8. **E.** The correct answer is E. There should be a small number of tall and narrow tables. Option A is incorrect because it does not include one table for equities and one for bonds. Option B is incorrect; this would lead to many small tables rather than fewer large tables. Option C is incorrect because it is missing the use of tall and narrow tables. Option D is incorrect because it includes Option B and not Option C.

9. D. The correct answer is D. The enterprise is building a data lake for large volumes of data that is not yet organized for analytics. Options A and B are incorrect because there is no information about how data will be queried or what data would be included. Option C is incorrect because Cloud Spanner is a global, horizontally scalable relational database designed for transaction processing.

10. A. The correct answer is A. Since data is being written to partitions, and the data modeler did not specify a timestamp or integer column as the partition key, it must be partitioned based on ingestion time. Options B and C are incorrect because they require a column to be specified that has a partition value. Option D is incorrect; clustered tables are not a form of partitioning.

11. B. The correct answer is B. FLOAT64 is not a supported cluster column type. Answer A is incorrect; the table is not external because data is loaded into BigQuery. Option C is incorrect; there is no such thing as a FLOAT64 partition type. Option D is incorrect; clustering keys do not need to be integers or timestamps—they can be data, Bool, geography, INT64, numeric, string, or timestamp.

12. C. The correct answer is C; comma-separated values, Avro, and newline-delimited JSON are supported. Options A and B are both missing at least one supported format. Option D is incorrect because the Parquet format is not supported in Google Drive, although it is supported in Cloud Storage.

Chapter 8: Understanding Data Operations for Flexibility and Portability

1. B. The correct answer is B. Cloud Catalog is designed to help data consumers understand what data is available, what it means, and how it can be used. Option A is incorrect; Cloud Composer is a managed workflow service. Option C is incorrect; Cloud Dataprep is used to prepare data for analysis and machine learning. Option D is incorrect; Data Studio is used for reporting and visualizing data.

2. A. The correct answer is A. Cloud Composer is a managed workflow service based on Apache Airflow. Option B is incorrect; Data Catalog is a metadata management service. Option C is incorrect; Cloud Dataprep is used to prepare data for analysis and machine learning. Option D is incorrect; Data Studio is used for reporting and visualizing data.

3. C. The correct answer is C. Cloud Dataprep is used to prepare data for analysis such as this, as well as machine learning. Option A is incorrect; Cloud Composer is a managed workflow service based on Apache Airflow. Option B is incorrect; Cloud Catalog is a metadata management service. Option D is incorrect; Data Studio is used for reporting and visualizing data.

4. D. The correct answer is D. Data Studio is the GCP tool to use for reporting and visualizing data. Option A is incorrect; Cloud Composer is a managed workflow service based on Apache Airflow. Option B is incorrect; Data Catalog is a metadata management service. Option C is incorrect; Cloud Dataprep is used to prepare data for analysis and machine learning.

5. B. The correct answer is B. CSV and JSON are the only formats supported for exporting compressed data from Cloud Dataprep. Option A is incorrect because it does not include JSON. Options C and D are incorrect because they include AVRO.

6. B. The correct answer is B. Extracted data sources work with a static snapshot of a dataset, which gives better performance than live connection data sources. Option A is incorrect because extracted connections are faster than live connections. Option C is incorrect because there is no compound connection. Option D is incorrect because blended connections are designed to query data from up to five data sources.

7. A. The correct answer is A. Live connections will update data in reports automatically. Option B is incorrect; you would need to update the extracted dataset manually in order to refresh data. Option C is incorrect; there is no such thing as a compound connection. Option D is incorrect because it includes extracted connections.

8. B. The correct answer is B. `conda install` or `pip install` can be run from within a Jupyter Notebook. Option A is incorrect; they do not have to go outside Jupyter Notebook to install the library. Option C is incorrect; the Linux package manager is not used to install Python libraries. Option D is incorrect; Python libraries are shared using Python-specific package managers, so users do not have to work with source code directly.

9. C. The correct answer is C. Cloud Composer is a workflow orchestration service that can perform all the tasks mentioned. Option A is incorrect; Cloud Dataprep is a service for preparing data for analysis and machine learning. Option B is incorrect; Cloud Dataproc is a managed Hadoop/Spark service. Option D is incorrect; Data Studio is a reporting and visualization tool.

10. B. The correct answer is B. Cloud Datalab is a managed Jupyter Notebook service that supports interactive analysis and ad hoc programming. Option A is incorrect; Cloud Dataproc is a managed Hadoop/Spark service. Option C is incorrect; Cloud Composer is a workflow orchestration service based on Apache Airflow. Option D is incorrect; Data Studio is a reporting and visualization tool.

Chapter 9: Deploying Machine Learning Pipelines

1. A. The correct answer is A. Cloud Storage is an object storage system that makes no assumptions about the internal structure of objects. Option B is incorrect; Cloud Spanner is a globally scalable relational database and provides for highly structured data schemas. Option C is incorrect; Cloud Dataprep is a tool for preparing data for analysis and machine learning but not for storage. Option D is incorrect; Cloud Pub/Sub is used for streaming ingestion, not batch ingestion.

2. D. The correct answer is D. Cloud Pub/Sub is designed for this kind of streaming ingestion, and it can scale to meet the expected growth in the number of sensors. Option A is incorrect; Cloud Storage is used for batch ingestion, not streaming ingestion. Option B is incorrect; the data will eventually be stored in Cloud Bigtable, but it should be written to a Cloud Pub/Sub topic that can buffer the data prior to having the data consumed by a Cloud Dataflow service. Option C is incorrect; BigQuery Streaming Insert should be used only when the streaming data is being stored in BigQuery.

3. B. The correct answer is B. The data is available in a data lake, so there is no need to ingest the data. Thus, the next step should be to understand the distribution and quality of data using Cloud Dataprep. Option A is incorrect; the data has already been ingested into a data lake. Options C and D are incorrect; the data should not be transformed until it has been evaluated.

4. B. The correct answer is B. Validation is used to assess the quality of model predictions when tuning hyperparameters. Option A is incorrect; training data is used to learn parameters of the model, not hyperparameters. Option C is incorrect; test data is used to measure the quality of a model after hyperparameters have been tuned. Option D is incorrect; there is no such thing as hyperparameter data.

5. A. The correct answer is A. The first thing to do is to explore the data to understand any quality issues and to perform feature engineering. Feature engineering can reduce the amount of time needed to train a model and improve performance. Option B is incorrect; visualizations of model evaluation metrics will not help with either the time to build or the quality of the model. Option C is incorrect; cross-validation is useful for evaluation, not for reducing the time to build a model. Option D is incorrect; it is too early to tune hyperparameters, and feature engineering should occur before that.

6. B. The correct answer is B. This is an example of underfitting. If the model performs poorly across multiple algorithms and when evaluating using the same data that was used to train the model, then that is underfitting and it is likely caused by too little training data. Option A is incorrect; the model is not overfitting the training data because, if that were the case, the accuracy would be high when evaluated with the training data. Option C is incorrect; the opposite is the likely cause of underfitting. Option D is incorrect; tenfold cross-validation for evaluation is a reasonable technique for evaluating the quality of a machine learning model.

7. C. The correct answer is C. The model is overfitting the training data, so adding a penalty factor using L1 and L2 regularization will reduce overfitting. Option A is incorrect; using confusion matrices will not change the model. Option B is incorrect; regularization is done during training, not evaluating. Option D is incorrect because it is not the best answer. Tuning hyperparameters may improve evaluation metrics but not as effectively as applying regularization.

8. B. The correct answer is B. There has likely been a change in sales patterns since the model was trained, and the model should be retrained with data that more closely reflects the actual distribution of sales data today. Option A is incorrect; if a model were overfitting, it would perform poorly initially, as well as several months later. Option C is incorrect; performance metrics, such as CPU utilization, will not help diagnose a quality of recommendation problem. Option D is incorrect; if the model were underfitting, it would perform poorly initially, as well as several months later.

9. A. The correct answer is A. The problem calls for analyzing images, not videos, and the task is identifying objects so one of the Object Detection services should be used. Since the data is used for analysis and long-term decision making, detection does not need to be performed at the edge. Option B is incorrect because analysis does not require a real-time result to make a decision at the edge. Options C and D are incorrect because this application uses images, not videos.

10. C. The correct answer is C. AutoML Tables is designed to build machine learning models using structured data. It also automates common tasks such as feature engineering. Options A and B are incorrect because they require machine learning knowledge to use. Option D is incorrect; AutoML Natural Language is used to classify texts and other natural language artifacts, not structured data.

11. C. The correct answer is C. BigQuery ML provides access to machine learning algorithms from within SQL, and there is no need to move the data from BigQuery. Also, BigQuery builds models faster than AutoML, so BigQuery ML best fits the requirements. Options A and B are incorrect because they require some machine learning experience to use. Option D is incorrect because AutoML Tables can take an hour or more to build, so C is a better option.

12. B. The correct answer is B. Spark MLib includes association rules for frequent pattern mining. Option A is incorrect; Cloud Dataflow is a stream and batch processing service. Options C and D are incorrect; BigQuery ML and AutoML Tables do not include algorithms for frequent pattern mining.

Chapter 10: Choosing Training and Serving Infrastructure

1. C. The correct answer is C. The requirements call for high-precision arithmetic and parallelization, so that indicates using a GPU. There is a small amount of data, and you want to work with it interactively, so a single machine with a GPU will suffice. Options A and B are incorrect because TPUs do not support high-precision arithmetic. Also, Option A requires more resources than needed for a small dataset. Option D is incorrect because this is an interactive workload, so there is no need for the high availability provided by a managed instance group and there are more resources allocated than needed for this workload.

2. D. The correct answer is D. The TPU strategy meets all of the requirements of synchronous training on TPUs. The other strategies all apply to GPUs and/or CPUs and therefore do not meet the requirements.

3. C. The correct answer is C. This is an example of a latency problem that might be resolved by serving the model closer to where the data is generated. Options A and B are incorrect because overfitting and underfitting are problems with model training not serving. Option D is incorrect; there is no indication that the volume of data processed is a problem.

4. B. The correct answer is B. The raw data does not need to be stored and with limited bandwidth; it is best to minimize the amount of data transmitted, so sending just the average is correct. Also, because the network connection is sometimes unreliable, you should use Cloud Dataflow to implement stream processing logic, such as handling late-arriving data and inserting default values for missing data. Option A is incorrect because it sends too much data. Option C is incorrect because it sends too much data and stores it directly in BigQuery without preprocessing for missing values and other business logic. Option D is incorrect because it stores data directly in BigQuery without preprocessing for missing values and other business logic.

5. C. The correct answer is C. Repeaters are used in networks to boost signal strength. There is no indication that this is needed, and in any case, that is a network implementation choice and not a comparable part of the IoT architecture of the other components. Options A, B, and D are all part of the standard IoT architecture.

6. C. The correct answer is C. Cloud Pub/Sub is a globally scalable messaging queue that can ingest large volumes of data and buffer it for other services. Option A is incorrect; Cloud Storage is not used for streaming high-volume data into GCP; it is used for batch uploads. Option B is incorrect; BigQuery streaming inserts are not used for ingestion in the reference model. Option D is incorrect; Cloud Bigtable is not used for ingestion.

7. C. The correct answer is C. Edge TPU is designed for inferencing on edge devices. Since the model is used to help autonomous vehicles improve their ability to track objects in adverse weather conditions, low latency is essential. Options A and B are incorrect because they serve the model from a central service rather than at the edge. Option D is incorrect; GPUs are used when training models, not when using them for inference.

8. D. The correct answer is D. Cloud Dataflow is a stream and batch processing service based on Apache Beam. Option A is incorrect; Cloud Storage is not used for stream processing—it is an object storage service. Option B is incorrect; BigQuery streaming inserts are for storing data in BigQuery partitioned tables. Option C is incorrect; Cloud Pub/Sub is used for ingestion, not stream processing.

9. B. The correct answer is B. This is a typical use case for TPUs because the model is built on TensorFlow using only basic operations and no custom operations, so TPUs are an option. The long training time on CPUs indicate that this is a good option for TPUs. Option A is incorrect; this would only cut the training time in half, assuming a linear speedup. Option C is incorrect because only CPUs are used and not TPUs. Option D is incorrect; App Engine is used for scalable web applications and not used for training models.

10. A. The correct answer is A. A Fortran library optimized for highly parallel, high-precision arithmetic that runs on GPUs would be a good option for training this model. Option B is incorrect; TPUs do not support high-precision arithmetic. Option C is not the best choice because it would not be as performant as a GPU-based solution, but it could be a backup option in case the Fortran library did not function on the GPU. Option D is incorrect; Cloud Functions do not run Fortran code and are not suitable to running workloads such as this.

Chapter 11: Measuring, Monitoring, and Troubleshooting Machine Learning Models

1. **B.** The correct answer is B. Sales price is a continuous value, so a regression algorithm would be used to predict it. Option A is incorrect; classifiers are used to predict discrete categories. Option C is incorrect; decision trees are used for classification. Option D is incorrect; reinforcement learning is a type of machine learning that learns from the environment.

2. **A.** The correct answer is A. The question is asking about building a binary classifier, so a logistic regression would work. Option B is incorrect; K-means clustering is an unsupervised learning algorithm, and this is a supervised learning problem. Options C and D are incorrect because simple linear regression and multiple linear regression are used for predicting continuous values.

3. **C.** The correct answer is C. The data being sent is time-series data, and they are trying to detect anomalies. Option A is incorrect; this problem does not call for partitioning the dataset. Option B is incorrect because K-means is a clustering algorithm, and this problem does not call for partitioning a dataset. Option D is incorrect; there is no learning from the environment.

4. **A.** The correct answer is A. The perceptron algorithm is used to train a binary classifier based on artificial neurons. Options B and C are incorrect; those algorithms can build classifiers but not ones based on an artificial neuron. Option D is incorrect; linear regression is used to predict a continuous value.

5. **C.** The correct answer is C. A baseline model is the simplest model, and it is used as a reference point. Options A and B are incorrect; this is a regression problem, not a classification problem. Option D is incorrect because the problem does not call for partitioning the data.

6. **A.** The correct answer is A. Bucketing maps continuous values to ranges, for example, from 0.00 to 10.00. Each bucket is a discrete value of the derived feature. Option B is incorrect because the problem does not call for reducing dimensions. Option C is incorrect because principal component analysis is a type of dimension reduction. Option D is incorrect; gradient descent is a technique used when training a model.

7. **C.** The correct answer is C. L2 regularization calculates a penalty based on the sum-of-the-squares of the weights. L1 regularization should be used when you want less relevant features to have weights close to zero. Option A is incorrect; gradient descent does not lessen the impact of a feature. Option B is incorrect; a large number of epochs will not reduce the impact of outliers, and it may actually lead to overfitting. Option D is incorrect; backpropagation is a technique used to train neural networks.

8. B. The correct answer is B. The model overfits the training data, and dropout is a regularization method for neural networks. Options A and C are incorrect and could actually make the overfitting problem worse. Option D is incorrect; ReLU is a type of activation function, not a regularization method.

9. A. The correct answer is A. The dataset is unbalanced, and undersampling legitimate products will lead to a more balanced dataset. Option B is incorrect; dropout is a regularization technique used with neural networks. Option C is incorrect; L1 regularization reduces the risk of overfitting. Option D is incorrect; AUC, or area under the curve, is a way to evaluate the quality of a model.

10. C. The correct answer is C. This is an example of reporting bias because the dataset did not reflect the population. Options A and B are incorrect; applying L1 regularization or dropout would not cause a model to perform well with training and test data but not with more representative data. Option A is incorrect; there is no indication that a human is involved in the decision making.

Chapter 12: Leveraging Prebuilt Models as a Service

1. A. The correct answer is A. The Cloud Video Intelligence API can identify objects and track objects across frames. Option B is incorrect because it cannot track objects across frames. Option C is incorrect because, although streaming traffic data is a form of time-series data, it does not support object recognition or object tracking. Option D is incorrect; Cloud Dataflow is a batch and stream processing service and may be used for its stream processing capabilities, but it does not have object identification or object tracking capabilities.

2. B. The correct answer is B. The Cloud Vision API supports explicit content identification, also known as Safe Search. Option A is incorrect since there is no requirement to support video on the site. Option C is incorrect; the site does need to analyze time-series data, which is what Cloud Inference API is used for. Option D is incorrect; Cloud Dataprep is used to prepare data for analysis and machine learning.

3. B. The correct answer is B. The Cloud Vision API supports up to 2,000 images per batch. Option A is incorrect because if the wrong function were called, none of the operations would succeed. Option C is incorrect since all buckets have the same access controls and some operations succeed. Option D is incorrect; images are loaded from Cloud Storage buckets.

4. D. The correct answer is D. Intents categorize a speaker's intention for a single statement, such as asking for a recommendation. Option A is incorrect; entities are nouns extracted from dialogue. Option B is incorrect; fulfillments are used to connect a service to an integration. Option C is incorrect; integrations are applications that process end-user interactions, such as deciding what to recommend.

5. C. The correct answer is C. Both changing the device specification to wearable and using WaveNet-quality voice will improve the output. Options A and B are both partially correct, but not a completely correct answer. Option D is incorrect; Base64 is an encoding for binary data, not text. Option E is incorrect because it includes Option C.

6. B. The correct answer is B. Google recommends a minimum sampling rate of 16,000 Hz. Option A is incorrect; WaveNet is used for speech synthesis, not speech to text. Option C is incorrect; SSML is also for text to speech. Option D is incorrect because it includes Option A.

7. C. The correct answer is C. The gRPC API is only available with the advanced version of the Translation API. Option A is incorrect; WaveNet is a speech synthesis option, not a translation option. Option B is incorrect; the basic version does not provide a gRPC API. Option D is incorrect because Option A is included in the choices.

8. A. The correct answer is A. The first two steps are to import libraries and to create a translation client data structure. Option B is incorrect because the translation client can't be created when importing the libraries first. Options C and D are incorrect because there is no need to pass a parameter into the API with the operation when there is a specific function call for translating.

9. A. The correct answer is A. The goal is to identify people, which are one kind of entity, so entity extraction is the correct functionality. Options B and C are incorrect because there is no requirement to understand the sentiment of the communications. Option D is incorrect because syntactic analysis does not help with identifying individuals.

10. A. The correct answer is A. Click-through rate (CTR) is the default optimization, and it maximizes the likelihood that the user engages the recommendation. Option B is incorrect; revenue per order is only available with the "frequently bought together" recommendation type. Option C is incorrect; conversation rate optimizes for the likelihood that the user purchases the recommended product. Option D is incorrect; total revenue is a metric for measuring performance, not an optimization objective.

11. C. The correct answer is C. Recommended for you predicts the next product with which the customer is likely to engage. Option A is incorrect; it provides a list of products that the customer is likely to purchase. Option B is incorrect; it provides a list of products often purchased together. Option D is incorrect; the recently viewed recommendation type provides a list of recently viewed items.

12. A. The correct answer is A. The Cloud Inference API is designed for this kind of time-series analysis and anomaly detection. Option B is incorrect; AutoML Tables is for working with structured, tabular data. Option C is incorrect; this is not a vision problem. Option D is incorrect; there is no such thing as the Cloud Anomaly Detection API.

Index

Online Test Bank

Register to gain one year of FREE access to the online interactive test bank to help you study for your Google Cloud Professional Data Engineer certification exam—included with your purchase of this book! All of the chapter review questions, the practice tests in this book are included in the online test bank so you can practice in a timed and graded setting.

Register and Access the Online Test Bank

To register your book and get access to the online test bank, follow these steps:

1. Go to bit.ly/SybexTest (this address is case sensitive)!
2. Select your book from the list.
3. Complete the required registration information, including answering the security verification to prove book ownership. You will be emailed a pin code.
4. Follow the directions in the email or go to www.wiley.com/go/sybextestprep.
5. Find your book in the list in that page and click the "Register or Login" link with it. Then enter the pin code you received and click the "Activate PIN" button.
6. On the Create an Account or Login page, enter your username and password, and click Login or if you don't have an account already, create a new account.
7. At this point, you should be in the testbank site with your new testbank listed at the top of the page. If you do not see it there, please refresh the page or log out and log back in.